Aids to Writing Latin Prose, With Exercises

ENGLISH SCHOOL CLASSICS

EDITED BY FRANCIS STORR, B.A.,
CHIEF MASTER OF MODERN SUBJECTS IN MERCHANT TAYLORS' SCHOOL.

THOMSON'S SEASONS: Winter.
With an Introduction to the Series. By the Rev. J. F. BRIGHT, M.A. 1s.

COWPER'S TASK.
By FRANCIS STORR, B.A. 2s.; or in Three Parts, 9d. each.

COWPER'S SIMPLE POEMS.
By FRANCIS STORR, B.A. 1s.

SCOTT'S LAY OF THE LAST MINSTREL.
By J. SURTEES PHILLPOTTS, M.A., Head Master of Bedford School. 2s. 6d.;
or in Four Parts, 9d. each.

SCOTT'S LADY OF THE LAKE.
By R. W. TAYLOR, M.A., Head Master of Kelly College, Tavistock. 2s.
or in Three Parts, 9d. each.

SCOTT'S MARMION.
By F. S. ARNOLD, M.A., Assistant Master at Bedford School

NOTES TO SCOTT'S WAVERLEY.
By H. W. EVE, M.A., Head Master of University College School, London.
1s.; WAVERLEY AND NOTES, 2s. 6d.

BACON'S ESSAYS. Complete Edition.
By FRANCIS STORR, B.A.

TWENTY OF BACON'S ESSAYS.
By FRANCIS STORR, B.A. 1s.

SIMPLE POEMS.
By W. E. MULLINS, M.A., Assistant Master at Marlborough College. 8d.

SELECTIONS FROM WORDSWORTH'S POEMS.
By H. H. TURNER, B.A., late Scholar of Trinity College, Cambridge. 1s.

WORDSWORTH'S EXCURSION: The Wanderer.
By H. H. TURNER, B.A. 1s.

MILTON'S PARADISE LOST.
By FRANCIS STORR, B.A. Book I., 9d. Book II., 9d.

MILTON'S L'ALLEGRO, IL PENSEROSO, AND LYCIDAS.
By EDWARD STORR, M.A., late Scholar of New College, Oxford. 1s.

SELECTIONS FROM THE SPECTATOR.
By OSMUND AIRY, M.A., late Assistant Master at Wellington College. 1s.

BROWNE'S RELIGIO MEDICI.
By W. P. SMITH, M.A., Assistant Master at Winchester College. 1s.

GOLDSMITH'S TRAVELLER AND DESERTED VILLAGE.
By C. SANKEY, M.A., Head Master of Bury St. Edmund's Grammar
School. 1s.

EXTRACTS from GOLDSMITH'S VICAR OF WAKEFIELD.
By C. SANKEY, M.A. 1s.

POEMS SELECTED from the WORKS OF ROBERT BURNS.
By A. M. BELL, M.A., Balliol College, Oxford. 2s.

MACAULAY'S ESSAYS:
MOORE'S LIFE OF BYRON. By FRANCIS STORR, B.A. 9d.
BOSWELL'S LIFE OF JOHNSON. By FRANCIS STORR, B.A. 9d.
HALLAM'S CONSTITUTIONAL HISTORY. By H. F. BOYD, late
Scholar of Brasenose College, Oxford. 1s.

SOUTHEY'S LIFE OF NELSON.
By W. E. MULLINS, M.A. 2s. 6d.

GRAY'S POEMS. SELECTION FROM LETTERS, with LIFE
by JOHNSON. By FRANCIS STORR, B.A. 1s.

Waterloo Place, Pall Mall, London.

AIDS TO WRITING LATIN PROSE

A New and Revised Edition.   Crown 8vo.   5s

Arnold's Practical Introduction to Latin
Prose Composition. *By* GEORGE GRANVILLE
BRADLEY, D D , *Dean of Westminster, late Master of University College, Oxford, and formerly Master of Marlborough College.*

RIVINGTONS
WATERLOO PLACE, LONDON

AIDS TO WRITING

LATIN PROSE,

𝔚𝔦𝔱𝔥 𝔈𝔵𝔢𝔯𝔠𝔦𝔰𝔢𝔰

BY

G. G. BRADLEY, D.D.

DEAN OF WESTMINSTER

LATE MASTER OF UNIVERSITY COLLEGE, OXFORD, AND FORMERLY
MASTER OF MARLBOROUGH COLLEGE

EDITED AND ARRANGED

BY

T. L. PAPILLON, M.A.

FELLOW AND TUTOR OF NEW COLLEGE, OXFORD

RIVINGTONS

WATERLOO PLACE, LONDON

MDCCCLXXXIV

PREFATORY NOTE

THIS book is a selection from materials prepared by the Dean of Westminster, while Master of University College, Oxford, for a treatise upon Latin Prose Composition: materials which, on finding that the duties of his present position preclude all hope of completing the work himself, he has intrusted to my hands, with full discretion as to their selection and arrangement. His original design was to frame an orderly series of introductory chapters or sections dealing with all the chief constructions of Latin Syntax; each chapter to be followed by two kinds of Exercise—the one elementary, consisting of short sentences, the other a continuous passage suitable for more advanced students; notes and hints being appended to either, as might seem convenient

The publication, however, of the revised edition of *Arnold's Latin Prose Composition* (virtually a new book under an old name) partly anticipated this design, so far as concerns the elementary exercises and detailed grammatical introductions. I have therefore, with his consent, abstained from attempting to make the present

... nor either systematic nor exhaustive, assuming that those who use this book will have already had such preliminary instruction as is provided by the other. My idea has been to arrange all the longer continuous Exercises under two or three comprehensive heads, presenting as a general Introduction such portions of the material placed in my hands as seemed from my own experience likely to be of practical use to undergraduates of the University, to boys in the upper forms of public schools, and—last but not least—to their teachers. I have placed at the foot of each Exercise references to such sections of this Introduction as may be helpful. The Exercises have all been carefully framed for educational purposes, and as the fruit of a long experience and of (*si parva licet componere magnis*) unequalled gifts of teaching, I feel sure that they will be found most valuable to many who are endeavouring either to acquire for themselves or to communicate to others that most difficult literary art—confessedly one of the surest tests of intelligent scholarship—the art of writing good Latin Prose.

In selecting the introductory matter I have as far as possible avoided repetition of what is already contained in Dean Bradley's revised edition of *Arnold's Latin Prose Composition*, but it was difficult to keep altogether clear of the same ground, especially as it seemed undesirable to make the possession of that book a *sine qua non* for those who wished to avail themselves of the assistance of the present work. Some few—a very few—direct references

are given to the book in question · but it may be profit-
ably consulted upon any points of Latin Syntax which
are not specially noticed here—such, *e.g.*, as the constructions of the Latin Cases ; and it will be easy to supplement
from it the few specimens of short-sentence Exercises,
which (for reasons there explained) are given below in
Part I. of the Exercises

Dean Bradley wishes me to repeat the expression of his
obligation to such works as Haacke's *Lateinische Stilistik*
and Draeger's *Historische Syntax,* as well as to Professor
Kennedy, Mr. Roby, and other writers.   For the selection
and arrangement of his materials I alone am responsible,
as also for the final correction of the proof-sheets.   I will
only add that it has been a grateful as well as an honourable task thus to assist in giving to others some results
of the teaching to which, in common with many former
pupils, I owe so much

T. L. PAPILLON.

New College, Oxford, 1884.

Four of the Exercises (Nos. xcviii , c., cxiv , cxv.) are contributed
by Professor S. H Butcher of Edinburgh University, formerly Fellow
and Tutor of University College, Oxford ; and eight (Nos LXI., LXIV.,
cv , cxvi., cxxix , cxxxvi., cxxxvii , cxxxviii) by myself   The
English of six Exercises (Nos. xlii., lxi , lxiv., cxvi., cxviii ,
cxxix.) has already appeared in Holden's *Foliorum Centuriae.*

TABLE OF CONTENTS.

INTRODUCTION.

INTRODUCTION

Value of Latin Composition—Order, Use, and Meaning of Words
—Substantives—Adverbs—Tenses—Moods—Participles—
Substantival, Temporal, and Concessive Clauses—Uses of
Qui—Causal and Conditional Sentences—Oratio Obliqua—
Rhetorical Questions—Specimen Lecture

INTRODUCTION

THE VALUE OF THE STUDY OF LATIN COMPOSITION.

THE most obvious purpose of this work is to assist those who wish to attain to the art of writing Latin Prose, not only in accordance with the rules of syntax but with some approach to the style of the best writers of the best or classical period of Latin Literature.

But I may at once state that this is by no means the only, I may even say that it is by no means the principal aim which I have set before me. The art of composing Latin sentences is not an end but a means, and if not valuable as an educational process it is of little value as an educational result. I do not require to be reminded that the task of reproducing in the form of an ancient language the thoughts and expressions of modern speech and literature is one that calls for the constant exercise not only of special linguistic and imitative gifts, but of the faculties of memory, observation, accuracy of thought and expression, concentrated attention, a clear perception of the precise meaning of language, a power of going below the surface, of grasping firmly its essence as distinguished from its accessories or its accidental form, a nice discrimination of the real and relative force of apparently synonymous expressions, some critical insight into the style and flow of an English or Latin author, much tact and delicacy alike of expression and of feeling, even some exertion of the higher qualities of reflection and imagination. All these are faculties which it is the very object of education to quicken and develop. But I am also aware that to attain to the highest excellence in this single department of a classical education is given to few, and these few seem to owe their success at least as much to special natural gifts as to systematic training. I am only too well aware that with the great majority of those who, under the ordinary teaching of English schools, have spent some portion of their weekly school-time in the regular writing of exercises in a dead language, the result is perhaps even more discouraging than that of some other of our recognised studies. Nor can one whose life has been given to the work of education refuse to give the most attentive hearing to those who urge that even when moderate excellence is reached in so laborious a task, it is purchased at the cost of devoting to a study which leads to no solid result time and powers which had better have been bestowed on some one of the many fresh fields of knowledge which the present age has opened to the human mind; and that even if the study of the language and literature of Rome is worth preserving, an attempt to force the mind of the young into the direction of using that language as a vehicle for thought is a wasteful and pedantic anachronism. These objections deserve the most respectful attention. But I venture to suggest some countervailing considerations which are occasionally overlooked. Among the many experiments in which those who have been interested in educating the young have borne a hopeful part, some have been most cheering, some more or less disappointing. All should be welcomed which give any sound promise of adapting our somewhat rigid educational system to the varied faculties and gifts of the human intellect, and to the complex requirements of our time. But amidst them all the study of language seems to hold, and to be likely to retain, if not an exclusive predominance, yet a position from which, in the present stage of educational experience, it is hardly likely to be dislodged. There are doubtless large classes of English society of both sexes for whom it may be well to choose as one main instrument of their educational training a modern language, such as German or French, the knowledge of which, as a spoken tongue, is more easily acquired, and which for the same reason has a practical and even commercial, as well as a literary and educational value. But those who have taken an active part in the advocacy and in the employment of such a substitute are perhaps the most keenly alive to the exceeding value of the instrument which they have laid aside. They find the new tool not ill adapted for its purpose. The modern languages, especially when supplemented with some study of the older forms of our own, do the work which is required from them sufficiently well; but nothing quite takes the place of a careful training in a language so exceedingly different (in spite of superficial resemblances) from our own as Latin, so rigorous in its rules, so suggestive in its syntax, so rich in its inflexions, so absolutely intolerant of imperfect knowledge, such a stern touchstone of obscure thought or superficial work.

And if this is so, it is of the last importance that so valuable an educational instrument should be used in the manner most adapted to secure the most perfect result. If a dead language is to be taught at all, let it be taught well and thoroughly. It may now-a-days be taken for granted that a child's memory has had its first training in the poetry of its own language. The days are passed, they once existed, when a boy of tender years could be called upon to begin his intellectual training with learning by heart the *Propria quae maribus* or *As in praesenti* without comment, explanation, or guidance. The burden laid upon memory in the indispensable work of thoroughly mastering the Latin accidence will still be severe, but when memory, at an age when that faculty is often powerful and retentive, and capable of almost indefinite cultivation, has done its full work, other faculties will come gradually into play. Side by side with the study of Latin should go the study of English. Memory here will be lightly tasked, but every step in the difficult acquisition of the first principles of Latin syntax may be made at once interesting and fruitful by some initiation into the structure and analysis of the English sentence, and even some information as to the earlier forms and history of English words. But above all, the stage of what is called "literal translation," that is, the rendering of Latin into the uncouth and unnatural English with which the ill-taught youth still shocks the University examiner, should be either materially abridged or absolutely annihilated. It is a practice that should be only tolerated in accommodation to tender years or unusual dulness, and to a necessarily imperfect acquaintance with ordinary English. But it is capable of growing into an evil more perilous and more antagonistic to

educational progress than all the false quantities and all
the false concords that were ever perpetrated. If a boy
is capable of reading Caesar and Virgil, he is capable of
reading some passages of good prose and poetry in his
own language. He should be taught from the very
commencement to translate either of these Latin authors
into a style in some degree suitable to each. Otherwise
he may contract a habit which will rob his study of the
great classical writers of all their value, degrade his
taste, and stifle or deaden the very powers of observation
which we wish to cultivate. He may be learning to
poison the springs of taste and imagination at their very
source. Those who have listened to young men rendering Homer and Plato, or Cicero and Virgil, into the same
mean and vulgar dialect of illiterate English, have not
been surprised at finding their attempts to write Latin
prose equally unsuccessful, though less depressing and
humiliating The youth who cannot reproduce the
thoughts of Cicero in any approach to idiomatic English
is scarcely likely to express English ideas in idiomatic
Latin. And yet there are teachers who, while they
neglect the training of their pupils in the one study, are
astonished at their want of success in the other!

And it is here, as it seems to me, when placed side by
side with careful and accurate, yet vigorous and idiomatic
translation from Latin authors, that the great value
of some form of Latin composition, as an aid to the real
and fruitful study of the language, asserts its true place.
No one would flatter himself that his knowledge of
German was otherwise than superficial, if he could not
write a few lines of German with moderate accuracy.

In French, even more than in German, the power of
writing a page or two that will not betray in every sentence the hand of the foreigner is an infallible test of some
real proficiency. But few things will give the learner so
clear an insight into the real nature of language generally as the attempt, if taught and practised with intelligence and care, on the part both of teacher and of pupil,
to reproduce in the form of the Latin author whom he is
studying the ideas and language of modern English.[1]
By such a process the likeness and unlikeness of the
mode of thought and expression of two great nations and
two distant periods will be brought home at every step.
Setting aside those sustained powers of undivided con-
centration on a process of reasoning which fall within the
province of mathematics, there is hardly a faculty which
education aims at stimulating which may not be appealed
to in the process. That combination of observation and
judgment which we call common sense will be tested at
every step. To begin with, the pupil will have to use,
to handle, and to analyse the materials supplied by
the English language. Its rich and varied vocabulary,
crowded with words which resemble in sound, but differ
wholly in sense from the Latin from which they are
derived; the innumerable and undefinable turns of expression which we have learned to substitute for the

---

[1] The boy whose Latin lesson is limited to the preparation of a
single chapter of Caesar's Commentaries should be encouraged and
aided to translate the language of a cultivated Roman into some
approach to the simplest but purest diction of a cultivated Englishman. His best Latin exercise will be English sentences so framed as
to need no further vocabulary than that which his Caesar will supply.
Specimens of such sentences would have formed no slight part of the
present work, had it been intended for a purely elementary manual.

simpler diction of an earlier period; its sentences following one another with no connecting link other than that
of punctuation; its comparatively simple and uniform
order; the loose texture of its longer sentences; above all
perhaps its rich and growing treasure of vivid and
picturesque metaphors, used consciously and unconsciously, for the possession of which it has drawn indis-
criminately on east and west, on dead and living tongues,
on ancient poetry and recent science, on Homer, Virgil,
or Horace, on David, or Isaiah, or St. Paul, will force
themselves gradually on his attention These he will
have to examine and re-cast before he can transfuse them
into the mould of a language differing at every turn from
his own; recalling in the richness of its inflexion an early
stage of language, yet moving onwards in its prepositional
and other usages in the direction in which we have
advanced so far; rigorous in its syntactical rules, subtle
and suggestive in its use of moods, tenses, and its
ubiquitous relative; often terse where English is diffuse,
and circuitous where English is direct; detesting ambiguity; sparing and timid in its use of metaphors;
loving the direct and concrete, and shrinking from the
abstract; connecting its sentences logically and carefully;
building up its symmetrical periods with a closeness
which often defies translation; and finally possessing the
power of varying the lights and shades of every sentence
by the almost illimitable freedom of its order; often, in
short, rich where we are poor, and poor where we are
rich.

All these points I have attempted to illustrate as simply
and plainly as possible in the following pages, and in

those of a more elementary volume[1] which has already appeared. I should regret deeply the time and labour which they had cost, had these been given merely to smooth the way to the acquirement of a graceful accomplishment, or to aid in an isolated and unfruitful familiarity with the rules of Latin syntax. If in any way they can contribute to increase the general value to the teacher, or the pupil, or the student, of a single department of that educational work to which so large a portion of my own life has been given, I shall not have laboured in vain. And I cannot but think that those who have followed the path marked out in these works may obtain, even if they never advance far towards perfection as writers of Latin, some solid and useful rewards in return for the exertions which they have made.

G. G BRADLEY.

---

[1] Arnold's *Latin Prose Composition*, edited and revised by G G. Bradley, D D , Dean of Westminster Rivingtons, 1883. Wherever in the following pages this book is referred to it will be designated simply as "Arnold, rev ed."

I.

The Order of Words and Clauses in Latin.

1. It may be assumed that those for whom this book is intended are familiar with the elementary principles of Latin order: but even fairly advanced students may be reminded of the essential difference in this respect between Latin and English. As a matter of fact, the two languages **very seldom correspond** Turn to the opening chapters of Caesar *De Bello Gallico*, and you will find that you must read through two-thirds of chapter I. before coming to a single sentence [1] which can be translated without some change in the order, while in chapter II. not one sentence is arranged throughout in the natural order of English. This difference is easily accounted for by the *inflexional* character of Latin; the relations of words to each other in a sentence being (in the case of substantives, adjectives, pronouns, and verbs) marked as a rule by inflexion, not by position in the sentence. "A brother loves his sister" may be expressed by *frater sororem amat, amat sororem frater,* or *sororem amat frater.* Here the *order* in Latin is immaterial, except as a matter of emphasis: the right *inflexion* of each word is essential

2. But for all this the order of words in the Latin sentence is a very important consideration; and both the ordinary rules and the principal variations from them should be carefully noticed in reading Latin authors What is the *natural* order of language?

The natural arrangement of a sentence is that which places the different images which its elements represent

---

[1] *Continetur Garumna flumine, Oceano, finibus Belgarum; attingit etiam ab Sequanis ab Helvetus flumen Rhenum , vergit ad septentriones . . . (Belgae) pertinent ad inferiorem partem fluminis Rheni; spectant in septentrionem et orientem solem.* Generally speaking, it is only in such short clauses as these that English order is adapted to Latin.

in the exact order in which we wish them to be conveyed to the mind of the reader or hearer. It is the order of *relative importance*. If a Roman were walking through a forest, and wished to call his companion's attention to the necessity of caution, and then to explain this by indicating danger from a wild beast, he would say *cave leonem*; if he wished promptly to call his attention to the presence of a lion, and *then* to the need of caution, he would say instinctively *leonem cave*.

In English we have not this freedom: we can say "beware of the lion!" but if we wish to use the word *lion* first, we must substitute an exclamation for the accusative case, and say, "a lion! take care!"

In English we, as a matter of course in ordinary languages, put the *subject* first; we say "I run," "he saw." But in Latin the unemphasised pronoun, so far as it is expressed at all, follows the verb: *curro* is "run I," *vidisti* "sawest-thou."[1] It does not follow that the English order is the more *natural*, because it is that to which we Englishmen are accustomed

In English we almost invariably place the object of a transitive verb after the verb:

"In the beginning God created the heavens and the earth"

In Latin this is not the rule but the exception. In English the adjective precedes the noun to which it is attached: "a good man," "an iron gate." In Latin the *general* rule is to place it after: *vir bonus, porta ferrea.*

3. Each of the two languages has an arrangement of words which it generally adopts. This may be called its *grammatical* or *usual* order. It places together those parts of speech which are grammatically connected with each other in the order in which, to the people who use that language, they would naturally occur to the mind.

---

[1] In *curro*, it is needless to remind those who are familiar with the elements of Comparative Philology, the element (*ma*) of the first personal pronoun "I" has been worn away, as from the corresponding Greek form (λέω)· but it survives in other forms (*curram, currerem*) of ordinary verbs, and in present indicative of *sum, inquam*

Each of the two languages substitutes for this grammatical order another which may be called the *rhetorical* order; which departs from the grammatical or usual order, with the view of giving special emphasis to certain parts or elements of the sentence, from various considerations— among them those of sound, harmony, and rhythm.

In English this is done in prose to a certain extent:

"Great is Diana of the Ephesians."
"Blessed are the peacemakers."
"Unto us was the gospel preached."
"For since by man came death, by man came also the resurrection."
"With his rod he smote the rock twice."
"Corrupt are they, and become abominable."
"A broken and contrite heart, O God, shalt thou not despise."

It is done of course far more in poetry, both on the grounds named above, and to meet the exigences of metre and rhythm.

In English, however, such inversions of the usual order, though often very effective, are far less common than in Latin. They can only be used within rather narrow limits, as owing to the absence of inflexions they are apt to cause ambiguity. Thus even in such a line as that of Gray—

"And all the air a solemn stillness holds,"

it is possible that doubt might arise as to which of the two nouns, "air" and "stillness," were the subject, which the object, to "holds." A Latin version would make it clear at once, not by the order but by the inflexions:

Et tacitas aures occupat alta quies.

Milton begins the *Paradise Lost* with an inversion in order to bring out his main subject with due prominence. "Of man's first disobedience," etc.,[1] but many lines follow without any marked departure from the usual English order.

---

[1] Cf. the opening of the *Iliad* and *Aeneid*. Μῆνιν ἄειδε, θεά—Arma virumque cano.

In Latin the rhetorical order constantly interferes with the more usual or grammatical order; it should not, however, be adopted without good cause.

A.—Order of Simple Sentences.

I. *The Subject.*

4. (1.) The **Subject**,[1] if separately expressed, comes as in English in its natural place, *i.e* either first or early in the sentence : for it is natural that we should place early the thing or person of which we are about to speak.

But it often yields the first place to words, phrases, or clauses, which mark the connection of the sentence with what goes before   Such are **pronouns** (especially the **relative**), **adverbs**, or **adverbial expressions**, of time and place, **ablative absolute**, etc.

Thus—*his de rebus certior factus ; quibus rebus cognitis ; eodem fere tempore ; dum haec Romae geruntur ; postridie ejus dici ; eadem nocte*, and innumerable similar expressions, and words or phrases such as *itaque, quamobrem*, are constantly used as the opening words in a Latin sentence They are much oftener found there than in English, as Latin seldom omits to express in words the connexion of thought between one sentence and another.[2]

5. In English this connexion has more often to be supplied mentally. In any continuous passage of good English prose the sentences are generally detached from each other, as far as their form is concerned ; but in Latin they are dovetailed, so to speak, into each other by the constant employment of *et, qui, quum, enim, itaque, neque,* or other connecting words or phrases. Each English sen-

---

[1] It is taken for granted that those who use this book are familiar with the terms Subject, Predicate, and others necessary to the logical analysis of a sentence.   They have been explained in Arnold, rev. ed., §§ 61 *sqq.*

[2] *Enim, vero, autem, quoque, quidem* (with of course the *enclitics, que, ve, në*), cannot be the first words of a clause.

tence will stand by itself apart from its context; but a
similar treatment of the successive sentences in a Latin
paragraph will give, to any one accustomed to good Latin
prose style, the impression of a string of sentences from
a "delectus" or exercise-book; the abruptness natural to
the one language being uncongenial to the other.[1]

6. Near the subject, and generally following it, are
arranged the accessories of the subject, such as words in
apposition with it, or relative or conjunctional clauses
which nearly concern it:

Caesar, qui nondum eorum consilia cognoverat .   .

In English we should probably say, " But though Caesar
had not yet ascertained their intentions," and repeat *he* in
the following and main clause. Latin gives greater prominence to the common subject of the subordinate main
clause by placing it early.

II. *The Predicate.*

7. Here the Latin order differs greatly from English.
We place the verbal part of the predicate early; its
accessories, such as its nearer and remoter objects, adverbs,
and adverbial phrases or clauses, after it.

In Latin this order is exactly reversed; the finite verb is
as a rule placed last, all words and phrases which qualify
it or depend upon it, such as those mentioned in the last
clause, together with *supines, gerunds,* and *dependent
infinitives,* come before, and lead up to, the final word, the
verb, which gives the predicate its full force and meaning,
and winds up the sentence.

---

[1] The opening paragraph of Gibbon's *Decline and Fall* contains ten
sentences separated from each other by full stops or colons, the last of
which alone is connected *verbally* (by a relative) with its predecessor.
yet the *mental* connection is plain throughout. In a Latin version this
mental connection would be expressed, in the majority of cases, by
such words as those indicated above For further examples of this
difference between continuous style in English and Latin, see below,
§ 25, and Exercise I.

We see the difference in such short English and Latin sentences as

"In the beginning God created the heaven and the earth."
"They have slain thy prophets with the sword."

The ordinary or grammatical order of such sentences in Latin would be

Initio (or *rerum in initio*) *Deus caelum et terras creavit.*
Prophetas tuos ferro occiderunt.

8. In Latin, therefore, far more than in English, the last place in the sentence is looked on as a place of the utmost importance. The attention is kept suspended till the closing word is reached; and when the verb does not occupy its usual place, that place is sure to be assigned to some emphatic, never to an unimportant or merely accessory word or phrase.

Not only would such conclusions to a sentence as

"Avoid the habits which these men have passed their lives *in*,"
"Envy is a vice that clever men are often guilty *of*,"

which are perhaps undesirable in English, be impossible in Latin, but it may also be said that we rarely see a Latin sentence from which the last word or words can be detached without destroying the grammar, at all events without destroying the life and force of the sentence.

Compare the Latin and English of one of the opening sentences of Caesar already referred to:

Hi omnes lingua, institutis, moribus, inter se differunt.
    These all (or, as we should say, *all of these*) differ from each other in language, institutions, habits

We have at one end the subject, *hi omnes*, at the other end the most important part of the predicate, the verb, with its most essential qualifying phrase *inter se* closely attached to it; between these, and in the less prominent part of the sentence, come the less important words of the sentence, viz, those ablative cases which point out the different points in which "all these differ from one another," but *the main point of the statement comes last.*

If you withdraw *different* from the Latin, the sentence
ceases to be a sentence, it has no predicate, and becomes
meaningless. Remove the last four words from the
English, and the sentence, though less clear and precise,
retains a perfectly grammatical and intelligible form It
is still a sentence.

This is the most fundamental difference between the
order of English and Latin.

9. One or two important exceptions may be noticed.

The very importance of the last place in the sentence
sometimes leads to the verb *sum*, especially in its mono-
syllabic forms, being banished from it Latin writers
preferred, on rhythmical grounds, to end their sentences
with words of some length and force (three-, four-, and even
five-syllabled words), rarely with monosyllables or un-
accented words.

(*a.*) Hence even when *sum* is used as a mere *auxiliary*,
though it sometimes ends a sentence in combination with
the participle :

diu acriterque pugnatum est, hostem . . . conspicatus est,

yet it is often separated from the participle and placed
between two other words quite out of what seems its
natural order ·

Qui in fortunae periculis sunt ac varietate versati.

It thus retires into the background and gives additional
emphasis to the words which it separates.

(*b.*) When used as a *copulative* verb it takes the same
place as in English, leaving the really important part of
the predicate to come last :

Spes est expectatio boni. Hope is the expectation of good.

This is entirely in accordance with the general principle
of Latin order.

(*c.*) When however *sum* is used in its most emphatic or *substantival* sense (denoting existence) it is almost always placed, not last, but first in the sentence, thus challenging the attention to the importance of its meaning.

> *Est coeleste numen.*   There is (or, there exists) a heavenly power.
> *Sunt ista quae dicis.*   What you say is true.

So in the pathetic use of the verb in Virgil's *fuimus Troes, fuit Ilium* (*Aen* ii. 325) the order is precisely that of prose.

10. But any verb will be made emphatic, *i.e.* have special attention called to it, by being placed first :

> *Tulit hoc graviter Cicero.*   It need not be said that Cicero felt this deeply.
> *Dicebat melius quam scripsit Hortensius*   Hortensius was better as a speaker than as a writer

In such cases the *subject* when removed from its natural place is generally granted the compensation of being placed last, as above.   So

> *Malum mihi videtur esse mors ,*

(*malum* is here an emphasised predicate, *esse* a mere copulative).

The verb is also often placed first in a series of short sentences representing a series of events as rapidly following one another.   Such instances are very common :

> *Tandem dat Cotta permotus manus ; superat sententia Sabini ; pronuntiatur prima luce ituros , consumitur vigiliis reliqua pars noctis.*—(CAES. *B. G.* v. 31.)

In all these instances we see how very much further Latin can go than our own language in producing a fresh effect by an alteration in the order of the words.

shall never see him more in this world" by *nec jam cum in hoc mundo visurus sum* instead of *in hac vita*

Mistakes of this kind can only be avoided by thought and observation; the real meaning, whether figurative or literal, of the English word must be thought out; and the use of Latin words as found in Latin authors must be carefully observed.

29. Again, if we compare the two sentences, "all the world believes," and *omnes homines credunt*, we shall notice that the English word *world* is a **metaphor**; *i.e.* is used in a figurative or transferred meaning; instead of meaning a mass or masses of matter of a certain shape and occupying a definite space, it is transferred to the human beings who inhabit the whole or a certain amount of its surface. Every language must make a wide use of metaphor; as a nation grows in knowledge and cultivation it has to find names, *i.e.* words, for fresh conceptions and ideas; and even at a very early stage it applies names drawn from material external objects to represent feelings, emotions, and perceptions. This is still more the case as time goes on: *si antiquam sermonem nostro comparamus*, says a later Roman writer, *pene jam quidquid loquimur figura est* (QUINTILIAN). The Romans, therefore, like other highly civilised nations, used metaphorical expressions both unconsciously in their ordinary words, as *impedire* (properly "to entangle the feet"), *vaccillari* ("to tread with shambling gait like a cow"), etc., and with more or less of purpose and intent.

30. But two things must be remembered: *First*, the metaphors of one nation are not those of another; and a warlike or trading, or seafaring or pastoral, a northern or southern, or highly imaginative race will have metaphors drawn from its own special circumstances or temperament. It does not therefore follow that a figure of speech which is recognised and familiar in English can be literally translated into any other language; least of all into one spoken so many centuries ago by a nation in so many points unlike our own.

A. W. L. P.   C

And, *secondly*, we must remember that the English language is both richer and bolder, so to speak, in its use of metaphors than the Latin. The Latin is an exceedingly clear and direct language ; but it is deficient on the imaginative and picturesque side as compared with the English ; and this arises partly from the temperament and habits of a nation of soldiers and politicians, and still more from their circumstances. Our language is enriched by whole streams of words and forms of expression which owe their source to springs outside the frontier of our own language or literature. The poets as well as the prose writers of ancient Greece and Rome ; the highly figurative Hebrew language, familiar to us through our version of the Bible, the literature and the science, and the fresh discoveries and experiences of the whole civilised world since the time of Augustus, have left their traces on our language, not only by enlarging its vocabulary, but almost as much by opening up fresh modes of regarding old conceptions, as well as by introducing fresh conceptions with fresh names of their own.

31. Two instances will be sufficient to illustrate such differences between the two languages as a young scholar might overlook. Such a sentence as "the young queen now succeeded to the crown, *or*, ascended the throne, of her fathers," might occur in the least imaginative historian ; and a beginner might be tempted to write *patrum coronae successit* or *solium conscendit ;* but any one familiar with Latin would at once condemn such Latinity as grotesque in the last degree. The reason is obvious : the words *crown, throne, fathers* are all three highly metaphorical expressions, and all three drawn (originally) from Eastern sources, and were too unfamiliar to the Romans to be adopted except in poetry. In Latin poetry they were freely used : but the gulf between the imagery of poetry and that recognised in prose was for many reasons greater in Latin than in English ; and the student must be constantly on his guard against importing into Latin prose either the poetical nomenclature or the poetical constructions which will meet him at every turn in Horace and Virgil.

What course must be taken then with such a passage? The answer is obvious: think what the passage really means, and discarding such expressions as *corona*, which means a festive crown, or one given as a mark of honour, substitute *regnum*, "royal power;" for *patres*, which in Latin prose writers means merely the last generation of our countrymen, substitute the Latin metaphorical expression for "ancestors," *majores* (the elders); and, thinking once more what the passage really means, substitute for *successit* the word *excepit;* and so write *regnum a majoribus traditum excepit.*

Again, such an expression in an English historian as "the political horizon seemed overcast with clouds," would call for no remark from an English reader, but any one acquainted with the style of the Roman historians would see at once that it could not be reproduced in Latin. The word "horizon," familiar enough to ourselves after generations of seamanship, of observation of the weather in a variable climate, and of some general acquaintance with elementary scientific terms, has no representative in Latin; and the imagery of the clouded sky as portending anything but a literal storm had hardly passed from the region of poetry into that of prose. The word *tempestas* is frequent as applied to the intestine convulsions of the state, but it is probable that the thought of coming dangers, which the English writer would clothe in a metaphor drawn from his own changeful skies, would in Latin take a simple shape, and that we had better write *reipublicae impendere undique pericula videbantur.*

32. Closely connected with metaphor, indeed a form of metaphor, is *personification, i.e.* the representation of inanimate objects or abstract ideas as living beings. A certain amount of this figure is common to all languages; otherwise few verbs representing any action at all could have for their nominative case any noun but that of a living agent. But the use of personification is far narrower in Latin than in English, and a careful reader of Roman authors will notice how often a substantive which in English would occupy the principal place, and by doing so add much of picturesqueness and vigour to the style, will by the rigour of the less imaginative language be banished to a subordinate position.

"The peril of the army struck terror into Caesar," or "Rome and Carthage were now at war," are two ordinary English sentences; but a Roman author would scarcely allow "peril" to be so personified as to be the nominative to such a verb as *commovit*, still less to *metum incussit* or *injecit*; nor, except in rare instances, would they so far personify a city or a country as to make them stand for the nation to which they belonged. He would write in the one case *hoc exercitus periculo Caesar graviter commotus est*, in the other *jam Romani* (or *Populus Romanus*) *Carthaginiensesque bellum inter se gerebant*.

33. We shall notice also that Latin is, if not deficient in, yet singularly sparing in the use of, a large number of nouns which denote to us very common abstract and general terms; it has no one word for "happiness," or "gratitude," or "certainty," or "patriotism;" but is obliged to use a combination of a substantive and defining adjective, such as *summum bonum; vita beata; ad beate vivendum; gratus animus; certum judicium; patriae studium, amor, caritas*.

Such general terms as "cause," "reason," "amount," "origin," it mostly expresses by a periphrasis; even in the verbal substantives which express agents, such as "teachers," "students," "learners," "slayers," it is constantly obliged to have recourse to a relative clause or a participle; and a large number of scientific or political words which English owes to Greek, such as "astronomy," "chronology," "geography," "etymology," "logic," "ethics," "politics" ("politician," "political"), "demagogue," "democrat," "oligarchy," and many others, had not found their way into Latin at the time when its best writers flourished.

These points of difference will be illustrated in the following sections; but no book and no teacher can supply the place of observation on the part of the learner, and no amount of practice in writing either a living or a dead language can compensate for a careful and intelligent study of its writers.

34. One further caution is of the greatest importance We have in English a large number of words obviously derived from Latin, and therefore resembling in form and sound their Latin derivatives. Some of these have come direct from Latin, either classical Latin, through the medium of literary men, or legal Latin, or later Latin, through the Vulgate or early Latin translation of the Bible, or through ecclesiastical writers or mediæval chroniclers: but the larger number have come to us through the French language, having previously passed through many changes as the Latin language was adopted successively by Gauls and Scandinavians. Some few of these words, especially those that are mainly confined to literature, retain the sense which they usually bore in classical Latin. But in the majority, and especially in those of most frequent use, the change in meaning which they have undergone is so marked as to make the external resemblance of sound almost a sure mark of a real difference in sense. Hence it is a good rule, though like all general rules it may be carried to excess, to avoid in translating from Latin into English the choice of the English word which is derived from or cognate to its apparent equivalent, and to look on resemblance in sound as the worst possible guide to the choice of a Latin word to represent an English one in composition. The former rule is at least as important as the last; so long as the mere jingle of sounds instead of the meaning of words is our guide in the choice of words in our native tongue, it is sure to mislead us in our attempts to express ourselves in the unfamiliar terms of a dead language.

The truth of what has here been said will be apparent at almost every attempt to render English into Latin: but

one short illustration may be given here.   In the sentence,
" The minister by resigning office at so fatal a moment
contributed seriously to the ruin of his nation," every
word that is not a monosyllable is of obviously Latin
origin; yet not one of these words could be translated
into Latin by the word from which it is derived without
substituting for the English a word like in sound but
wholly unlike in sense.

A few obvious examples are subjoined (i.) of English
derivatives whose meaning is different from that of the
cognate Latin word: (ii.) of political, scientific, or literary
terms derived by us from Greek, for which Latin has no
literal equivalent.

35. English Derivatives differing in meaning from their Latin original[1]

" To acquire " is not *acquirere*, but *adipisci* or *consequi*.

" To act," " acts," is not *agere*, *acta*, but *facere*, *facta*.

" Alien " is not *alienus*, but *externus*, *advena*, etc.

" To be astonished " is not *attonitum esse*, but *mirari*, *ad-
mirari*, *demirari*.

" To attain to " is not *attinere ad*, or *attingere*, but
pervenire ad.

" Barbarous " (cruel) is not *barbarus*, but *crudelis*.

" To cease " is not *cessare*, but, if turned literally, *desinere*
or *desistere*.

" Class," not *classis*, but *genus*.

" Commonly " is not *communiter*, but *persaepe*, *saepe*, etc.

" Country " is no one word exclusively, but will vary with
the meaning of the English: *rus*, *fines*, *civitas*, *respublica*, *patria*; *cives*, *populus*.

" Crime," not *crimen*, but *scelus*, *flagitium*, etc.

---

[1] In each of these instances it has been left to the reader to ascertain
the true meaning of the rejected Latin word.

"I desire," not *desidero*, but *cupio*, *iubeo*, etc., according to its meaning (*i.e.* "wish" or "command").

"It is destined," not *destinatum est*, but *in fatis est ut*, etc.

"To expose to," not *exponere*, but *obicere*.

"Famous" is not *famosus*, but *praeclarus*, etc.

"Fatal" is not *fatalis*, but *perniciosissimus*, etc., or expressed by the verb *noceo*, etc.

"Fathers" (=ancestors) is not *patres* (a Hebraism), but *majores*.

"Fury" is not *furor*, but *ira*.

"Heart" (metaph.) is not *cor*, but *animus*, *ingenium*, etc.

"Heaven" (metaph.) is not *caelum*, but *Deus*, *Di Immortales*, etc.

"Injury" (damage) is not *injuria*, but *damnum*, or the verb *noceo* is used.

"Mortal" (wound) is not (*vulnus*) *mortale*, but *mortiferum*.

"Nation" is not *natio*, but *civitas*, *respublica*, etc.

"To obtain" is not *obtinere*, but *consequi*, *adipisci*, etc.

"I am obnoxious" (hateful) is not *obnoxius*, but *odio sum*.

"Office" is not *officium*, but *magistratus*, *honores*, etc.

"To oppress" is not *opprimere*, but *vexare*, etc.

"To provoke" is not *provocare*, but *animum irritare*, etc.

"Rome" (nation) is not *Roma*, but *Romani*, or *populus Romanus*.

"Ruin of" is not *ruina*, but *interitus*, *pernicies*, etc.

"Scene" (place), never *scena*, but must be either *locus*, or paraphrased in some other way.

"Secure" (safe) is not *securus*, but *tutus*, etc.

"Triumph" (victory) is not *triumphus*, but some form of *vincere* or *victor*.

"To urge to" is not *urgere*, but *agere cum* . . . *ut*.

"Vile" is not *vilis*, but *turpis*.

"World" is (generally) not *mundus* (material universe), but, according to its meaning, *omnes homines*, *nemo quin*; *orbis terrarum*, *ceterae gentes*, etc.

"Study," not *studium*, but *cognitio*.

36. POLITICAL AND PHILOSOPHICAL TERMS, ETC.

A.—*Political.*

" Aristocracy," never *patricii*; the distinction between patrician and plebeian families had long ceased to be a social or political distinction.

Nobiles and *nobilitas* denote the families of more or less hereditary office-holders, and are often used invidiously by Cicero, who was a *novus homo. Optimates* is the word which he uses in a good sense.

Such expressions as "an aristocratic form of government" would be *civitas, quae optimatium arbitrio regitur*, or, *in qua penes optimates est summa rerum*, etc.; " an oligarchy," *civitas . . . penes paucos (ac praepotentes).*

" Democratic party" (democracy), never *plebeii*, but *ii qui causam popularem suscipiunt, homines populares.* For " demagogues" the terms are mostly those of abuse, *turbulenti cives et vulgi turbatores; homines qui auram popularem aucupantur*, etc   For the form of government Cicero uses the term *civitas popularis;* or in a bad sense *multitudinis dominatus*, " ochlocracy."

" Despotism" (tyranny), *unius dominatus*, or *imperium;* " Monarchy," *regnum (singulare imperium* is also used); *civitas in qua penes unum* (or *regem*) *est summa rerum.* So for "a republic," substitute *populum*, or *cives ipsos*, for *regem.*

" Constitution" is also *respublica;* "constitutional," *e r. p.;* " unconstitutional," *contra r. p.*

" Politics," " political life," is always *res publica* (sing.): *rempublicam attingere*, to meddle with *politics; ad r. p. accedere*, to enter *political life; r. p. capessere, gubernare, procurare*, " to administer the *government;" reipublicae procuratio*, " the government;" *in republica versari*, " to be a politician."

It will be noticed that none of these Latin words are borrowed, as our own are, from the Greek.

B.—*Philosophical and other Terms*

Nor, though the list of Greek words adopted by the Romans is fairly long, did they use more than a fraction of those which are in common use in English.

An "atheist" was *qui deos esse negat*, an "atom" *corpusculum*, a "dogma" *praeceptum*, *enuntiatum* (never *doctrina* for "doctrine," still less *doctrinae*, but either *praecepta* or *disciplina*, "the system"), "drama" is *fabula*; "a dialogue," or conversation between more than two, is *sermo; heros* is a "demigod," and should not be used as we use "hero, heroic," but other words or phrases should be substituted, such as *vir magnus, summus*, etc.; *heroicus* is rather "mythical," *aetas heroica*

Historia is used for "history" in its most general sense; but other phrases are more common: not *annales*, which is simply "year-books" (*libri*) of the main events of each year, nor *Fasti*, a kind of (religious) almanac, including the names of the chief magistrates, but *antiquitatis*, or *rerum gestarum*, *memoria*. So *post hominum memoriam*, "since the dawn of history;" *rerum scriptores*, "historians."

Scena is always the "stage" literally, as *scenicus* is "theatrical:" never in the sense of place, as in "scene of the battle."

Schola is a place of higher instruction, rarely a philosophical sect; *stoici*, or *stoicorum disciplina* (system), "the stoic school." *Stigma* is hardly used for "stigma" or "brand," but *nota, ignominia: notam ei inurere, ignominia notare. Thesaurus* is only a treasure-place or house, not "a treasure."

Tyrannus, etc, are rarely used in prose; see "despotism." *Tragoedia, tragicus*, are used as "tragedy" in the strict sense, and *tragicus* as applied to, *e.g.* an orator, not to events, as in English.

Besides these, *philosophia* is used (with *sapientes, sapientia*) freely ; *philosophorum more*, "philosophically," *ad philosophiae rationes revocare*, to insist on the scientific treatment of . . . "Moral philosophy," *ph. quae est de (vita atque) moribus.* "Logic" is *disserendi ars*, or *ratio*, etc. ; "logical nicety," *disserendi subtilitas*, so *disserendi elegantia*, "logical correctness," etc, occasionally only *dialectica (-orum,* or *-ae).* "Mathematics," *Mathematica, -ae,* but *mathematici* is oftener used : *qui omnia necessaria mathematicorum ratione concludi volunt,* " who ask everywhere for demonstrative and mathematical proof."

"Physics" is *physica(-orum):* also *naturae cognitio*(study); *rationes physicae,* " principles of natural science " "Poetry " is *poesis,* or *ars poetica* · the terms *poema, poeta, poetice* (ποιητική), being also naturalised. "Prose" is *oratio,* or *oratio soluta.*

Exercises II and III. will afford useful practice in the rendering of English derivatives from Latin, English political terms, etc.

III.

Use of Substantives in Latin and English.

A.—Apparent Omission of Subject.

37. Every sentence in Latin, as in English, must have a **Subject** and a **Predicate** (nominative case and verb); but, whereas in English the subject must almost always be expressed, there are many cases in Latin where it is apparently omitted.

The **Personal Pronoun**, for example, which, in however mutilated a form, is expressed by the **person-endings** of a Latin verb, need never be expressed, except for the sake of emphasis, distinction, or contrast. Whenever, accordingly, in a Latin (or Greek) sentence the pronoun is expressed, it should be carefully marked in translation, and often requires some emphatic English phrase ("for my own part," "as regards himself," "it was I who") or, at the least, such stress as we can give by the tone of the voice in speaking, or by the use of "italics" in writing or printing. In a continuous passage, narrative, or otherwise, a change of subject from that of a previous sentence will often necessitate its expression by a personal pronoun; and in the third person, as our English "he" is ambiguous (*e.g.* "*he* told *him* to come to *him* as soon as *he* could"), it will often be necessary to substitute for the Latin *hic, ille,* etc., the proper name or substantive to which it refers.

38. The first and second persons, which must always refer to the speaker and person addressed, naturally dispense with an expressed nominative more readily than the third, which is vaguer (*he, she, it*).

But the third person plural is often used with an unexpressed indefinite nominative answering to our "they," "you," "men," "we," "one," used (like the French *on* or the German *man*, which have no corresponding word in English or Latin, and must often be translated by the passive) to express "men" in general:

> *Ferunt, dicunt, tradunt, eum haec fecisse.* There is a story, a report, a tradition, that he acted thus.

There is a similar use of the second person singular, but only with the subjunctive mood:

> *Credas, credideris, crederes, victos esse.* You (*i.e.* any one) would believe, would have believed, that they were conquered.

Also, as in English, of the first person plural:

> *Ut apud Ciceronem,* or *rerum scriptores, scriptum legimus.* As we find in the writings of Cicero, or historians.

39. *Impersonal* verbs, strictly so called (*miseret, pudet, piget, paenitet, taedet,* and such expressions concerning the weather as *illucescit, vesperascit, tonat,* etc.), have no apparent subject; the impersonal "*it*" being of course contained in the terminations. [Other so-called "impersonals" (*accidit, decet, refert, oportet,* etc) have always a neuter pronoun, or infinitive, or *ut*-clause for their subject.]

The same is the case with the frequent impersonal use of intransitive verbs, by which many abstract or semi-abstract substantives in English may be represented; *e.g.*

> *In urbe trepidatur.* There is confusion in the city.
> *Diu pugnatum est.* The battle was long.

Attention may here be called to the familiar, but often forgotten, fact, that the large class of transitive verbs which in grammatical phraseology "govern a dative"—*i e.* having no *direct* object in the accusative case, as transitive verbs, are only used with a dative of the *remoter* object—can in the passive voice **only be used impersonally.** Hence *tibi favetur,* not *tu faveris; parcitur mihi,* not *parcor;* and similarly with *noceo, suadeo, ignosco,* and many others. This is of course an elementary rule, but it is ignored or forgotten by too many young scholars.

B.—LATIN AND ENGLISH SUBSTANTIVES.

40. It has already been noted (above, sect. **33**) that Latin has no equivalent for many English nouns of *abstract* or general meaning, and this comparison may be extended to substantives generally. In writing Latin, we have constantly to set aside an English substantive and supply its place in some other way. It will be useful to recall a few obvious examples of this contrast between the two languages.

Adjectives and **Participles** (the adjectival form of the verb) are often used precisely as substantives : *amicus, adolescens, decretum, majores, praeceptum, portentum.* The adjective is eminently concrete, indicating a quality as seen in some person or thing; it is therefore likely to be much employed in a language which so much prefers concrete to abstract expressions. Thus many abstract ideas, expressed by English substantives, are often expressed by the neuter singular or plural of Latin adjectives, *e.g. utile, honestum, rectum, verum* (*i.e.* "expediency," "duty," "right," "truth"); *vera et falsa* (truth and falsehood); *futura, praeterita* (the future, the past). So too the participle :

> *Suadenti tibi obsecutus sum.* I deferred to your desire.
> *Indignantium voces audires.* One might have heard cries of indignation (*indignationis* would be absurd, as personifying *indignatio*).
> *Malevolorum minas contempsi.* I despised the threats of malice (*malevolentia* could not be personified as "malice" is).

Even where Latin can use an abstract noun, an adjective or participle is often preferred. Thus . *arrogantis est sibi confidere,* "arrogance is self-confident;" *stulti est nugis delectare,* "folly delights in trifles" (where *arrogantiae, stultitiae* would be permissible).

The English genitive of definition is often set aside for a corresponding adjective in Latin : *res alienae* (not *aliorum*), "the affairs of others."

The process however is sometimes, and not unnaturally, reversed, for in both languages the genitive or "of" case is eminently "adjectival," *i e* fitted for adding or attaching to another substantive   Thus:

In tanta rerum obscuritate.   In such obscure matters.

In hac magnificentia rerum.   In the midst of this splendid scene

41. Oftener still, the substitute for the English noun is to be found in the Latin **Verb**, used either alone or in various combinations.   Thus .

Respondere, to give a reply ; *eligere,* to make choice of , *mentiri,* to tell a lie ; *tecum pugnat,* he is in conflict with you.

The English verbs "answer," "choose," etc, can no doubt, and *sometimes* would, be substituted for the longer expressions given ; but in Latin the verb would always be preferred.

Very often the substantive will be expressed by the combination of a neuter (generally plural) adjective or pronoun, and the verb :

Haec praecepit   These were his maxims

Haec fremebat vulgus.   Such was the popular cry.

Often the English verbal noun must be expressed by the impersonal use of the Latin intransitive verb:

Ad arma concurritur.   There is a rush to arms

This is far more common than *ad arma concursus fit.*

There are no doubt a large number of verbal nouns in -*tio, -sio,* and in -*tus, -sus;* but they are by no means so widely used as the English verbal nouns derived from them, or answering to them (such as those in -*ing*) Their use should be carefully watched.   A few instances will be given at the end of this section.

42. The English noun will often be expressed by the **infinitive,** either the *substantival* or the *dependent* infinitive :

Liberius dicere mihi non licuit.   Greater freedom of speech was not permitted me.

Sperat se brevi liberatum iri.   He hopes for freedom at an early date.

Mori satius fuit.   Death would have been better.

Sometimes a clause is necessary; *e.g.*

(1.) A dependent interrogative :

Quid tempus postularet parum vidisti. You were blind to
the requirements of the crisis.
Ubi ceciderit incertum est. The place (or "scene") of his
fate is uncertain.

(2.) A relative clause :

Qui patrem meum occiderunt. My father's murderers.

(3.) A conjunctional clause (*quod, ne, dum, ut,* etc., *si*) :

Id egi ut salvus esses. Your safety was my aim.
Dum Roma absum, bis causam meam egisti. During my
absence from Rome you twice pleaded my cause.

43. The **participle** is often used (in the oblique cases)
to represent both a class of persons and an abstract noun;
e.g.

Adstantium clamoribus perterritus conticuit. Terrified by
the shouts of the bystanders, he became silent.
Jam querentium et indignantium audiri voces. And now
expressions were being heard of remonstrance and
indignation.

N.B.—Such expressions as " tears of grief," etc., may often
be turned by two substantives, *cum dolore ac fletu* (or *lacrimis*) :
never by *lacrimae doloris*.

Assentantem te aversatus sum, minantem contemno. I turned
with disgust from your sycophancy ; I despise your
threats.

So the ablative absolute :

Te repugnante. In spite of your resistance.
Nerone regnante. In the reign of Nero.

The English verbal noun followed by " of " is often
represented by a passive participle or gerundive conjoined
with a substantive :

Propter amissam classem condemnatus est. He was condemned for the loss of the fleet (*amissionem classis*
would be inadmissible).

In the majority of these instances it will be noticed how often the Latin shrinks from the *abstract* or more general expression, and uses the *concrete* form—one, that is, which applies to the individual *person*, or *thing*, or *event* concerned or described.

44. There are a great many abstract nouns in Latin, yet even these are often illogically, as it seems to us, divested of their abstract nature and used in the plural Thus *turpitudines, furores, amicitiae,* and many other plurals, are used to denote the idea either of *various kinds* of baseness, etc., or the general idea of madness or friendship when seen in *more than a single case*.

> *Multorum hominum inimicitias ac furores pertuli.* I have endured the hostility and madness of many.

We may compare the English "virtues," "vices," "abilities," etc. ; the last word is in Latin always singular, *ingenium,* unless more than one person is spoken of; we cannot say *hujus viri,* but only *horum* (*hominum*), *ingenia.*

C.—On the use of Participles as Substantives and Adjectives.

45. As already noticed, the present participle is sometimes, the past participle frequently, used as a substantive : *e g. amans, infans, adolescens, candidatus, praefectus, jurisconsultus, acta* ("measures"), *merita* ("services"), *peccatum, responsum.* The future participle is only so used in *futurum, futura* ("the future").

The number of participles, both present and past, which are used precisely as **adjectives** with degrees of comparison is very large.

The present participles so used are mostly those of intransitive verbs. Where transitive participles are so used they often are joined as adjectives with a genitive of definition in place of the accusative of the nearer object.

(*a.*) Intransitive verbs:

> *Abstinens,* self-denying; *audens,* daring (in good sense, *audax* rather in bad); *fidens,* trustful; *confidens,* presumptuous; *florens, -ntissimus,* at the height of fame or prosperity; *florentissima republica,* in the "palmy" or best days of the nation, *nocens, -ntissimus,* guilty; *praesens,* ready, instant (*animus, paena*).

(*b.*) Transitive verbs:

> *Amans (mei,* etc.), *-ntissimus,* attached: *appetens,* "selfish," and with genitive "desirous of;" *experiens, -ntissimus,* active.

Such participial adjectives are largely represented in English:

> A smiling prospect, *aspectus amoenus;* burning heat, *aestus fervidus,* threatening letter, *literae minaces,* appalling cruelty, *crudelitas nefaria;* moving story, *narratio flebilis* or *movendis animis apta,* etc.

The number of **passive** participles used as **adjectives** is very large; such are:

> *Absolutus (omnibus numeris),* 'perfect' (in every respect); *confertus,* crowded; *doctus, eruditus, litteratus,* learned, highly cultivated, literary; *erectus (animus),* high-strung; *victoria parata,* easy victory; *reconditus,* deep, recondite; *res abstrusa ac recondita,* so deep and mysterious a question.

So entirely have some participles passed into adjectives that they are used with the negative prefix *in,* which is never combined with verbs: *infans, impotens, innocens, insipiens, inauditus, incultus, indomitus, imperitus, invidus.* Even *intactus* and (later on) *immutatus* were used in the sense of unbroken, unchanged, not as the participles of *infringo* and *immuto.*

D—On Substantives in -tor, -sor, -tio, -sio.

46. The English verbal substantive in *-er* (*doer*, *murderer*, etc.), or (derived from Latin) *-tor*, *-sor* (" vindicator," " liberator," " successor," and many other masculine substantives) can rarely be turned by the Latin substantive of like signification in *-tor*, *-sor*.

Such Latin words denote not merely the momentary presence in an individual of the action or state indicated, but its existence as a permanent or exceedingly characteristic quality

They are used, therefore, to denote an office or profession, *dictator*, *censor*, *mercator*, *pictor*, *gubernator*, *rerum scriptor* (historian), or a person in whom a special act is so prominent that it may be used as a distinguishing title. Thus Brutus and Cassius might be called either *Caesaris interfectores* or, on the other hand, *patriae liberatores*, but neither of the words would be used in an ordinary case. So *bellator* is one great in war, *venator*, a passionate hunter,[1] *proditor*, one capable of betraying his city or country So Fabius was called *cunctator*.

Cicero thus uses *emendator ac corrector noster* ironically = " this would-be improver and reformer." So *concionator*, one who speaks in the style of the hustings, as opposed to *orator*, a real speaker.

The commonest exception is *auctor*, which is constantly used as the " prompter,' " suggester," " adviser," " asserter," of great or little matters ·

> *Te auctore hoc feci.* I did this at your suggestion.

In all ordinary cases, the English noun in *-er*, *-tor*, *-sor*, will be represented by a *qui*-clause or some one of the substitutes mentioned above , *e.g.*

> His predecessors on the throne *Qui ante eum regnaverunt*
> The champion of my cause. *Qui meam causam* (or *causae meae patrocinium*) *suscepit.*

---

[1] Cp. Virgil's *bellator equus* (*G.* ii. 145, *Aen* x. 891, etc), *venator canis* (*Aen* xii. 751), where *bellator*, *venator*, are equivalent to adjectives descriptive of characteristic quality.

47. The use of substantives in -*tio* and -*sio* in Latin authors is not nearly so wide as that of their English derivatives in -*tion*, -*sion*, and they rarely answer to the English verbal substantive in -*ing*, though, as denoting originally the action of the verb, they in some respects resemble it.

Among the commonest are *admiratio*, *dubitatio*, *existimatio* (good name), *expectatio*, *conjunctio*, *disjunctio*, *exercitatio* (facility acquired by practice), *occupatio*, *obsessio*, *op-* and *ex- pugnatio*

Also *dictio*, mode of speaking, style ; *defensio*, mode of defence ; *educatio*, mode of educating ; with *divinatio*, power of foretelling ; *explicatio*, expository power. So they often express "*means of ·*" *neque valetudinis curatio, neque navigatio, neque frugum fructuumque perceptio et conservatio ulla esse potuisset, omnem ei excusationem adimere volui ;* this is natural, as their true meaning is the *act* or *process* of doing that which the verb denotes.

48. Verbals in -*tus* are derived both from transitive and from intransitive verbs   Such are *afflatus*, inspiration ; *discessus*, departure ; *habitus*, demeanour ; *incessus*, gait (mode of walking) ; *vestitus*, mode of dressing , *sensus*, consciousness, power of feeling ; *aditus*, means of approach   Often the forms in -*tio* and -*tus* are used side by side ; some verbs have one, some another, some both, many neither. Thus :

> *Est enim interitus quasi discessus et secretio ac diremtus earum partium quae ante interitum conjunctione aliqua tenebantur.*

We may use *consensus*, and supply its place in the dative singular and in the plural by *consensio ;* so with *dominatus* and *dominatio*. But we must carefully distinguish *ambitus* and *ambitio*, *status* and *statio*, *quaestus* and *quaestio*, *visus* and *visio*.

Both classes are used sometimes to express neither an act nor a state, but a *result* or *product*. Thus :

> *Cogitationes, adumbrationes, lucubrationes meae.* My (i e the result of my) meditations, sketches, nightly labours.
> *Belli apparatus omnis.* All the material of war.

See Exercise VI , on the Use of Substantives.

IV.

Use of Adverbs in Latin and English.

49. The Adverb is so called because its main function is to qualify the verb. It is the proper satellite of the verb or "instrument of predication," as the adjective is of the substantive, the preposition of the noun:

He ran *swiftly* *Fortiter pugnavit.*

But as an adjective indicates by its nature some special quality as seen in or attached to a person or thing, so many adverbs will naturally be combined with adjectives to express the amount or degree of the quality expressed by the adjective; *e.g*

"Very good," "truly great." *Vir vere magnus.*

It may even qualify an adverb, adding a qualification of *degree* to one of *kind:*

Very negligently. *Admodum sapienter.*

50. So far the two languages agree. In both languages adverbs are formed largely from oblique cases of nouns, though the inflection is often obsolete, or altered by long use.

Thus "needs," "always," are old genitives; "seldom," a dative; "there," "here," "where," locatives So *certo, diu, improbe, certe,* are existing or old ablatives; *multum, palam, sensim, saltem,* accusatives; *ubi, ibi,* locatives. In both languages a preposition with a case is often equivalent to an adverb: "on a sudden," *ex improviso.* Compare "aloft" (on), "betimes" (by), "indeed," "of old," "to-day," "perchance," with *de integro, admodum, per vim.* In both also adverbs are formed by adding a *suffix* to an adjective: "likely," "fairly," *graviter, divinitus;* and in both the adverb is sometimes a compressed sentence, *i.e.* contains a verb: "how-be-it," "to be sure," "may-hap," *scilicet* (*scire licet*), *videlicet* (*videre licet*). Sometimes we have an obvious compound: "notwithstanding," "nevertheless," *quotidie, imprimis.*

51. In both languages also there is an endless variety of phrases used as adverbs. "He did this to the great benefit of the nation" contains a long adverbial phrase as obviously as *hoc cum summo reipublicae emolumento fecit.*

In both languages also the adverb is sometimes identical with the preposition—"on," "up," "before," "after," "above," etc., *ante, post, supra, circa,*—and may be used as either; *e.g.*

> "After many years," "many years after." *Post multos annos, multis post annis.*

In both, the adverb is often used as a conjunction. In "when did you come?" *when* is an interrogative adverb, but in "I ask when you came," *when* is a conjunction; so with *ubi* or *quando*, etc.

In both the number of *pronominal* adverbs is very large. "Where," "when," "there," then," are obviously derived from interrogative and demonstrative pronouns; but so also in Latin are *ubi* (*quubi*), *quum, quando, cur, quâ, quo, eo, ibi*, and many others, most of which are used both as adverbs and conjunctions.

52. In both, also, the most important in meaning is the negative *non*, "not," as the modification which it attaches to the verb or adjective is that of absolute contradiction.

In Latin, as in English, the old negative was *ne*. The English "not" is a shorter form of the stronger and compound negative *nôght, nought, no whit;* it is analogous to the French negative *ne . . . pas* (a step), or *point* (a point).

So in Latin it is well to remember that *ne*, which in Classical Latin is either prohibitive or a conjunction meaning "lest," is the old negative. We see it in *ne . . . quidem,* and the compounds, *nefas, nemo* (*ne-homo*), *nullus, nunquam*, etc. *Non* is a compound, *ne-unum*. Of *haud* we know less. Its main use is with adjectives and adverbs and the verb *scio* (*haud scio an*).

Finally, in both languages adverbs may be classified as adverbs of *quality, quantity* or *amount* (including numeral adverbs), *place* and *time*.

In spite, however, of so much agreement, the right rendering of English adverbs and adverbial phrases into Latin requires care and observation, and it must never be assumed that an adverb in one language is best translated by an adverb in the other.[1]

53. A Latin adverb, for example, will often be sufficient to express an English phrase, or even clause:

Prudentissime abfuisti. You showed great wisdom by absenting yourself.

Parum e republica haec dicis. Your present language is far from constitutional.

Or two Latin adverbs may take the place of an adjective and substantive in an English adverbial phrase:

Modice ac sapienter. With a wise moderation.

Constanter ac sedate. With a calm courage, *or* with an undaunted calmness.

The Latin adverb may express the English adjective:

Prospere rem gessit. He carried on a successful campaign.

I will pay careful or zealous attention to this matter. *Hujus rei diligenter, studiose rationem habebo.*

I will take earnest heed . . . *Enixe (summo opere) operam dabo ut or ne . . .*

So—*Nullo privatim periculo.* With no personal danger.

Ego ille pacis semper laudator. I, once the invariable eulogiser of peace.

(In these two instances the adverb seems to qualify a substantive; in both cases, however, an adjective in the form of *nullo* and *ille* (pronominal adjectives) is combined.)

---

[1] See Arnold, rev. ed., §§ 61-64.

54. On the other hand, the English adverb or adverbial phrase must sometimes be translated by the Latin adjective, or participle·

> *Aversos aggressus est.* He attacked them from behind.
> *Invitus, imprudens, huc veni.* I came here reluctantly, or unawares.

Sometimes the English adverb attached to a verb or adjective is represented in Latin by two verbs or adjectives:

> *Oro atque obsecro.* I urgently or earnestly entreat.
> *Perfecta et absoluta virtus.* Absolutely (or ideally) perfect virtue.

Sometimes the English adverb can only be represented by a clause: "undeniably," "indisputably," by *negari, dubitari, non potest, quin;* "fortunately," *opportune accidit ut;* "mysteriously," "unaccountably," by a verbal phrase, *nescio quomodo;* by a verb: "you are apparently setting out," by *proficisci videris;* by an impersonal phrase: "you are *obviously* wrong," *errare te manifestum* or *perspicuum est;* sometimes by a phrase, as *salva fide,* "honourably," etc.

See Exercise VII., on the Use of Adverbs. The meaning of some of the adverbs in ordinary use is explained below, after the Exercises.

V

Tenses in Latin and English.

55. It is the office of a Verb to combine together, in the form of an assertion (or else of a question or command), two separate objects of our thoughts.

But in order to make an assertion clear and precise, the verb requires other aids than this power of combining together two words or tenses.

One of the most essential of these is that of *Time;* and hence wherever we find a verb, we find it endowed with power, greater or less in different languages, of modifying its form so as to express relation of time What we call *tense* is simply an English form of the French word *temps,* "time"

In some languages the verb can do this by a series of changes in its form to a very large extent; others call in very largely the aid of auxiliary verbs. Greek, for instance, has a great number of tense-forms, both in the active and passive verb, and in all moods; Latin requires the help in some of the passive tenses of the verb *esse;* the English verb can distinguish between one present and one past tense without external aid, but calls in very largely the aid even there, and always in the future, of auxiliary verbs. "I see," "I saw," but "I am seeing," "I was seeing," "I have seen," "I had seen;" "I shall see," "You will see," etc.

Time or tense is not an absolute, but a relative notion. The same moment, say noon, may be either future, past, or present, according to the moment taken as the point of comparison it would be absurd to say, "Mid-day is past," unless we were speaking in the afternoon.

The most obvious point of comparison then for all languages is the moment at which language is being used, the time of speaking, all time must of necessity be either *simultaneous* with this, or *before* or *after* it.

These three divisions, then, of time mark the most obvious division of tenses into **Present, Past,** and **Future.** "I run," "I ran" (or "have run"), "I shall run:" *curro, cucurri, curram.*

[We may notice with interest that Latin forms its past tense either by a change within the word itself, such as reduplication, *canit, cecinit;* or as in *vĕnit, vēnit;* or by the addition of a final syllable or suffix, *amat, ama-vit, dic it, dic-s-it,* to the *stem* of the verb (that part of the verb to which inflexions are affixed); that English also either makes a similar change, "I see," "I saw," or adds a suffix, "I love," "I loved." It is interesting also to know that these terminal additions are fragments of auxiliary verbs attached to the end of a word —loved = love + did, *amaveram = amavi + eram*—exactly as the case-termination is the remains of an old prepositional word analogous to our where*to*, where*by;* and that the internal changes probably arose from and are contractions of reduplication, *veni = veveni*, the root of the verb being repeated twice to mark completion of an act, and so past time. But these are not questions with which we are at present concerned, though some knowledge of them adds greatly to the interest of the study of grammar.]

56. So far all is simple enough. But though all languages with which we are familiar have **tenses,** or a construction equivalent to a tense, to express **present, past,** and **future,** yet no two languages entirely coincide in their use of tenses; it is almost impossible for an Englishman to use one or two French tenses with perfect accuracy, and as great, or greater, care is required for the choice of the right tense in Latin.

Notice, first, that Old English had no future; it used the present for the future till it called in the aid first of *shall,* then of *will,* one expressing *obligation,* another *will* or purpose; and we constantly use a present in English where Latin more correctly uses a future : " I *go* to Rome next year;" "If you *see* my brother to-morrow, tell him to come to me if he *can.*"

But this is not nearly all the difference between the two languages. If we keep to the classification of tenses as denoting time compared with the moment at which we are speaking, we shall see some points of agreement, many of disagreement.

57. Both languages use the present in some extended and half-figurative sense; language cannot strike out a fresh tense for every shade of difference. Both use the present—(*a.*) in general assertions true of time present, but also of past and future summer follows winter; *fortes Fortuna adjuvat;* (*b*) in citing an author whose works remain: "St Paul says;" *scribit Thucydides; apud Platonem* (in, *or* in the works or pages of, Plato) *Socrates loquitur;* (*c*) in an animated narrative of past events, both English and Latin substitute present for past time This is a natural figure of speech, as things that are present move and stir us more than things that are past

But Latin employs this **historic present** far more widely and more freely than English In good English prose it is used sparingly, and when used is continued through the whole paragraph, and not intermingled with past tenses in either co-ordinate or subordinate clauses. But in the very best Latin writers the point of view will be shifted from the present to the past, and *vice versa*, with the greatest rapidity, and apparent irregularities will arise from such idioms as the use of past verbs in clauses dependent on present verbs, which will seem to set all rules at defiance, unless we remember that the historic present is often precisely equivalent to the historic past. *Scribit ut iis qui a Verre venissent, responderent* is literally, "he *writes* that they *were* to apply to those who *had* come from Verres;" in English we must either say *he wrote*, or, keeping *writes*, say *are* and *have* for *were* and *had*.

58. The Latin **Present** is also used, though not *nearly so often as the English*, in an anticipative and figurative sense for the future. *hoc ni propere fit,* . . . "unless this is done with speed," *antequam dicere incipio,* "before I begin to speak."

The Latin verb, however, is rich in future forms, which are used much oftener and more accurately than our own future. (See below, §§ 64, 65.)

But our own verb has a large number of compound present tenses formed by the aid of auxiliary verbs with which Latin cannot compete. "I see," "am seeing," "do see," our *indefinite, continuous*, and *emphatic* forms of the present tense are all represented by the Latin *video*.

The Latin present also, in combination with words or phrases expressing duration of time, answers to our continuous or progressive form of the present perfect:

> *Jam pridem*, or *tres jam menses, te videre cupio.* I have been long, *or* for full three months, desiring to see you.

Compare the French *depuis longtemps je parle;* the Greek πάλαι λέγω.[1]

In past time, the Latin imperfect answers here to our *continuous* pluperfect:

> *Multos jam annos domicilium Romae habebat Archias* Archias had now been resident at Rome for many years.

59. The future and past tenses exhibit more marked differences between the Latin and English tense-systems.

Thus far, in roughly dividing tenses into *present, past*, and *future*, the moment of speaking has been taken as the point of comparison. "I see," "I saw," "I shall see," at, before, after the moment at which I speak.

But language also takes sometimes a past, sometimes a future moment as the centre of comparison, and coins fresh tenses to denote a time simultaneous with, before, or after, that *other moment.*

We shall see this more easily by the use of English examples, though we must remember that the English verb forms much more precise and definite tenses by the aid of auxiliaries, and that we use them with less discrimination, and more sparingly, than is the case in Latin. Let us first consider *past* time.

---

[1] Arnold, rev. ed., §§ 181, 328.

60. If we are narrating an event as simply having happened in the past, we use the ordinary tense for narrative or history—the English *preterite* or *indefinite past;* adding perhaps some adverb or adverbial phrase of time to mark its exact place in the past. " I reached the summit at five o'clock." If we add to this, " Two men *had ascended* before me, and *were conversing,* a third *arrived* after me," we see that the verb " I reached" forms a point of comparison which we use as a measure of time for three other verbs : " had ascended," *i.e.* before that point of comparison; " were conversing," *i.e.* simultaneously with my reaching the summit; " came up," subsequent to that ' fixed point.

Now Latin and English agree in possessing two separate tenses (though English for both of these tenses, and Latin for one of them, in the passive voice, calls in the aid of an auxiliary verb) for the ideas of time, time *prior* to and time *coincident* with a point in the past, designated by a past tense, *perveni.* These two ideas are represented in Latin by the two tenses, *adscenderant, colloquebantur,* and these tenses are called the *pluperfect* and *imperfect.* The two languages also agree in possessing no tense to mark time subsequent to a past time; Latin being content to use the simple past tense, *advenit, intervenit,* adding where necessary an explanatory adverb or adverbial phrase—*mox, postea, tum,* etc.

We have here then two fresh tenses, commonly called the *pluperfect—plusquam perfectum,* " more than (complete or) past"—and *imperfect* or not fully complete tense. These two tenses are often called *secondary,* because the point of time with which they are compared is not the obvious and *primary, i.e.* first and principal one of the present moment, that *at* which, but another, that *of* which we are speaking. So far the two languages resemble each other, though they often differ in the application and use of these tenses.

61. If we now turn to future time, it is clear that we may also, by the use of the simple or indefinite English future (formed by the aid of an auxiliary), fix on a point in the future, which we may also define by some adverb or adverbial phrase, and round which we may group other tenses on a similar principle: "You *will be* in London next Tuesday." "I *shall be staying* at such or such a place, and *shall have done* my business, and *shall be* free to go on with you."

Here, as in past time, the indefinite future is used as the point of comparison round which are grouped *three* other ideas of time. one coincident with it, "I shall be staying;" one prior to it, "I shall have done," a third, for which we have again no separate form, subsequent to that point, "I shall be free." Now Latin has no two tenses to discriminate between the indefinite and the simultaneous future, "You will arrive," "I shall be staying," for *laudabo* means both "I shall praise" and "I shall be praising:" and, like English, it has no tense to mark time *subsequent to* a point in the future But it agrees with English in having a separate tense to mark **time, future as regards the present, but past as regards a future point of time** ; and it can express this in the active voice, not by the somewhat awkward circumlocution of "shall have," "will have," but by a single word or **true tense** (formed by annexing the future of *esse* to the past tense, *confeci*, *confecero*), and it differs **from English in using this tense far oftener than we use its English representative, and with the greatest nicety and precision.** This tense (*amavero, amatus ero*) is called the future perfect (*futurum exactum*) or the second future, and is one of the most characteristic tenses of the Latin language. (See below, §§ **64, 65.**)

We have thus added to the simple **present, past,** and **future** tenses, an **imperfect,** a **pluperfect,** and a **second future ;** and this without mentioning the Latin periphrastic or third future, formed by the participle in *-rus* and the verb *esse.*

62. But one tense constantly used in English and in Greek has not been mentioned.

The Latin past tense *cucurri* may be translated by " I ran," and " I have run;" by a simple tense, and by a *periphrastic* or *compound* tense: and the difference between these two English tenses is very great.

" I ran" is in modern English simply a past tense. It is the tense of narrative or history: " I saw him yesterday ;" " In the beginning God created the heavens and earth." The time in the past to which it refers is in itself, without the aid of the context or some explanatory word or words, quite vague; it does not imply (like the perfect proper, " I have done") any result or effect continuing to the present moment; and it is called in English Grammars the *preterite* or *simple past* tense, or sometimes the *indefinite* or *aorist* past (ἀόριστον). In French, where its use is in many points very different, it goes by the opposite name, *passé défini*. But side by side with this there has been formed in English, as in Greek (compare γέγραφα with ἔγραψα), another tense, which we sharply discriminate from this vague past tense by a different form of words. The words, " I have run," " I have seen," resemble " I ran," " I saw," in referring to past time; but the tense which they represent belongs not to the past only but to the present; it indicates not only a past state or action, but a *present result ;* the past is represented as completed (*perfectum*), and its result or effect as coming down to the moment of speaking: " I *have been* young, and now am old ;" " He *has killed* his brother," *i.e.* his brother is *now* dead ; " I *have written* my letter," which is *now* therefore finished. Hence we only use this tense of **those past events, the effect or result of which we may consider as still existing.** We should not say, " Cain has killed Abel," or " The Normans have conquered England ;" nor should we say, " God has created the world," unless we intend to add some effect or purpose of this act, which we look at as still present, " in order to give man a field of action," etc.

63. We express this tense mainly by an auxiliary which denotes possession, for possession implies previous existence of what we now possess, and we see some traces of the same process in Latin, *hoc cognitum habeo*,[1] " I have ascertained this," " I am in possession of this," as a point ascertained; as also in Greek, κρύψας ἔχει   But, great as is the difference between this tense, which we may call the true perfect, and the simple past tense, Latin (as indeed did early English) uses the same tense for both. *Dixi* means both " I said " and " I have spoken," *i e.* have finished my speech, *vixerunt*, "they lived" and " they are no more ;" *amatus sum*, " I have been loved " and " I was loved," and which of the two meanings the so called Latin perfect bears, whether in the indicative or subjunctive, must be decided by the context.[2]

This **perfect** tense, then, as expressing completion, belongs at once to present and past time   It is usually classed in modern English Grammars as a present tense, and in Latin Grammars as the past or (so-called) perfect. *Scripsi* when used as a true perfect is classed with the present and future as a *primary* tense, *i e.* as representing past time, not vaguely but in distinct reference to the *moment at which* we *are* speaking   This is in all probability the earliest sense of the English past and Latin perfect tenses, or rather of those which are formed by an internal change, and not by a suffix, *e.g.* "I saw," "I ran," *cecidi, veni*, as compared with I told, I walked, *ama-vi, cae(d)si, mon-ui*.

In Greek we see the difference at once:

γέγραφα γέγραμμαι.
ἔγραψα ἐγράφθην.

---

[1] In such phrases, at any rate during the classical period, *habeo* does not wholly lose its possessive sense. We may compare it with such phrases as *urbem jamdiu obsessam tenet*, "He has long been closely besieging the city," or with *hoc me sollicitum habet*, "This keeps me anxious." But that in the popular dialect, especially in the provincial speech of the later Empire, *habere* and *tenere* came to have a merely auxiliary force, is probable from the extensive use in the " Romance " derivatives from Latin of *avoir*, *avere* (Ital.), *tener* (Span.), as simple auxiliaries.

[2] The same tense in form, *j'ai ecrit*, is used so differently in French that it goes by the name of the *passé indéfini*.

64. It remains to compare the use of each of these tenses in Latin with that of their English representatives.

The first future is used in Latin where we use either the indefinite or *continuous* future: *scribam,* "I shall write, or shall be writing;" but the latter is the meaning which, as contrasted with that of *scripsero,* "I shall have written," it constantly bears where it is not necessary to express this in an English translation.

It is used in Latin in this sense where we use the present in a figurative and anticipative sense:

> *Naturam si sequemur ducem, nunquam aberrabimus.* If we follow Nature as our guide we shall never go wrong.

Here *sequemur* means if, or as long as, we shall be following; and implies time coincident with that marked by *aberrabimus.* So

> *Quem haec civitas, dum erit, laudabit.* Whom this nation will praise as long as it exists, or "shall be in existence."

We must be careful, therefore, to examine the real force of our English present in all subordinate sentences where the principal verb is in the future; in all probability a Latin future will be required.   So

> *Vel ducam vos, quo voletis, vel sequar.* We should say where or whither you wish.

In Latin the word used means "shall wish," or "be wishing."

So, too, where we use the present in a clause subordinate to a command or wish relating to the future, Latin prefers the more accurate future:

> *Tu si poteris mihi occurras velim.* Do you (on a future occasion) meet me if you *can,* or *are* able.
>
> *Tum vero ii qui poterunt se recipiant.* When that time comes (marked by the emphatic *tum vero*) let those who *can* retreat.

Latin uses the future, as does English, in a figurative sense for the imperative : *hoc animadvertes,* "you *will* notice this," a strongly-expressed statement as to the future, especially in the second person, being almost equivalent to a command : just as our "shall," implying properly obligation, passes from the simple future of the first person into a threat when used in the second "You shall go to prison."

65. But the precision with which the Latin speaks of future time as compared to the very loose language of English is seen still more in the case of the *future perfect.* Its English representative, "shall have," is too cumbrous a form to be often used; we mostly substitute the present or the perfect.

For instance, we say, "he who *does* this shall be punished;" but *does,* though a present tense, represents a time *future* as regards the present, but *past* and *complete* as regards the future time fixed by the principal verb "shall-be-punished."

Future Perfect, or Future II

The Romans, therefore, neither used *facit* for "does," nor *faciet* for "shall do"—the one would imply "is doing," the other "shall be doing"—but *fecerit : qui hoc fecerit, poenas dabit.* Thus ·

(a) *Quod nisi facis in vincula te duci jubebo*
(b)   „   *facies*   ·,   „
(c.)   „   *feceris*   „   „

are all three good Latin. But (*a.*) means "unless you are doing this," *i e* are ready to do it at once; (*b*) unless you shall be doing this at a fixed time, while (*c*) *feceris* answers to our "unless you *do* this I will order you to be imprisoned."

But this tense represents not only the English loosely-used *present,* but also, where the principal verb is in the future or imperative, the English *perfect* ·

    Quae cum fecero, Romam ibo, or . . *ad me veni.* And when
        I have done this I shall go to Rome, *or* come to me.

We see here that the English perfect is far more loosely used than the corresponding tense in Latin.

66. Hence the extremely common use of this Future perfect tense in Latin subordinate clauses, though we rarely meet with it in English.

Its ordinary place is in *subordinate* clauses, after a conjunction or relative, but it is sometimes, by a figure of speech, used in the *principal* clauses to express certainty or promptness. The act or state which it expresses will be over by a fixed time, often unexpressed.[1] *Recte feceris,* "you will have done right," *i.e.* "you will find that you have acted rightly; you will certainly do right;" so *vicero,* "I shall, if something happen, prove the conqueror."

Another common use is in postponing a decision: *mox videro,* "I will look to this hereafter," *i.e. in good time;* so, probably by an extension of the same idea, in handing over a decision to others, *viderint posteri* or *alii,* or *tu videris,* "I *leave* to posterity, or to others, *or* to you *to decide."*

Observe :

This tense *only exists in the indicative mood.* In the subjunctive its place is taken by the *perfect subjunctive,* which resembles it in form in all persons but the first, *scripserim, scripsero ;* but when it passes over into *oratio obliqua* as dependent on a *past* verb *sentiendi et declarandi* in past time, **its place is taken by the pluperfect subjunctive.** Thus *si hoc feceris* (fut. ii.) *in vincula te duci jubebo* will become after *dicit* (he says) *te si hoc feceris* (perf. subj) *in vincula duci,* etc., *jussurum esse :* after *dixit* (he said) it becomes *te si hoc fecisses, in vincula duci jussurum esse.*

---

[1] Compare the use of the same tense in Greek to express a strong denial :

οὐ γὰρ Κρέοντος προστάτου γεγράψομαι, *i.e.* I shall certainly not be enrolled as a client of Creon. "I shall not find myself enrolled."

67. But, besides these two future tenses, Latin employs a third, the periphrastic future, or **future iii**, formed of the participle in *-rus* and the appropriate tense or mood of the verb *esse*, which in some of its uses resembles a fresh *mood* rather than a mere tense. *Hoc facturus sum, eram fui, fueram, ero*, means, " I am, was, had been, shall be, either about to do (*i.e.* on the point of doing) this ; or intending to, or likely to, or even destined to do this ;" *e.g.*

> *Hoc anno neminem in vincula duci sum passurus.* I do not intend to suffer any one to be imprisoned in the present year.
>
> *Jam urbem expugnaturus erat consul.* The consul was just on the point of taking the city by assault.
>
> *Nemini persuasurus es.* You are not likely to persuade any one
>
> *Quoquo modo nos gesserimus, fiet quod futurum est.* In whatever manner we behave, that which is to be will come to pass ; " what will be shall be."

The last example is a good instance of the use of all three forms of the future.

Owing to this wide range of meaning, the periphrastic future in past tense often takes the place of a pluperfect subjunctive :

> *Arma tradituri fuistis* You would have surrendered your arms.

It differs from *tradidissetis*, as expressing the same idea more vividly (" you were on the point of doing so"), and is very largely used (in the perfect tense) to express the same idea in the subjunctive mood :

> *Quaesivit num arma tradituri fuerint* (not *tradidissent*). He asked whether *they would have* surrendered their arms.
>
> *Adeo territi sunt ut arma tradituri fuerint* (not *tradidissent*) *ni, etc.* They were so alarmed that they would have surrendered their arms had not, etc

N.B.—**This tense is not, as in fut. ii., confined to the indicative, but takes the place of a non-existent future in the subjunctive, and forms the ordinary future of the infinitive mood.**

Past Tenses of the Indicative.

68. The difference between the two English tenses, the **preterite** or **aorist**, " I wrote," and the **true perfect**, " I have written," has been already explained; and it has been shown that one tense has to play the part of both in Latin.

Conticuerunt tuae literae may mean, according to the context, either " your letters have become silent," *i.e.* " no longer speak to me," " have ceased," or " became silent " at some indefinite time in the past.[1]

The Latin perfect, however, is more commonly used as an aorist or simple past tense.   In itself, when so used, it is the natural tense of narrative, and implies nothing as to continuance, or repetition, or place before or after another past event.   We may say *diu restitere*, " they held their ground long;" or *saepe dixit*, " he often said;" or (and this is the usual form) *postquam venit*, " after he came," or had come; or *tum venit*, " then he came."

But though colourless in itself, it gains, when contrasted with the imperfect tense, the meaning of a *point* of time rather than of a *continuous period*, and *relates*, without enlarging on, a fact, which the imperfect is used to *describe;* and **this distinction is of great importance both in the indicative and subjunctive moods.**

69. The imperfect is the tense of *incomplete* as opposed to *completed*, of *continuous* as opposed to *momentary*, action ; of *description* as opposed to *recital ;*[2] of *surrounding circumstances* as opposed to the *main fact ;* of *repetition*, or *habit*, or a *series* of acts, as opposed to a *single* act ; and hence it answers to such English phrases as " began to," " proceeded to," " tried to," " continued to," " were seen to,"

---

[1] *Novi* (*nosco* is not used in prose) means always, " I *have* ascertained," " I know ;" so *memini, odi ;* so *actum est de*, " it *is* all over with."

[2] *Perfecto procedit, imperfecto insistit oratio*, " the narrative goes on in the one tense, pauses in the other," says an old grammarian.

" were in the habit of," " used to," " would," etc., and also to
ideas conveyed, sometimes by these phrases, but oftener
not expressed at all in the English. For in English,
from our not having, as so many other languages have, a
true imperfect tense (but only a substitute), we include a
large number of these ideas, unless we wish to emphasise
them, under the simple preterite or aorist, but in translating English into Latin we must **never substitute the
Latin aorist perfect for our preterite without asking ourselves whether the imperfect is not required.** (See Arnold,
rev. ed., 183, 184.)

70. The imperfect, denoting time simultaneous with
some point in the past, is constantly used in a narrative
to describe the circumstances or feelings which *accompanied* the main fact as *stated* by the aorist perfect, where
in English we should make no distinction :

> *Tum montem conscendere incepimus* (the main statement);
> *erat summa altitudine et negabant ducrs id posse fieri*

Fuit would here be used in an independent statement,
but *erat* describes the circumstance which then caused
us such difficulty ; so with *negabant*. In English all three
verbs would be in the same tense.

So a sentence in Caesar begins : *Caesar armis rem gerere
constituit ;* this is followed by *videbat* and *reputabat,*
introducing the reasons which influenced him in this
determination to decide the question by arms; an English
writer would use the same tense throughout.

71. This characteristic of the imperfect, as describing
simultaneous and continuous action in the past (the two
ideas are closely connected), is of great importance not
only in the indicative but in the subjunctive mood. Thus
in a subordinate clause :

> *Quaesivi cur hoc faceret.* I asked why he was doing this
> *Quaesivi cur hoc fecerit.* I asked why he did (*aorist*) this
> *Quaesivi cur hoc fecisset.* I asked why he had done this.

Historic Infinitive.

In an animated narrative, as the place of the **aorist
perfect** is often taken by the "historic present," so
the "historic infinitive," *i.e.* the infinitive used independently after a subject in the nominative, often takes
the place of the **descriptive imperfect**, especially where a
series or rapid succession of events is described. It is a
means of introducing variety into a narrative; and it is
used by the best Latin writers, when they wish to give a
lively picture of past events, side by side both with the
imperfect, the aorist perfect, and the historic present.
Instances will be found repeatedly in Caesar (*e.g.B.G.* i. 16),
and Cicero and Livy make abundant use of it. As a rule,
at least two or three such infinitives are used in succession :

> *Clamare omnes, ego instare.* A general cry arose, I pressed
> the point.

Pluperfect.

72. This tense has been already defined. It does not
differ widely in its use in Latin from our own use of the
same tense, except that **it is the regular tense in a subordinate clause following a relative or conjunction by which
frequency or repetition in the past is expressed.**

> *Quos viderat ad se vocabat.* Whomever he saw, he would
> call to him.
> *Quoties eo venerat, loco delectabatur.* As often as he came
> there he was charmed with the situation.

It corresponds in such clauses to the imperfect in the
principal clauses.

It mostly gives place to the aorist perfect indicative
after *postquam, ubi*, etc., but with *quum* represents in the
subjunctive the absent past participle of Latin active
verbs. Thus, *ubi* or *postquam pervenit*, but always *quum
pervenisset*, for "having arrived."

TENSES OF THE INFINITIVE.

73. The Latin infinitive, though asserting its *verbal* nature by the possession of tenses, is naturally, from its *substantival* character, not so rich in them as the indicative. Of its three tenses in the active voice, one (the future) has to be formed by the aid of an auxiliary verb and the participle in -*rus*, and as all verbs have not this participle it has often recourse to a somewhat awkward periphrasis.

The present infinitive expresses time strictly contemporaneous with the verb on which it depends, whether that verb be in present, past, or future time. Thus:

> *Dico, dicam, dixi, me otiosum esse.* I say, shall say, *or* said, that I am, *or* was, at leisure.

Here we see that in English the use of the conjunction *that* with a finite verb after a principal verb in a past tense involves a past tense in the dependent clause, so that the Latin present infinitive represents an English imperfect. Again:

> *Hoc facere poteram, possum, potero,* I was, am, *or* shall be able to do this,

where the English present infinitive is also used with all three; but if we substitute in the past and present tenses the English *might* or *could* we see a difference; for these English auxiliaries do not retain enough of their original past sense to dispense with the aid of a past tense in the infinitive to make their meaning clear, and we say, " I might do " for present, but " I might *have done*," " I could *have done*," for past time. So we translate *hoc facere debui* by " I ought to *have done* this," as " ought," though a past tense, is now used in a present sense : " I *ought* to do or be doing this." **This important difference between the two languages must be carefully noticed.**

The Latin past or perfect infinitive denotes time *prior* to that of the verb on which it depends, but it includes under one form the meanings both of the aorist and true perfect indicative and also of the pluperfect :

> *Dico eum me fefellisse.* I say that he deceived, has *or* had deceived me.

In each case *fefellisse* denotes time *prior* to that of *dico*, but the context or some other words must decide as to the precise relation of the time.

74. For the future the Latin infinitive has no one definite tense. With active verbs that have a participle in *-rus*, it forms its future of this participle and the verb *esse* or *fore,* and uses this whenever the time expressed by the verb in the infinitive is subsequent to that of the verb on which it depends, whatever the tense of the other verb :

> *Credo, credam, credidi eum venturum esse.* I believe, shall believe, that he will come ; I believed that he would come.

Latin also, which is more precise in marking future time than English, uses the future infinitive after verbs of hoping, promising, etc.

" He hopes to do this" is not *sperat facere hoc (se),* which would mean " he hopes, flatters himself, that he *is doing* this," but *sperat se hoc facturum esse.*

Many verbs have no future in *-rus,* and the Latin has no passive future participle. In both cases the want is supplied by the periphrasis *fore,* or *futurum esse, ut :*

> *Credo fore ut convalescat,* or *ut urbs capiatur.*
> *Credidi fore ut convalesceret,* or *ut urbs caperetur.*
> I believe that he will get well, *or* that the city will be taken.
> I believed that he would get well, *or* that the city would be taken.

With passive verbs there is also another substitute for the missing future infinitive passive, viz a combination of the supine in -*um* with the impersonal *iri*, e g · *credidit urbem expugnatum iri:* an expression which can only be literally translated by the uncouth phrase, "he believed that there was a going to take the city." The accusative *urbem* is governed by the supine, which has an active force, and is itself an accusative of motion towards.

The infinitive of *esse, fuisse*, with the participle in -*rus*, is also used to supply the place of an infinitive to the potential mood, to express our "would" or "would have." As *facturus sum* is very near in sense to *hoc faciam*, "I would do this," *facturus fui* is very near in sense to *hoc fecissem*, "I would have done this," so we must translate, "I believe, *or* believed, that you would do this," by *hoc te facturum esse credo, credidi;* "I believe, *or* believed, that you would have done this," by *hoc te facturum fuisse credo, credidi;* while for the passive we are obliged to use a long periphrasis :

> *Credo* or *credidi futurum fuisse ut urbs expugnaretur.* I believe, *or* believed, that the city would have been stormed.

The infinitive of the future ii , *scripsero*, is rarely needed. It can however be expressed in active and passive verbs by a combination of *fore ut* with the perfect subjunctive :

> *Credo fore ut antequam tu veneris ego epistolam perscripserim.* I believe I shall have finished the letter before you come ;

in the passive, *fore ut epistola perscripta fuerit ;* and in deponent verbs by such a combination as *sperat se adeptum fore*, "he hopes to have obtained."

NOTE ON CONSECUTIO TEMPORUM (SEQUENCE OF TENSES).

75. Though familiarity with the ordinary rules on this point is assumed throughout this book, it may be convenient to recapitulate them here.

A.—After a *present, future,* or even the more rare *true perfect* tense, in the principal clause we use—

(1.) A present subjunctive to denote contemporaneous (or vaguely used future) time :

> *Mitto, mittam (misero) qui tibi subveniant.* I send, will send, men to aid you.
> *Sunt qui dicant.* There are persons who say.

So—*Ita vixi ut non frustra me natum esse intelligam.* I have so lived that *I* see that I was not born into the world in vain.

[But very often this perfect is treated as a past tense:

> *Haec dixi ut intelligeres.* I have said this that you may perceive; *i.e.* that you might while I spoke.]

(2.) The perfect subjunctive to express previous time :

> *Adeo crudelis est ut nemini unquam pepercerit.* He is so cruel that he never spared any one.
> *Oblitus sum quid initio dixerim.* I have forgotten what I said in the beginning.

B—If the principal verb is in an *historic* tense, *i.e.* aorist perfect, imperfect, pluperfect, the dependent verb will be—

(1.) If it denotes time contemporaneous, in the *imperfect:*

> *Imperavit ut obsides darent* (proceed to give). *Fuere qui dicerent.* (There were some who said at the time.)
> *Quaesivi quis vellet mecum ire.* I asked who was (at the time) ready to go with me.
> *Tanti erant fluctus ut jam desperaremus.* The waves were such that we were now beginning to despair.

(2.) If it denotes time previous to that of the principal verb, in the pluperfect. The pluperfect is used in such combinations as—

> *Quaerebam, quaesii, quaesiveram,   quis hoc fecisset.*
>   I asked,   had asked, who *had* done this.
> *Erant quibus haec olim placuissent.* There were some whom this course *had* once pleased.
> *Oblitus eram quid initio dixissem.*   I had forgotten what I had said in the beginning.

[But very often for the sake of liveliness of expression the perfect subjunctive is used in place of the pluperfect, the point of comparison being shifted from the past time of the principal verb to present time:

> *Dixit se eundem esse qui semper fuerit.* He said that he was the same as he always had been (literally, " has been ").]

VI.

The Use of Moods.

(See Arnold, rev. ed., Ex. XIX.)

76. Every verb, when used as a **verb** in the full sense of the word, and not as a **noun** (infinitive, participle, etc.), implies a connection between *two* objects of our thoughts, a *subject* and a *predicate*.

Now this connection of two separate objects, or terms of a proposition or statement, may be looked on by the mind in various lights, and therefore expressed in language in different *manners* or *modes*, irrespective of those which regard time, and which are therefore called tenses.

For instance we may use a verb simply to assert an agreement between two objects of thought, *i.e.* to make a *statement*: He is good, or bad, etc. But we may also ask a *question*: "Is he good?" or we may address a *command* to a person, "Come here," or a *prayer*, "Grant me this," or an *exhortation*, "Let us show courage," or we may state a fact with *hesitation*, "It may be so," or ask a question with a form implying *perplexity*, "What am I to do?" or we may express a *wish*, "Would I were there!" and we can imagine a language which expressed such and all other conceivable modes of uniting two different terms, not by an alteration in the order of the words, nor by importing an auxiliary verb, nor by anything in the tone or accent, but by **modifying the form of the verb itself. A "mood," then, is a change effected in the form of the verb** to represent some special condition of the mind of the speaker when he uses a verb; *i.e.* when he combines together two separate objects of thought, and uses language to express such combination.[1]

---

[1] "*Modi sunt diversae inclinationes animi* (movements, variations of the human mind), *quas varia consequitur declinatio* (inflexion) *verbi.*"—(Priscian, A.D. 500.)

77. The number of moods is greatest in the languages of uncivilised tribes without a written literature. In Latin the number of moods is limited to three —1 The expression of *fact* or reality ("**Indicative**'), 2. The expression of *conception* or supposition,—condition, contingency, wish, purpose, etc. ("**Subjunctive**"); 3. The expression of *command* ("**Imperative**") [1] These are the three moods of the Latin verb, and though Greek has nominally a fourth, the "Optative,' the group of tenses which bear that name are really part of the mood of conception, answering in many syntactical uses to the "historic," as the "subjunctive" group answers to the "primary" tenses of the Latin subjunctive. English has in one sense three moods, but the imperative is confined to the second person, and the subjunctive is gradually disappearing, its place being taken either by auxiliary verbs, or by the indicative, as shown below

78. Of the three Latin moods, the use of the **indicative** and **imperative** requires no comment; in the expression of simple assertion or command there is no essential difference between Latin and English The most important characteristic of the Latin as compared with the English verb is the **subjunctive mood**, the correct use of which is one of the greatest difficulties in Latin composition, and one of the best tests of a knowledge of Latin syntax.

This arises from the fact, that while the Romans used this mood very largely, it has almost disappeared as a parate mood, that is, as a distinct form of the verb itself, from modern English.

Its use is occasionally retained in clauses beginning with " though " and " if " " Though he *slay* me, yet will I trust in him," would probably be expressed in more recent English prose by the aid of an auxiliary verb, " Though he *were* to slay me ." but we still say, " If

---

[1] The term " Subjunctive " is retained throughout this work as the most familiar general name for the mood of conception or supposition, " Conjunctive " or " Hypothetical " being preferred by some modern scholars.

The right of the " Imperative " to be called a mood is disputed, but here too it seems best to follow traditional nomenclature.

he *fail*," " If he *be* the man to do this," and we are conscious that the forms *slay, were, fail, be*, convey a sense of contingency or doubt greater than that implied by *slays, was, fails, is*, and additional to that implied by *though* or *if*.

We also form, by the aid of auxiliary verbs followed by the infinitive, a compound mood that answers to some senses of the Latin subjunctive : " May I be there ! " (a wish.)   " Let us go " (hortative) ; " Let him go " (a command) ; " I *may* or *might* go ; " " I *should* or *would* go " (potential and conditional).

79. But the subjunctive is used in Latin again and again where we should not use either this combination of two verbs, or what remains to us of the older and true subjunctive ; and careful study is required before we can either account for its systematic use in Latin authors, or use it correctly ourselves in writing Latin.

For instance, it would never occur to any one who knew no language but English to use the subjunctive in such expressions as " Tell me why you *did* this," " It happened that I *was* absent," " He was a man whose courage never *failed*," " He was so much injured that he *died* ; " but these are only some of the most obvious cases where the subjunctive is essential in Latin.

It was called the *subjunctive* (or *conjunctive*) mood by grammarians, from being the form of the verb which was very largely used in *subjoined* or *conjoined* clauses, in which no doubt it is most frequently employed.

But as there are many kinds of subjoined or subordinate clauses in which the subjunctive would be quite out of place, so it is also frequently found in the principal clause of a compound sentence, and also in simple or independent clauses :

> *Hoc faciat, si velit.*   He would do this if he cared to.
> *Hoc ausim dicere.*   I would venture to say this.

And though in the former instance it is *con*joined or linked to a subordinate clause, and in the second it is easy to supply such a clause as, " if circumstances allowed," etc., yet its origin as a distinct form of the verb is probably older than that of the construction of compound or complex clauses.

80. It is, in fact, largely used as an apparently independent mood in simple or merely co-ordinate sentences, where it is neither *subjoined* nor *conjoined* to any other verb, and it is used in this manner both to state a **fact**, to ask a **question**, and to express a **command** or **desire**.

(i.) In making a *statement*, it differs from the indicative by doing this in a somewhat hesitating or modest manner; answering to the so-called potential mood, formed in English by the aid of the auxiliaries "may," "might," "would," 'could,' or to the Greek optative with *ἄν*.

Notice that this use of the potential mood occurs mainly either with the *first person* or with an *indefinite* subject, *e g* "you," for "any one" in the second person, *aliquis, quispiam,* etc., in the third.

With a *definite* subject such assertions are made either by the indicative with *fortasse,* or the subjunctive with *forsitan, nescio an,* or with the infinitive after *credo,* etc.; not, or rarely, by a mere subjunctive.

"*Some one* may say," *dixerit quispiam;* but "*your father* may say," *dicet fortasse,* or *dicat forsitan pater tuus;* not *dicat* or *dixerit* simply.

Vix crediderim, "*I can* scarcely believe, ' but not *vos, judices, hoc rerum esse vix credideritis,* rather *hoc . . . credere potestis,* or . . . *credere vos posse arbitror.*

(ii.) It is also used in apparently independent *questions.* Sometimes the question denotes *perplexity* (*modus dubitativus*):

> *Quid agam ? quid agerem ?* What *am* I ? what *was* I to do ?

It is possible here, but by no means obvious, to supply "if occasion arose." Also in questions denoting *indignation* or *surprise,* or when the answer "no" is expected :

> *Hoc tu dicere audeas, auderes ?* Would you dare, *or* have dared, to say this ?
> *Quis hoc facere audeat, auderet ?* Who would dare, *or* have dared, to do this ? No one.

[*N.B.*—The imperfect subjunctive should be used rather than the pluperfect, "Would you *at that past time* have dared ?" and is more natural in Latin than *ausus fuisses,* which means, "Would you have dared *prior to that past time* ?"]

(iii.) It is also used very largely in an *optative* or *jussive* sense, to express a *wish, exhortation,* or *command.*

In the first sense it answers to the Greek optative; in the others it completes or takes the place of the imperative mood, whose use is naturally often avoided, even where it exists

A *wish* or *prayer* is expressed by the subjunctive with or without *utinam:*

> *Quod Di bene vertant!* May the gods bring this to a good issue!
>
> *Ad quam senectutem utinam perveniatis!* At this old age may you arrive!

The negative of a wish is expressed by *ne: hoc ne videatis utinam,* "may you not see this!" If *non* is used, it merely negatives the single word to which it is attached.

[Though as a simple mood, as opposed to combination of the infinitive and an auxiliary verb, the subjunctive is nearly extinct in English prose, it is still largely used in German and French, as well as in Greek and Latin. German resembles Latin in using it when a statement is made on the authority of some one else; French in certain uses after the relative. "I must have men who *are* capable of storming a city," would be in Latin *militibus mihi opus est qui urbem expugnare possint;* in French "j'ai besoin de soldats qui *soient* capables de," etc. In both these languages the subjunctive is used because the relative points not to certain soldiers of whom this capacity is predicated, but to a class of whom it might be predicated: "*such as.*"]

81. The *tenses* of the subjunctive retain the force which they have in the indicative.

But the meaning and use of them all is enlarged, owing to the absence of any true *future* tense in the subjunctive mood, the resources of Latin being here limited to the periphrastic future (*laudaturus sim, essem,* etc.), which often expresses other ideas than those of mere time, viz. intention, probability, etc. Hence the *present* subjunctive is used both of present and future time, where no ambiguity can arise:

> *Cras veniat!* May he come to-morrow!
> *Vereor ne veniat.* I fear he will come.
> *Oro ut hoc facias, idcirco te eligo ut hoc facias.*

In such cases the idea of *wishing, fearing, entreaty, purpose,* removes ambiguity, and the absence of a future tense is not felt. Where ambiguity can arise, the future in -*rus* is available. Thus *dubito num adsit* would naturally mean, " I doubt whether he *is* on the spot (now) ;" *adfuturus sit* would therefore be used if the doubt refers to his future coming So too with *vereor*, if the future is emphasised :

Vereor ne venturus sit.   I fear he is likely to come.

82. The *imperfect* subjunctive will represent, not only time exactly contemporaneous with a past moment, but also continuous time from a past moment up to the present, and the other ideas of *repetition, beginning, proceeding* to, etc., which fall under its indicative senses.

Hence *quid facerem*, " what was I to do," or " proceed to do," at a *past* moment, answers to *quid faciam*, " what am I to do," or " proceed to do," *now ;* so *accidit ut abessem*, " it happened that I was absent" (at that *past* moment), answers to *accidit ut absim hodie*, " it happens that I am absent *now*."

So also *misi qui dicerent*, " I sent (past tense) men who *were to* say (at some time in the past);" *veritus sum ne veniret*, " I was afraid he would come," not at the moment denoted by *veritus sum*, but at a moment now past to the speaker.   Each of these exactly corresponds to *mitto qui dicant*, and *vereor ne veniat*, in present time.

Sometimes there is apparent ambiguity . *e.g. utinam adesset*=" would he *had been* present," *during*, say, that battle or debate, *or*, " would he had been present in the moment just past," *i.e.* " would he were, *or* had been, present, *as he is not*, even now ;" but the context will leave little doubt.   The former is the more common, but the main point is to remember that the meaning of this tense **can never extend beyond the present into the future.**

Hence *nec tu si Atheniensis esses unquam clarus fuisses*, " and you, had you been (*i e. through* previous time and *up to now*) an Athenian (=were you an Athenian), would never have been (*at any moment previous to the recent past*) famous."

Si Atheniensis sis would mean " if at any moment from the present *you were to be* an Athenian ;" *nunquam clarus sis,* " you never *would* be famous." As such suppositions, when applied to the known past, are more in the teeth of facts than any as regards the unknown future, the imperfect subjunctive after *si* naturally carries with it an idea of a very remote or impossible supposition.[1] It is the same with wishes; if we can represent them as applied to the past we bring out more strongly the fact of their not having been realised : *utinam adesses,* " during the time I have been making this speech," implies more strongly than *utinam adsis* the absence of the person alluded to.

83. The *perfect* also has its domain extended in the subjunctive. It is used—

1. As a simple aorist :

Quaero quid dixeris. I ask what you said.

In such dependent interrogative clauses it is the usual tense (Arnold, rev. ed., 173), the imperfect being less common.

2. In a potential form (generally in the 1st person):

Vix crediderim. I could scarcely believe (*or* have believed).

3. With *ne* as a mild prohibition :

Ne hoc feceris. Do not find that you have done this: *i.e.* do not allow yourself to do it.

4. As a true perfect, or where English at least would employ that tense :

Vereor ne jam advenerit. I fear he has come already.

5. Side by side with the imperfect, to denote a past result in a more striking and vivid manner, as an event that still strikes the senses ; or as a single fact opposed to a series of facts ; or momentary as opposed to continuous

---

[1] In English we may notice the identity between a past tense of the indicative and the form often used to express a remote contingency : " if he attempted this he would fail "=" if he were to attempt this in the future."

time (the precise effect of the aorist in many constructions of Greek syntax):

> *Adeo crudelis fuit, ut captivos omnes trucidaret, ne fratri
> quidem suo pepercerit* . . . "And actually did not
> spare even his own brother" (the latter fact being
> emphasised by the tense).

6. With the participle in *-rus*, and the modal verbs
posse, debere, etc., to express a contingent result in past
time (instead of the more usual pluperfect):

> "I was so terrified that I would have done anything;"
> *adeo territus sum ut quidvis facturus fuerim; adeo territi
> sunt milites ut exercitus deleri potuerit,* ". . . that the
> army might have been destroyed."

7. To represent the indicative second future (70, 71)
when the subjunctive mood is required, *e.g.* by *oratio
obliqua:*

> *Si hoc fecero, vincam.* I shall win the day if I do (shall
> have done) this.
> *Dico me, si hoc fecerim, victurum esse.* I say that I shall
> win the day if I do (have done) this.

Here the full meaning of *fecero* (time at once *future,*
and, as regards the future, *past*) cannot be reproduced in
the subjunctive, but its *past* sense is preserved.

84. The *pluperfect* subjunctive preserves the meaning
of the tense, viz. time *prior to a point in past time,* with
only some slight extension:

1. It is used in wishes of a time prior to a past event:
utinam adfuisses, "would you had been there" before some
other things happened); but, as contrasted with *adesses,*
it expresses *simple* as opposed to *continuous* past time.
So Cicero says:

> *Quam vellem ad illas pulcherrimas epulas me invitasses;
> reliquiarum nihil haberemus.* Would that you had
> invited me to that glorious banquet (Caesar's assassina-
> tion); we should have had (now) no "leavings."

Invitasses, "once for all," "before the occasion;" *haberemus,*
"up to this moment."

2. It is constantly used after *quum* as the substitute for the non-existent past participle of active verbs: *quum venisset,* " having come."

3. As the verb in the principal clause it is used to express our potential mood, " would have :" *hoc dixissem,* " I would have said this," which is equivalent to and often expressed by *hoc dicturus fui.*

Hence to prevent ambiguity it is set aside in a dependent question (where we in English use the potential form) in favour of a periphrastic form: *quaesivi quid dixisset,* " I asked what he *had* said," but *quaesivi quid dicturus fuisset,* " I asked what he *would have* said."

4. **It has an exceedingly common use as the representative of indicative future ii. in oratio obliqua when the verb sentiendi vel declarandi is in past time.** Thus the words *si haec fecero vincam,* which after **dico,** etc., would become *si haec fecerim me victurum esse* or *fore ut vincam,* will after **dixi,** etc., be expressed by *si haec* **fecissem**[1] *me victurum esse* or *fore ut vincerem. Fecissem* here denotes a time prior to *victurum esse,* which at the present moment is past, but future as regards *dixit.* In English we simply say, " that I should conquer if I *did* this," not " if I *shall have* done it."

5. It has been pointed out that in *consecutive* clauses this tense gives way to the future participle with the *perfect subjunctive.*

USES OF THE INFINITIVE.

85. The *infinitive,* though sometimes called a " mood," is really, as both grammar and philology show us, a **verbal noun** with the properties both of noun and verb: of noun, in its substantival use (Arnold, rev. ed., Ex. xiii.), to denote the action of the verb in general; of verb, in

---

[1] Occasionally (often in Caesar) *fecerim* is substituted, with the same object as that of the use of the historic present, for greater liveliness. " He said that if he *does* this he would perish " would be bad English, but an analogous construction is common in Latin.

admitting inflexions of voice and tense, in governing the case of a verb, in being qualified by adverbs and not by adjectives, and in its use to mark statements in *modo obliqua*. It is only in this last case that it acts as a true verb by joining two conceptions (above, **55, 76**), nor does it then do so in any one distinctive *modus* or manner (as fact, supposition, or command). It represents, for example, either the indicative of fact or the sub-junctive of conception, [1] and, while sharing the functions of both of those moods, has no distinctive modal function of its own. When, therefore, it is spoken of as the " In-finitive *Mood*," that term is used loosely and irregularly to denote a group of verbal forms, just as in Greek grammar (if the view expressed above, **77**, be correct) a group of strictly " subjunctive " tenses is spoken of as the " Optative Mood."

86. The infinitive in English is used by itself after auxiliary verbs, " I *can, will, shall, must, would, should, dare*" (*dare* itself is sometimes a mere auxiliary, " I *dare* say "). After *might* and " modal " verbs, such as *hasten, begin, cease*, etc., it is mostly used in what we may call a gerundial form, *i e* with *to* prefixed; with this prefix of *to* it often represents the abstract noun [2] (" to be or not to be "); indeed it has the widest possible range; it is used without *to* after verbs of sense, " I saw him fall," " I heard him cry," exactly like the Latin infinitive, it represents a **purpose**, like the Latin supine in -*um*, " I come to bury Caesar, not to praise him," the **aim** with an adjective, " swift to shed blood," " slow to speak " (Latin gerund and gerundive); it qualifies an adjective like the Latin supine in -*u*, " fair to see ; " it answers to the Latin gerund, " power to forgive," and to the gerundive, " he is to blame " (*ignoscendi potestatem, culpandus est*).

---

[1] Thus *valeret si adesset* becomes in oratio obliqua *iturum fuisse si adesset* (Arnold, rev. ed , 519)

[2] In the nominative case, as a rule, but Spenser can say (*Ruines of Time*, l. 429) .

> " For not to have been dipt in Lethe lake,
> Could save the sonne of Thetis from *to die*."

87. In Latin prose, as distinct from poetry, the range of the infinitive mood is far more restricted, and its use differs in one or two important points from the English infinitive.

When used as a noun it still, as in English, asserts its verbal form, and completes its sense when transitive with an accusative case :

> To praise thee boots not.   *Laudare te nil juvat.*

It has also three tenses, one of them, however, formed by the aid of an auxiliary verb . *laudare, laudavisse, laudaturum esse, fore, fuisse.*

But its use after verbs of sense and assertion is far wider than in English or any other kindred language.

Such constructions as " I saw him die," " I felt myself grow faint," " I bade him go," are almost confined to certain verbs of sensation and command. After " I know," " I say," and the like, English and all modern European languages employ for the most part a conjunction with a separate clause (*that, que, dass*) ; and even Greek fluctuates between the infinitive and ὡς, ὅτι, with indicative or optative. But in Latin the construction natural after verbs of pure sense is extended not only to all transitive verbs, but even to phrases implying assertion or knowledge in their widest range. We say not only, *vidi eum perire* (" I saw him die "), and *scio eum periisse* (" I know *that* he perished "), where we can understand the accusative as being the object to the verb in the indicative ; but the construction is transferred by analogy to such expressions as *eum periisse certum est*, where there is nothing in *certum est* " to govern " an accusative as in the words *scio, audivi;* and the accusative case has become so attached by habit to the infinitive mood, that, even when used as a noun, if a subject is to be expressed at all, that subject must be in the accusative: *te hoc facere turpe est,* " *Your* doing this, or *for you* to do this, is disgraceful."

So when used as a pure exclamation : *te hoc facere !* " your doing this !"

In fact the infinitive mood is never combined with a nominative, except where it is used as a substitute for a finite verb in a graphic narrative, *jam Romani loco cedere*, or when it is closely joined with a modal verb, *possum, volo, incipio*, etc , *Romanus esse*.

88. The most widely extended and most characteristic use of the Latin infinitive, that in Oratio Obliqua (123), is closely connected with its characteristic use after verbs of assertion. When a speech is reported not *dramatically*, i e. in the first person, as in Shakespeare, but, as is usual in historians, in the third person, it entirely takes the place of the indicative mood in all principal clauses which convey an assertion, as though the word *dixit* or *dixerunt* were perpetually repeated In English we use the third person and a past tense : compare, *e.g.*

> The language of the Etruscans was somewhat bolder ; *they had* a right (they said) to be angry, etc. *Paulo ferocius (locuti sunt) Etrusci , iure se nasci.*

(The words in brackets are in neither language essential.)

89. As a verbal substantive of the neuter gender the infinitive is used (1.) in the *nominative* to *est, fuit*, etc (rarely as subject of other verbs), or to an impersonal verb, or verb used impersonally ; (2) in the *accusative*, as subject to another infinitive, after *verba declarandi et sentiendi*, etc. [In the genitive and dative cases, and with the accusative after a preposition, the gerund or gerundive is used.] But this substantival infinitive retains its *verbal* nature (*a*) in keeping the tenses of a verb, (*b*) in " governing " the case of a verb, (*c*) in being qualified by adverbs. The following sentence illustrates these idioms :

> *Haec fecisse et pati in miserrime carere non solum mihi turpissimum est sed etiam inimicis placet. Neque enim mihi contigit redeundi facultas, et impar sum recuperandae libertati.*

This infinitive, either by itself, or combined with object, subject, adverbs, or adverbial phrases, is in constant use in Latin as the subject to adjectival or substantival predicates, such as *aequum, verum, honestum, credibile est,* "it is right (*or* just), is true, is honourable, is credible," as well as to *fama, opinio est,* "there is a report or impression that," *manifestum est,* etc.; and to such nouns as *facinus, nefas, scelus est,* with many others; *e.g.*

> *Non mihi operae est hoc facere.* It is not worth my while to do this.
>
> *Ejusmodi rebus immisceri non meae est consuetudinis.* It is not my practice to meddle with other people's concerns.
>
> *Nihil negotii est res gestas tuas perscribere.* There is no difficulty in writing an account of your achievements.
>
> *Me* (not *mihi*) *ad mortem abire tempus est.* It is time for me to go away to death.
>
> *Haec neglexisse ei exitio fuit.* The neglect of (*lit.* the having neglected) these points was his ruin.

Also to a large number of impersonal verbs, and to some passive verbs *sentiendi et declarandi* used impersonally.

90. Even with the aid of the infinitive, Latin, and even English, often find it difficult to find an expression for the abstract idea involved in a verb.

We use in English the periphrasis of "the idea" or "the notion;" "the very idea or meaning of happiness" may be expressed by *illud ipsum, beate vivere,* or by *omnis,* or *tota, beate vivendi ratio,* or *vis* (see **33**).

91. There are several uses of the infinitive which fall under those already enumerated, but not quite so directly as might appear at first sight. The following examples may therefore be studied with advantage.

Obsides dat se intra biduum rediturum esse

Inter omnes convenit diem praeterisse.

Defendit se nihil contra legem commisisse

Prae se fert omnia se tibi debere. He openly avows (wishes every one to know)

Certum est deliberatumque omnia experiri.

Se Orestem esse perseverat.

Omnibus innatum est et quasi in animis insculptum esse Deos.

Mihi satis est consulem fieri. ⎫

Satis habeo consul fieri.   ⎬ I am content *or* satisfied

Satis habeo me consulem fieri ⎭ with being consul.

Si sociis fidelissimis subvenire non laboratis (curatis).

Aut mori aut vincere obstinaverant animis.

Vitam beatam in voluptate positam esse volunt.

In hostium fines ducere occupat.

Interfici praestat quam hoc dedecoris admittere.

Tu consilium cepisti hominis propinqui fortunas funditus evertere.

Dicaearchus vult efficere animos esse mortales.

NOTE ON INDIRECT PREDICATION (ACCUSATIVE AND INFINITIVE).

92. By "indirect predication" we mean such statements as are made not *directly* or in the usual manner, *i.e.* by a finite verb with its subject in the nominative, as *homo sum*, "I am a man;" but *indirectly*, *i.e.* by a verb which is itself dependent upon another verb (or phrase) of assertion or knowledge, or some similar meaning, as *aio* ("I affirm"), or *scitis* ("you know"), *me hominem esse*, "that I am a man."

This "indirect predication" is a form of *oratio obliqua* (see **123**). It is so called either as being an *indirect*, as opposed to a *direct* or straightforward, mode of making a statement, or from the constant use of an *oblique* case, the accusative, in place of the *casus rectus*, or nominative, as subject to the verb.

93. In English we introduce such statements by the conjunction "that." When this conjunction is omitted, as in older English, in poetry, and in conversation, we place the two clauses side by side: "I know he did it." In all modern European languages a similar conjunction, *que*, *dass*, etc., is used. In Greek, ὅτι or ὡς, the infinitive mood, or even the participle, is used according to circumstances In Latin alone **the use of the infinitive with the accusative** case in statements dependent on verbs of this class (*declarandi et sentiendi*), and even on phrases conveying the same idea (see 87), is **invariable.** It was not till Latin had become the language of foreign races that such conjunctions as *quod*, *quia*, or even *quoniam*, followed by a finite verb, were used after such verbs.

Such a sentence as *vides ut alta stet nive candidum Soracte?* (Hor. *Od.* i. 9. 1) is no exception; for *ut* here is an interrogative, not a demonstrative, conjunction, and must be translated not by *that* but by *how*.

94. Observe, (i.) that the pronominal nominative case, so often (apparently) omitted in the direct statement, is always expressed in the indirect.

Currit, "he runs," becomes after a verb of these two classes not merely *currere*, but either *se currere*, if the subject of the two verbs is the same, or *cum*, *hunc*, etc., *currere* if they are different: *nobiscum pugnat ; ait se* or *cum* (according to the person meant) *nobiscum pugnare.*

(ii.) That the English verb "say," when followed by a negative in the *that*-clause, is generally represented in Latin by *nego*, the following negative being omitted :

> *Negat se consulem esse.* He says that he is not the consul.

(iii.) That this infinitive construction must be used in Latin, not only where "that" is omitted in English, as in "I knew he had done it," but also where the verb or phrase of *knowledge, assertion,* etc , is in English inserted as a parenthesis ; such insertions are much rarer in Latin than in English.

" He is, I believe, a good man," must not be translated by *est, credo, vir bonus,* for a parenthetic *credo* is almost always ironical in Latin, but by *credo cum virum bonum esse.*

[The one great exception to the construction of *verba declarandi* is *inquam . . . inquit* This is never used to introduce *oratio obliqua,* but is always inserted after the first one or two words of a speech quoted exactly as spoken without affecting the construction of the clause. *Tum ille, haec omnia, inquit, faciam,* "thereupon the other, I will do, *says he,* all this," is a more lively form of saying *tum ille omnia illa se facturum esse respondit,* . . . "thereupon the other replied that he would do all this. . . ." This direct quotation is as a rule confined to *inquit,* and not used with *ait, dicit,* etc If we quote the words of an *author,* we may insert *ut ait Cicero,* or *ut Ciceronis verbis utar,* or *inquit Cicero*

Inquam is also used where a word is repeated for emphasis . *tu, tu inquam, haec fecisti.*]

95. With regard to the *tense* in such statements, it need only be remembered **that the present infinitive represents both the present and imperfect tenses of the indicative ; that the past infinitive represents the true perfect and aorist, and also the pluperfect ; and that Latin far more than English insists on a future tense, where possible, to represent time really future (see 64, 65),** though in the infinitive mood it has only one future to represent different ideas of the future ; such as that he will run, will *be* running, will *have* run.

Thus, while in English we say, " he said that he *was* in Asia," we must not translate this by *dixit se in Asia fuisse,* unless by *was* we mean some time prior to that meant by " he said ;" *e g.* if the sentence went on " thirty years ago ;" but by *dixit se in Asia esse* if *dixit* and *esse* refer to the same time. This is a mistake constantly made by beginners and the unobservant. Thus:

> *Dico me in Asia esse.* I say that I *am* in Asia.
> *Dico me in Asia fuisse.* I say that I *have* been, *was* (at some past time), or *had* been, *before* some past time.
> *Dico me in Asia futurum esse* or *fore.* I say that I *shall* be, or *shall have* been, in Asia.
> But—*Dixi me in Asia esse.* I said that I *was* in Asia (at the time of my speaking).
> *Dixi me in Asia fuisse.* I said that I *had* been, or was *at*, *before* some previous time.
> *Dixi me in Asia futurum esse* or *fore.* I said I *should* be, *at* or *before* some future time.

96. Observe also that where in the infinitive clause any ambiguity can arise from the *subject* and *object* of a transitive verb being in the same case, the passive voice should be used.

Aio te, Acacida, Romanos vincere posse is an oracular line *intended* to have a double sense.

If a prose writer had meant to say that Pyrrhus would conquer the Romans, he would have said *aio a te Romanos vinci posse;* he would thus avoid defeating the main object of language, which is to convey our thoughts clearly.

It is extremely common, where a statement or denial is made, to prefix *hoc, id,* or *illud*, in the accusative case after the principal verb, and then to explain the neuter pronoun by an infinitive clause:

> *Hoc, id,* or *illud negat se multis annis Romae fuisse.* He *asserts* that he has *not* been at Rome for many years. What he says is that, etc.

We may remember how often we begin an English sentence by an indefinite *it*, which we then explain by a clause in apposition: "*it* is strange *how* often," etc.

VII.

Use of Participles in Latin and English.

97. The use of the Latin participle as a substantive or adjective has been noticed above (**40, 43, 45**). When used as a true participle, in apposition to the subject or object of a verb, it forms a substitute for adjectival (or relative) and adverbial (or conjunctional) clauses.

Sometimes, in combination with a finite verb, it represents what in English would be expressed by two finite verbs connected by the co-ordinating conjunction " and ; " *e g.*

> *Militem arreptum trahebat.* He seized the soldier and began to drag him along.
> *Patrem secutus ad Hispaniam iter fecit* He followed his father and travelled to Spain.

But much more commonly it represents adverbial clauses of *time, cause, circumstance*, etc, such as are introduced in English by the conjunctions " when," " while," " after," " as," " since," " although," etc ; *e g.*

> *Haec locutus* ("after he had spoken") *sublimis abiit.*
> *Omne malum nascens* ("at its birth"=a temporal clause), *facile opprimitur ; inveteratum* ("when it has grown older") *fit robustius.*
> *Plato scribens* ("while he was writing") *est mortuus.*
> *Non hercule mihi nisi admonito* ("after having been warned") *venisset in mentem.*
> *C. Servilius Ahala Sp Maelium regnum appetentem* ("who," or "inasmuch as he was aiming at ").
> *Occupatum* ("when he had caught him") *interemit.*
> *Urbem oppugnaturus* ("when on the point of assaulting ") *constitit.*
> *Hanc virtutis speciem intuens* ("so long as," *or* "if you keep your eye upon ") *nunquam errabis.*

Notice that in all these instances the participle (as also the gerundive, gerund, and supine) enables Latin to compress into the limits of a simple sentence what would otherwise be expressed by two clauses—either two coordinate, or one main and one subordinate clause.

98. Attention should be paid to certain differences of idiom between Latin and English.

1. In Latin the *present* participle always denotes action going on contemporaneously with that of the verb to whose subject or object it is in apposition:

> *Hoc moriens dixit.*   He said this while he was dying (*or* "while dying").
>
> *Haec ambulans meditor.*   I think of these subjects when I am walking (*or* "when walking").

In English it is used much more vaguely as regards time: "Mounting his horse, he galloped off to the camp," *i.e.* he first mounted and then rode off; *conscendens equum* would mean "while in the act of mounting," and the real Latin equivalent for "mounting" is *quum equum conscendisset*. The past participle, however, of deponent or semi-deponent verbs (*veritus, ratus, ausus, confisus*, etc.), or of passive verbs used in a middle or reflexive sense (*conversus, projectus*, etc), are often equivalent to the present participle in English; *e.g.*

> Caesar, fearing danger, drew off his troops.   *C. periculum veritus* (or *quum p. timeret*) *milites abduxit.*
>
> Turning to me he spoke as follows.   *Ad me conversus in hunc modum locutus est.*

2. Certain elliptical uses of the present participle in English cannot be literally translated by a present participle without grammatical absurdity. Thus in the expressions, "while dying," "when walking," used above, there must be an ellipse of the pronoun and auxiliary verb ("he was," "I am"), for no conjunction in English, any more than in Latin, can be really constructed with a participle. But in Latin the tenses expressing contemporaneous action (present and imperfect) are not formed by auxiliary

verbs, the equivalents for "was dying," "am walking," being *moriebatur, ambulor* (not *moriens erat, ambulans sum*). An elliptical phrase, corresponding to "while dying," cannot therefore arise in Latin, and *dum moriens, quum ambulans* are impossible absurdities.

Again, in such English phrases as "those returning," "those departing" (a class of undefined persons), we have an ellipse of the relative pronoun and auxiliary verb, "those (who are) returning." But as the Latin equivalent for the full expression is not *ii qui redeuntes sunt*, but *ii qui redeunt*, the literal equivalent to "those returning," viz. *ii redeuntes*, is impossible; though a false association of the Greek usage of article with participle (οἱ κατερχό-μενοι) helps sometimes to betray young scholars into so egregious a blunder. A moment's reflection, however, that Latin has *no* article, and that (in the literary or "classical" dialect at any rate) the pronouns *is, ille*, were never employed as such, should protect them from this too common error. If the Latin participle be used to denote a class of persons, it stands by itself, *e.g. male dicentibus ne respondeas*, "do not answer those who revile you" (= *iis qui male dicant* or τοῖς κακὰ λέγουσι); this usage, moreover, being confined to the oblique cases, or but very rarely found with the nominative.

Thus the English present participle in ordinary narrative may be represented in various ways; *e.g.*

> "The Sicilians hearing this, and fearing lest Verres should be angry . . ."

> 1. *Sicilienses, quum hoc audivissent, et vererentur* (continuous) *ne irasceretur Verres . . .*

> 2. *Sicilienses, hoc audito, veriti ne . . .*

or by use of the causal relative (111):

> 3. *Sicilienses, qui, hoc audito, vererentur ne . . .*

Sometimes, when the English participle represents a personal characteristic, by an appositional phrase with *vir, homo:*

> The king, being of a passionate nature. *Rex, homo iracundus* (=*qui facile irasceretur*).

ABLATIVE ABSOLUTE.

99. One of the commonest uses of the participle is that known as the "ablative absolute," by which a participle and noun agreeing together in the ablative case are equivalent to a distinct (subordinate) clause, introducing some detail of *attendant circumstance, cause, condition,* or *contrast;* and answer most nearly to such English phrases as " in," " with," " during," " on," " after," " not-withstanding," " in spite of," etc (or after a negative, " without "), used with a substantive or verbal noun in *-ing.*[1] *e.g.*

> *Regnante Tiberio.* In or during the reign of Tiberius.
> *Morte proposita.* With death in view.
> *His auditis.* On or after hearing this.
> *Te repugnante.* In spite of your resistance.
> *Hoc me dicente.* In the midst of my speech.
> *Te dissuadente.* In the teeth of your advice.
> *Te non adjuvante.* Without your help.
> *Re infecta* Without success.

Note that the time denoted by the participle depends upon the principal verb, the present participle denoting time contemporaneous with, the past participle time prior to, that of the principal verb, whether past, present, or future. Thus *his adstantibus* may=*hi quum adstarent, adstant,* or *adstabunt; his constitutis* may=*haec quum constituta essent, sint,* or *fuerint,* according to the time of the principal verb in each case.

The very frequent occurrence of this idiom in Latin is owing partly to the absence of a past participle active. It is only with a limited number of verbs that the Romans had any corresponding phrase to "having conquered the enemy," "having heard this." Besides this,

---

[1] The nearly obsolete English absolute case (once a dative, now a nominative), though not wholly disused by good authors, and still common in certain phrases, such as " this said," " this done," etc., had better be discarded altogether in translation from Latin (or Greek) prose.

the use of the ablative absolute in place of an additional
subordinate clause beginning with *cum* or other conjunction enabled the Latin writer to give variety to the long
periods of his language.

100. Certain limitations to its use should be borne in
mind.

1. The ablative absolute cannot be used if the subject of the participle is either the subject or the object
of the principal verb. Thus, "Caesar after taking the
enemy massacred them" must be translated *Caesar hostes
captos trucidavit*, not *captis hostibus Caesar eos trucidavit*.
"As I was reading this I saw you" must be translated,
haec legens te vidi, not *me haec legente te vidi*.

[Exceptions to this rule in classical writers may generally be
accounted for, *e g* by the desire for emphasis, *nemo credit invito te
provinciam tibi decretam*; or by the use of an established phrase to
mark time, *multa me consule a me ipso scripta recitasti*]

2. It cannot be applied to the past participle passive of
intransitive verbs, as this only exists in the neuter used
impersonally; *e g.* we cannot say *Caesare periento*, "on
Caesar's arrival," as there is no such form as *perientus
sum*. We must substitute a temporal clause, *quum pervenisset Caesar*; or *Caesar postquam*, or *ubi pervenit*.

[Such a sentence as *convento mihi Hirtio opus est* seems, but is
not, an exception, *convenire* being sometimes used as a transitive
verb: "I must have an interview with Hirtius"]

3. It is rarely used unless when the verb in the
participle forms the whole, or nearly the whole, of the
predicate. The participle in this construction may
occasionally govern an accusative: as above, *haec me
dicente*, or with deponents, *militibus ducem sequentibus*;
but if it requires a substantive, or adjective, or participle,
in apposition, the construction with *cum* is substituted:
e g. not *Caesare imperatore salutato*, but *cum Caesar Im-
perator salutatus esset*; not *haec te invito faciente*, but *cum
haec invitus faceres*.

[Caesar, however, who uses the ablative absolute at every step of
his narrative, writes *quibus oppressis inopinantibus* (*B. G.* vii. 8)
and even longer phrases]

A. W. L. P.   G

4. Where a deponent verb will express the idea the appositional participle is of course used :

Caesar, cohortatus milites, signum dari jussit.
Haec locutus statim abiit.

And the *quum*-clause, the meaning of which is almost or quite as various, will constantly take its place.

It is always to be borne in mind that the use of this last idiom is so widely extended in Latin that its precise force in each passage must be determined (like that of the Greek participle) by the context; that to translate it literally when found in a Latin author is almost invariably to translate it awkwardly; and that to translate it by "when" is almost certainly to mistranslate it.

For use of Participles, see Exercise XII.

VIII

Substantival Clauses with *Ut*.

101. The usual constructions of *ut* require no comment, viz. *final* or *consecutive* ("in order that," "so that"), with subjunctive mood; *temporal* ("when"), *relative* or *comparative* ("as"), *interrogative* or *exclamatory* ("how"), with indicative mood.

In its ordinary final or consecutive construction, the *ut*-clause is adverbial. But frequently after "*verba imperandi vel efficiendi*," though perhaps originally an adverbial clause (final or consecutive), it is practically *substantival*, standing in the relation of an object case to the verb of the principal sentences; *e.g.*

Oro ut hoc facias = hoc te oro. I entreat this of you

Or it may be regarded as explanatory of, or in apposition to, the actual object of the verb:

(Hoc) militibus Caesar imperavit ut pugnando desisterent.
Gave them this order, viz., to desist from fighting

One great difficulty of the young composer is to know when to use this *ut*-clause, and when the infinitive mood, to represent the English infinitive. He has learned **(87, 93)** that after *verba sentiendi et declarandi*, and many expressions of analogous meaning, the English "that" . . . must be translated by the Latin infinitive; after many other verbs he will be tempted to use the infinitive where it is inadmissible in Latin, particularly where he finds the English infinitive "to" . . . **(86)**

102. Thus after most verbs of *asking, commanding, advising, striving, effecting, entreating*, the English infinitive must be rendered by *ut* or *ne* with the subjunctive; such verbs implying some aim or result. Exceptions are *jubeo*, scarcely ever followed by an *ut*-clause, except in

its technical legal use for a vote of the Roman people
(*populus jussit, ut,* or *ne* . . .); and in most cases *sino,
veto, patior* (" I allow "), *volo.*

Many verbs expressing desire or purpose, which are
usually joined with an *ut*-clause, are used with infinitive
when the subject of both verbs is the same, *i.e.* when the
desire or purpose relates to the nominative of the principal verb.   Thus:

Decrevi, statui, cupivi, ut hoc faceret pater meus.
But—*Decrevi, statui, cupivi hoc facere* (to do it myself).
So—*Statuit Caesar in Italiam redire.*
 Statuit Caesar ut legiones suae in Italiam redirent.
 Curavit ne hoc facerem.   He took care that I should not
   do this.
But—*Neque hoc facere curavit.*   Nor did he care to do this.

103. The same verb may be used either as a verb
sentiendi or *declarandi,* in which case it will be followed
by the accusative and infinitive; or as a verb *imperandi*
or *efficiendi,* in which case it will be followed by an *ut*-
clause.   In English the same difference of construction
exists, but with this difference, that **where we use the
infinitive Latin uses the subjunctive,** and *vice versa :*

Moneo adesse hostem.   I warn you *that* the enemy *is* at
   hand.
Moneo ne hoc facias.   I warn you not *to do* this.
Mihi persuasum est ita rem se habere.   I was persuaded
   that the case *was* so.
Mihi persuasum est ut locum relinquerem.   I was persuaded
   to leave the spot.
Attico scripsit se venturum esse.   He wrote to Atticus *that*
   he meant *to come.*
Attico scripsit ut ad se veniret.   He wrote to Atticus *to*
   come to him.

Obs.—It should be noticed that as in the phrase *hoc facias velim,*
the omission of *ut* is the rule in the second person with *velim, nolim·*

(only followed by a subjunctive in this idiom), and also with *oportet*, *licet*, *necesse est*, when used with the subjunctive, so also *ne* is omitted after *cave* with second person : *cave (ne) hoc facias*, "take care not to do this"= do not do this

The phrases have become so familiar that the full construction is dropped; as the English, "I dare say," compared with "I dare to say

104. Notice also the following phrases.

Id egit ut tibi placeret. He made it his aim to please you.

Hoc ne faceres citare potuisti. You might have avoided doing this.

Non committam ut hoc faciam I will not allow myself to do this.

Dabo operam ut tibi satisfaciam. I will take care or try to satisfy you.

Impetravere ne arma traderent Their prayers not to surrender their arms prevailed.

Ut or *ne consul fieret assecutus est*, or *effecit*, or *evicit*. He succeeded in being made consul, or in not being made consul.

Vide ne haec temere dicas Is it not possible (be on your guard lest) that you are speaking hastily ?

A rege postulatur ut reipublicae prosit A king is expected to benefit the nation

Non ut nihil agas auctor sum, sed ne quid temere agas. I do not advise you to do nothing (to be idle), but against doing anything rashly.

Notice also, in phrases denoting either *prayer*, *effort*, or similar ideas, two verbs are often used where we use one with an adverb or adverbial phrase:

Oro atque obsecro ut (ne). I earnestly beg
Contendo et elaboro ut (ne). I use every effort.
Instare et flagitare ut (ne). To urge with importunity.
Orando et instando. By urgent entreaties

105. One of the most idiomatic, and at the same time commonest, uses of *ut, ut non*, is that in which, corresponding to an *ita* in the main clause, they are used in a *restrictive* or *limiting* sense:[1] "so *only*, so far *only*, as to."

This combination answers to many English phrases, especially (*ut non*) to the English "without," followed by the gerundial infinitive in *-ing*:

> *Cujus ingenium ita laudo ut non pertimescam.* "I praise or admire his abilities *without fearing* them;" or, "*though* I admire his abilities, I have no dread of them;" or, "I admire his abilities, *but* have no dread of them."

Ita haec facere te oportuit ut consulem te esse meminisse deberes might be translated "You ought not to have done this *without remembering* that you were a consul;" or, "though acting thus, *or* even in acting thus, you ought to have remembered that you were a consul."

Where the contrast is greatly emphasised a *tamen* may be inserted with the *ut*:

> *Verum haec ita praetereamus, ut tamen respectantes relinquamus.* Though we pass by this subject, yet let us leave it with many glances back.

Sometimes, as in the following example, the force of the *ut* is rather final than consecutive, as is shown by the use of *ne*. It is then equivalent to "on the understanding that," "on condition that:"

> *Ita rem tuam augere licet ut ne quid ceteris noceas.* "You may increase your own property on condition of doing no injury to others;" or "the increasing your possession is only allowable on condition of its not injuring your neighbours."

---

[1] Compare the limiting sense of *tantus* = "only just so much," "so little;" *e g* CAES. *B. G.* vi. 35 (*ad fin.*):

> *Praesidu tantum est ut ne murus quidem cingi possit.* They have not force enough even to man the wall.

Cp. Cic. *Fam.* i. 7. 4 (26 Watson's *Selection*); VIRG. *Ecl.* vi. 1C

Substantival *Ut*-Clause with Impersonal Verbs and Phrases.

106. Most of the *ut-* and *ne-* clauses above noticed, though practically substantival, are originally adverbial, and may be referred to the *final* sense of *ut* (*aim* or *purpose*).

But a large number of *ut*-clauses stand in the relation of nominatives to impersonal verbs and impersonal phrases, such as *est* with a noun or neuter adjective.

> *Accidit ut abessem*   It happened that I was absent
> *Proximum est ut de te loquar.*   The next point is for me to speak of you.

In these clauses there is no trace of any sense of *end* or *aim ;* only that of *result*, or often of *mere fact ,* hence *ut non* is used as the negative in place of *ne*, and they are more nearly allied to the *consecutive* than to the *final* sense of *ut*.

Their meaning is often so similar to that of the substantival infinitive with the accusative as to be freely used in place of it with some impersonal and other phrases.

Thus such phrases as *verum est, verisimile est*, etc., are usually joined with (*i.e.* have for their subject or nominative case) an **infinitive mood**, but occasionally an **ut-clause** is substituted: the *ut* exactly answering to our "that" used in a *defining* sense.

This is especially the case where the *ut*-clause stands in apposition with, and defines, a preliminary neuter pronoun, such as *hoc, illud*

> *Sin autem illa vemera, ut idem interitus sit animorum et corporum.*   But if the other view is true, I mean that soul and body perish alike.

So *oportet, licet, necesse est* are occasionally joined with a subjunctive (the *ut*, however, being omitted).

107. But the use of the *ut*-clause to express a fact is not optional, but (practically) universal, with certain impersonal words and phrases, *e g. fit, evenit, accidit, contingit, usu venit, potest fieri;* all of which are used in the sense of *happening* or *taking place*

So *accedit* (or *huc accedit*) *ut* (or *quod*, see **108**), "there is the additional fact that:" *accedit* being never used with the infinitive.

Also with *restat, sequitur, reliquum est*, or other neuter adjectives with *est*—e.g. *integrum est*[1] *ut hoc faciam*, "it is still in my power to do this."

It is also used with *tantum abest*, "so far from."—This idea may also be expressed by *ita non* (or *adeo non*) . . . *ut* (consecutive); or by two co-ordinate sentences, *non modo non . . . sed potius* (or *sed ne . . . quidem*): so that we may render the sentence, "So far from approving your language, I do not at all care to listen to it," by

(1.) *Tantum abest ut ista probem, ut nullo modo audire velim.*

(2.) *Adeo non ista probo, ut nullo modo audire velim.*

(3.) *Non modo non ista probo, sed ne audire quidem velim.*

[Note that in (1.) *ut . . . probem* is a substantival clause, the subject of *abest*; *ut . . . velim* an adverbial clause explaining *tantum*.]

108. Substantival clauses of a very similar nature are sometimes introduced by *quod*, followed by the *indicative*.

Thus, *accedit* or *accessit quod*, "there is" or "was the additional fact that," is at least as commonly used as *accedit ut*. *Accessit quod* is the rule where the fact is in the pluperfect tense: *accessit quod equitatus se receperat,*

---

[1] *Integrum*, literally an "untouched" or "entire matter;" so *res integra =* "an open question," one that may be decided either way.

The phrases *mos est, moris est*, are generally followed by an *ut*-clause on the analogy of *accidit*, etc , less frequently (in poets and Tacitus) by an infinitive, on that of *solet;* e.g.

Negavit moris esse Graecorum ut in convivio virorum accumberent mulieres.—Cic *Verr.* ii. i. 26, 66.

Id morum Tiberii fuit, continuare imperia.—Tac *Ann.* i. 80.

" there was the additional fact that the cavalry had retreated ;" or where the *fact* is also a *reason* · " there is, *or*
was, the additional reason or motive." It is often equivalent to " moreover " or " besides."

But *quod* is also used with *accidit*, etc (107), to denote a *fact* happening, especially when some *judgment*
is pronounced on the fact by the addition of an adverb
Thus :

> *Accidit ut abesses.* You happened to be absent
> But—*Perincommode accidit quod aberas.* Your being absent was
> most *inconvenient*, or, Your absence was most unfor-
> tunate.
> *Magnum est hoc, quod victor victis pepercit.* It is no small
> thing his having spared the vanquished when vic-
> torious.
> *Omitto illud, quod regem patriamque prodidit.* I pass over
> the fact of his having betrayed his king and country.

This *quod* with indicative will be found, as well as the
infinitive mood, very useful in translating the English
verbal substantive of the perfect tense, *e g* " your having
said this," and such expressions as " the circumstance
that," " the fact that"

See Exercises XIII., XIV

107. But the use of the ut-clause to express a fact is not optional, but (practically) universal, with certain impersonal words and phrases, *e.g. fit, evenit, accidit, contingit*, *non evenit, potest fieri*; all of which are used in the sense of *happening or taking place.*

... additional ... that the cavalry had re-
... where the *fact* ... a *reason*; " there is, or
... tional reason ... motive." It is often equi-
... reover" or " ...."

... also used with *accidit*, etc. (107), to de-
... happening, especially when some *judgment*
... on the fact ... the addition of an adverb.

... abesses. You ... pected to be absent.
... umale accidit quod ... es. Your being absent was
... incommode ut ... es, our absence was most unfor-

... est hoc, quod ... in ... peperit. It is no small
... his having spa... the vanquished when vic-

... llud, quod regem patriamque prodidit. I pass over
... of his having betrayed his king and country.

... with indicative ... ll be found, as well as the
... mood, very useful in translating the English
... stantive of the ... tense, *viz.* "your having ...
... and such expressions as "the circumstance
... he fact that."

See Exercise xH.; XIS.

IX.

Uses of *Qui*.

109. *Qui* is used with the *indicative* mood:

1. In ordinary **relative** (adjectival) sentences, subordinate to a clause in *oratio recta*, such as are introduced in English by " who," " that."

2 When it introduces not a subordinate adjectival sentence but a **fresh fact**—*i.e.* a co-ordinate clause. The relative is sometimes so used in English—" He saw the Queen, who at once granted his prayer,"—but much more frequently in Latin, and under circumstances where English does not employ the relative, *e.g.* after a full stop has intervened : " He saw the Queen. She at once granted his prayer." The Latin in either case could use the relative : *quae veniam dedit precanti*,—such phrases as *quae quum ita essent, quibus rebus cognitis, quod ubi confectum est,* etc., being among the very commonest modes of beginning a new period.[1]

---

[1] We may notice a very common instance of an apparently pleonastic use of *quod* at the beginning of sentences ; mostly referring forwards, to something yet to come, such as an *ut*-clause, or other substantival clause, and answering to our "and indeed," " whereas," or "inasmuch as ."

Quod ferme fit ut secundae res negligentiam creent. And indeed it (=*nam illud*) often happens that success breeds carelessness.

It is also common with *ubi* and *cum, utinam,* etc.:

Quod ubi consul vidit nulla parte moveri Ligurum signa.

It is especially common before *si* and *nisi,* answering generally, but not always, to our *but if, and if,* etc. :

Quod nisi pater affuisset. And, indeed, had not his father been present.

In neither of these cases, however, has the relative any
real influence on the mood which follows it and when
the subjunctive is demanded, it is in obedience to general
laws of the language—*e.g.* that which forbids the use of
the indicative in subordinate clauses of *oratio obliqua*, or
that which demands the subjunctive mood for the expression of a wish In such clauses as *cujus sceleris
poenas dabis,* "and you will be punished for this
crime," and *cujus sceleris poenas des,* "and may you
be punished . . ." the mood of the verb is determined
quite independently of the relative pronoun with which
they begin.

110. But besides these two uses of *qui* as introducing
adjectival and **co-ordinate** clauses, in which the relative
has no effect whatever on the mood of the verb, the same
pronoun has many uses which either **absolutely require**
or **usually involve** the employment of the subjunctive
mood.

All these uses come under one explanation. **The
relative introduces a clause which, though in form adjectival, is really adverbial.** It is no longer a mere
relative, but, in addition to its relative force as referring
to some antecedent word, it expresses some further idea
of *design, result, cause, contrast,* etc.; and, in order to do
this fully, it requires the aid of the subjunctive mood to
mark that the apparently adjectival clause is not, what it
at first sight appears to be, a simple statement of fact,
but either tells us of a *design* or *aim,* or, if it introduces
a fact, states that fact not as a mere fact, but as coloured,
so to speak, by being either the *result* of something else
(consecutive), or else a *cause* of, or a *contrast* to, some
other fact. The relative, in short, takes the place of
various conjunctions, such as *ut, quia, quamvis,* etc ,
"so that," "because," "although," and in proportion
as it departs from its simple use as a relative it needs
the aid of the subjunctive mood to mark such departure.

111. Thus *qui* may denote *purpose* (= *ut is*) or *conse-quence* (="such as to,"[1] very frequently in the phrase *is qui*); or it may introduce a *causal* (="because he") or *concessive* (="although he") sentence. In the two former cases the subjunctive must *always*, in the two latter almost always, be employed; the exceptions being cases in which the writer may prefer to emphasise the *fact* which *qui* introduces, and leave the reader to infer the relation of *cause* or of *contrast* in which it stands to the other fact. Hence *habeo tibi gratiam, qui vitam meam servâsti*, " I am grateful to you, for you have preserved my life," is as good Latin as *servaveris*, though less usual ; but the indica-tive asserts more emphatically the fact "that you *have* preserved my life." So *expectantur Kalendae Januariae, quas non expectat Antonius*, "we are waiting for the new year, but (*or* though) Antony is not doing so." The indica-tive denies emphatically Antony's waiting, and leaves the reader to point the contrast, while if the subjunctive were used the "although" would be made more pro-minent, the fact which it introduces less so.

It must be remembered, too, that whereas ideas of *consequence* and *purpose* are habitually expressed in Latin by the subjunctive mood, this is not the case with clauses introduced by the *causal* conjunctions *quod* and *quoniam*, or by some *concessive* conjunctions, as *quanquam* and *etsi*. (114, 145, 146.)

For, while *qui causal* is so often followed by a sub-junctive, other causal words, *i.e. quod, quia, quoniam, quandoquidem*, are regularly followed by the indicative. *Qui* and *quum* are the only causal words which in themselves, when purely causal, require a subjunctive. (114.)

---

[1] It should be noted, however, that *qui* is used in place of *ut* after *tam, adeo, tantus*, etc., only in a *negative* or *interrogative* sentence. We can say *nemo est* (or *quis est*) *tam ferreus qui haec faciat*, "no one is (or who is ?) so hard-hearted as to do this," but not *nec homo tam ferreus est qui haec faciat*, "this man is," etc. ; *ut haec faciat* will he rebe the correct Latin phrase.

112. An exceedingly common use of *qui* with the subjunctive resembles that of *quum* with the same mood.

It is used with the imperfect and pluperfect tenses to express the ideas which are often expressed by the English, and still more often by the Greek, participle, *i.e.* the circumstances *under which, owing to which,* or *in spite of which,* the action described by the principal verb takes place:

> *Tum Caesar, qui haec omnia explorata haberet, redire statuit.*
> Thereupon Caesar, having (as he had) full knowledge of all these circumstances, determined to return.

The context will generally show that the *qui* with the subjunctive in such passages has, like *quum,* a more or less causal meaning. (115.)

Occasionally, however, it will, like *quum,* mark a *contrast* and be used in a concessive sense; in such cases *tamen* will generally be added. Thus the same *qui*-clause might have a different sense:

> *Tum Caesar, qui haec omnia explorata haberet, tamen redire statuit.* Thereupon Caesar, *in spite of his having* full knowledge, etc., determined to return.

In such cases, as with the Greek participle, the context must be our guide in translation: no mechanical rule can be given.

113. The distinction between *is qui* with the indicative and with the subjunctive should be carefully noted. With the **indicative** the *qui*-clause **states a fact about a definite antecedent;** with the **subjunctive it refers the antecedent to a general and indefinite class** of persons or things:

> *Hi sunt quos odisse debetis.* These are the people (*i.e.* certain definite persons, A, B, and C) whom you ought to hate.
> *Hi sunt quos odisse debeatis.* These are the kind (*or* class) of people whom you ought to hate.

So, when Cicero says, *Quae pax esse potest cum eo, in quo est incredibilis crudelitas, fides nulla?* he is speaking of a definite person (Antony), but if *sit* be substituted for *est* the reference is generalised. English cannot mark the difference so simply, and "What possibility is there of peace with one whose character is marked by a cruelty past belief and a total want of honour?" would represent either form of the Latin. We might say for the latter, "with *men* whose character is marked by . . .," etc.

In such sentences as (*a*) *eam complexus est causam, quae senatui, quae populo grata esset*, (*b*.) *id iniit consilium quod nemini, qui bonus esset civis, probari posset*, a general rather than a specific description is given to the *causa* and *consilium* by the use of the subjunctives *esset* and *posset*. We may translate correctly—(*a*.) "he embraced a cause which was in favour with both the senate and people," (*b*.) "he formed a design which could have won the approval of no patriot;" but this does not really distinguish with precision the Latin use of the subjunctive (*esset, posset*) from the indicative (*erat, poterat*), and we must if necessary have recourse to periphrasis, *e.g.* in (*a*.) the insertion of some such idea as "naturally in favour with," in (*b*.) "such a design as could . . ." or "a design of such a nature that it could . . ." Compare, again, these two sentences :

> (*a*.) *Scriptor haud ita diligens, sed qui optimis auctoribus usus est.*
> (*b*.) *Probus homo, sed qui omnia negligenter agat.*

In (*a*:) *qui . . . usus est* states a fact about a particular *scriptor* ; in (*b*.) *qui . . . agat* refers the *probus homo* to the class or category of habitually careless people, and may be translated, "but one of those who act with habitual carelessness."

See also Exercise xv.

X.

Causal Sentences.

114. Causal clauses are introduced by (*a*) *quod, quia, quoniam* (= *quum jam*, "since now"), *quandoquidem;* (*b.*) *quum, qui* (*quippe qui*). The relative conjunctions under (*a*) often have a demonstrative particle corresponding to them in the main clause, to emphasise the cause or reason: *idcirco, ideo, propterea, hanc ob causam,* etc Such causal conjunctions, inasmuch as they introduce a *fact* on which another fact is grounded, **are naturally joined with the indicative mood.**

The subjunctive may, however, be required —

(1.) If the whole sentence is in *oratio obliqua.*

(2.) If the cause alleged is in "virtual *oratio obliqua,*" *i e.* is reported as a reason felt or alleged by the subject of the principal verb :

> *Iratus erat Caesar, quod inim sibi inimicissimum defensurus esset Cicero.* Because Cicero, *as he* (Caesar) *said,* or felt, was intending to defend his deadliest enemy.

Defensurus erat would state Cicero's intention as a fact, on the writer's own authority. So

> *Mirabile videtur, quod non rideat haruspex, cum haruspicem viderit.*—(CIC.) It seems strange that an augur does not smile when he sees a (fellow) augur.

Rideat, not merely the fact, but the fact as part of what we look on as strange : "It seems strange when *we think of* the fact that;" *mirabile videtur* being equivalent to *mirabile esse existimamus.*[1]

---

[1] By a curious idiom the construction of virtual *oratio obliqua* is some-times preserved even when a word such as *dicere* is used

Rediit, quod aliquid oblitus esset, "he returned because (as he alleged) he had forgotten something," would be entirely in accordance with the rule given. But instances are not uncommon of such constructions as *Rediit quod aliquid se oblitum esse diceret.*

(3.) When a fictitious or possible cause is brought forward and contradicted (*non quo*, . . . *non quod*, etc.):

> *Non quo te errare existimem, sed quod monere te volo.* Not that I think you in the wrong, but that I wish to warn you

So even *non quin* (= *non quod non*). Such clauses are often so detached from any principal clause as to form separate sentences in themselves; a fresh period after a full stop beginning with *non quo* (precisely as in English).

(4.) When *qui* or *quum* are used in a causal sense. (111, 117.)

N.B.—The Latin causal conjunction will often be represented in English by such phrases as "seeing that," "inasmuch as," "under the impression that" (subjunctive), etc. Often, too, the English construction will be either *participial*, "hoping," "being," etc., or *prepositional*, "owing to," "on account of." Thus :

> *Quod sperabat.*　On account of his hoping.
> *Quod volebat.*　From a wish.

XI

Temporal Clauses (*quum, ubi, ut, postquam, dum, donec, priusquam, etc.*).

115. The indicative is the natural mood for such clauses, unless there is some special reason to the contrary (*e.g.* subordination in *oratio obliqua*); for they explain that the fact stated in the principal clause was *preceded*, or *accompanied*, or *followed* by something else:

Antequam }
Ubi } *haec audivit abiit.* { Before } he heard this } he departed.
Postquam } (or *audierat*) { When } (or had heard) }
{ After }
or On hearing this . . .

But with the commonest of the temporal conjunctions *quum*, when used with imperfect or pluperfect tense, the subjunctive mood is the rule, indicative the exception:

Quum haec audiret (audiisset), abiit. On hearing this, he departed

The reason for this idiom is that when a writer or speaker mentions certain circumstances as accompanying (*imperfect*) or having preceded (*pluperfect*) the main fact which he relates, he implies in the majority of cases that these circumstances more or less influenced that main fact; that it happened either in consequence of or in spite of those circumstances; or, at least, that the relation between the main fact and the circumstances mentioned was in some respect closer than that of mere priority or nearness of *time*. And as with the relative *qui* the Romans used the subjunctive mood, whenever that pronoun conveyed meanings beyond that of a mere relative (purpose, result, cause, contrast; see 110, 111), so whenever the relative conjunction *quum* (originally an adverbial form of *qui*) was used to indicate not only cause or contrast (= "because" or "since," "although"), but **the circumstances which led up to or attended a fact, it was** their practice to use the subjunctive mood, even when the actual effect of the circumstances on the main action could have been very slight, and when to all appearance *quum* denoted nothing more than the relation of time.

116. Hence a very common mode of beginning a fresh chapter or period in a Latin narrative is by *quum* with imperfect or pluperfect subjunctive, or by its equivalent, the ablative absolute:

> *Quae quum audivisset (audiret) Caesar* . . .
> or—*Quibus auditis Caesar* . . .

But no careful scholar will translate such a *quum* by "when," or the ablative absolute literally. Our equivalent for this expression of the relation of one event to another is either the simple participle, "having heard (*or* "hearing") this, Caesar . . ." or the phrase "on" or "after" combined with the verbal substantive "hearing," or "in consequence of," or "in spite of," with the same verbal substantive, according to the context.

117. *Quum* is thus mainly a conjunction of *attendant circumstances* (="whereas," "since," "because," "although"), and **as such is invariably used with the subjunctive mood;** this usage, especially with imperfect or pluperfect tense, being extended to clauses denoting mainly or only *time.*

It is in one of these senses, where the idea of *time* is blended with that of *contrast* (*when* and *although*), that one of its most idiomatic uses occurs. Joined with the right tense and mood of *posse* and *debere, quum* often answers to the English "instead of" as combined with the English gerund, or verbal noun, in -*ing.* Thus:

> *Quum in senatu adesse posset (deberet), rus abiit.* Instead of taking his place (as he *might, ought to,* or *should* have done) in the senate, he went off into the country.

Of course this idiom can only be used when the neglect of either an *opportunity* or *duty* is implied; otherwise such expressions as *adeo non* with *ut, non modo non . . . sed,* etc., must be used (107).

118. Thus the use of *quum* is exceedingly different from that of the other temporal conjunctions; and it will be borne in mind that even these (*ubi, ubi primum, simul ac* or *atque, postquam, posteaquam, ut* in its temporal sense) do not merely answer to the English conjunctions or phrases "when," "when first," "as soon as," "after that," but often correspond to such English as "no sooner than," "the moment that," etc.

Note that *postquam* is properly a comparative phrase, and is often (as also *priusquam*) written and treated as two words:

> *Septimo post die quam urbs oppugnari coepta est.* On the seventh day after the beginning of the siege.

Almost any chapter in Caesar or Livy will give instances of the great use made of *postquam, quum,* and participial clauses, to give variety to a description and form a compact period. Thus:

> *Quod postquam barbari fieri animadverterunt, expugnatis compluribus navibus, quum ei rei nullum reperiretur auxilium, fuga salutem petere contenderunt.*

The other temporal conjunctions need cause little difficulty if we bear in mind the true meaning and use of the *tenses* of the indicative (**55** *seq.*), and that **the indicative mood is used unless some other idea than that of time is introduced, or unless the clause falls under** *oratio obliqua.*

119. *Dum* requires some care. Its proper meaning is purely *temporal,* "during the time that," "while." Its own and the main clause represent two periods as simply contemporaneous; but though contemporaneous they may, or may not, be of equal duration. We may say, "While I live, I hope," or "While I was at Athens I had a severe accident." In the first case the *while*-clause period is of the same duration as the other, in the second the time that I was at Athens was longer than the time at which my accident occurred.

In both these senses *dum* is used in Latin with the
indicative, but the difference of meaning is marked by a
difference of *tense*.

When *dum* means "while" in the sense of "during the
whole time that," and connects two periods of time the
equal length of which is asserted, the indicative is used with
various tenses:

> *Aegroto, dum anima est, spes esse dicitur.* As long as there
> is life, men say, there is hope.
> *Vivet ejus memoria dum civitas haec manebit.* His memory
> will live as long as this state shall endure, *or* endures.

Quamdiu (often answering to a *tamdiu*) is used in a precisely
similar sense, only it rather implies that the period is a long one ; it
might be substituted for *dum* in either of the foregoing examples,
not in those that follow.

Donec is usual in poetry and later writers in the same sense, rarely
in Cicero, etc. ; its meaning is "all along," or "always," *until*.

Quoad means rather "up to the end of," and "so far as," and is
not confined to *time; quoad potui,* "to the utmost extent of my
powers," though it often expresses time : *quoad vixit,* "to the end of
his life."

120. But *dum* has another use peculiar to itself. When
two periods in past time are not represented as of equal
length, but one as covering a period *during which* the
action takes place which is narrated in the principal
clause, the *dum*-clause is, as a rule, in the (historical) *present
indicative*, **even though the surrounding verbs are in past
tenses, and even in spite of the principal clause being in
oratio obliqua :**

> *Dum Romani ea parant* (not *parabant*) *jam Saguntum
> oppugnabatur.* Whilst the Romans were making these
> preparations, Saguntum was already besieged.
> *Allatum est praedatores, dum latius vagantur* (not *vagarentur*),
> *ab hostibus interceptos fuisse.* News was brought that
> the plunderers, while wandering too far, had been cut
> off by the enemy.

This construction of *dum* may often be conveniently
rendered by the English elliptical idiom, "while doing,"
i.e. "while (they are, *or* were) doing."

121. *Dum* = "until" (so too *donec, quoad*) is used with the indicative mood when no idea but that of time is denoted :

> *Mane hic, dum rediero (redibo).* Stay here till I return
> *Usque eo timui donec ad portum perventum est.* I was in a fright, up to *the moment that* the harbour was reached
> *In senatu fuit, quoad senatus dimissus est.* He was in the house *till* the house adjourned, or *till the last moment that* the house sat

Quoad lays great stress on the idea of an *end* or *limit*, and therefore implies, more than the others, that with that end the *action of the other verb ceased*, *e.g.* that (in the last example) he then went away.

But when, in addition to the idea of time, some further idea of *expectation*, or *purpose*, or *watching* is implied, the subjunctive is used [so too with *donec, quamdiu, quoad*] .[1]

> *Num expectatis dum testimonium dicat ?* Are you waiting till he gives his evidence ?—*i.e.* waiting in order to hear him, waiting with *an end in view*.

Dum as a *conditional* conjunction (" provided that,' " so long as"), with or without *modo*, is always used with subjunctive mood, the negative used with it in this sense being *ne :*

> *Veniam dum sinas (or dum ne prohibeas).* I will come provided that you will allow me (or " do not prevent me").

---

[1] Good instances of the difference of mood after the English " until" may be given from poetry :

> *Delicta majorum immeritus lues*
> *Romane, donec templa refeceris*, etc.—Hor. *Od.* iii 6. 1.
> *Et duxit longe, donec curvata coirent*
> *Inter se capita.* —Aen. xi 860.

In the first instance *donec* is purely temporal, in the second partly final, " till he saw "

The subjunctive after *donec* in Livy's description of the elephants at the ferry :

> *Nihil sane trepidabant, donec continenti velut ponte agerentur* (xxi 28),

is probably a *frequentative* subjunctive, adopted by him from the Greek ; cp 139.

An excellent instance of *dum* with the indicative is to be found in Cicero's translation of the inscription at Thermopylae (*Tusc. Quaest.* i. 42 101) ·

> *Dic, hospes Spartae, nos te hic iacisse iacentes,*
> *Dum sanctis patriae legibus obsequimur.*

122. *Antequam, priusquam,* when implying mere priority of time, are used with the indicative, but if some *end in view,* some *act of will,* or *prevention of a result* be implied, with subjunctive (as in final or consecutive clauses) : *e.g. priusquam pugnaretur non intervenit* (came on and so prevented the fight) ; *priusquam se hostes ex terrore reciperent, in fines eorum exercitum duxit* (*i.e.* he aimed at preventing their rallying).

In negative sentences, *priusquam* often = English "until," " without :" *non prius respondebo, quam tacueris,* " until you are silent" (future perfect, see **65**) ; *prius ire noluit quam judicum sententias audiisset,* " without hearing the verdict" (*audiisset,* subjunctive in virtual *oratio obliqua,* **127**).

" Not until " may also be expressed by *tum demum (denique) . . . quum ; tum demum respondebo, quum tacueris; tum denique ne se velle (dixit), quum . . . audiisset.*

See also Exercises XVI., XVII.

XII

Oratio Obliqua.

123. In reporting another person's language we may
either (1.) profess to give his actual words in the form in
which he spoke them, or, as it is technically called, in
"*oratio recta*" (coming *directly* from his lips); or (ii.)
insert or imply a verb of saying, asking, etc., and report
what was said *indirectly*, in the third person—*i e* in *oratio
obliqua*. Both methods are equally familiar in English
and in Latin, but in both languages the tendency is to
reserve the former, or *direct* report (particularly in the
case of long or continuous speeches), for those which are
in some way especially striking or important, and to
adopt *indirect* or "oblique" narration as the more usual
form of reporting another person's words   Each language
has its special rules or formulæ for *oratio obliqua*, and
it is the difference of Latin *oratio obliqua* from that with
which we are all familiar in English, rather than any
special complexity of its rules (which are really few and
simple), which makes it a bugbear to young composers.
In some points, indeed, there is practically no difference,
and no one who reads intelligently the Parliamentary
reports in an English newspaper ought to have a moment's
doubt as to, *e g.* the conversion of first and second personal pronouns into the third (Arn, rev. ed, 517), or (in
the most usual form of *oratio obliqua*, that which depends
on a past tense of narration) of "primary" into "historic"
tenses (*ib.* 524). As "*I* will go if *you are* willing to
follow," becomes in English *oratio obliqua*, [he said
that] "*he* (A) would go, if *he* (B) *was* willing to follow;"

so, "*Ego* ibo si *tu vis* sequi" becomes (dixit) "*se iturum
esse si ille vellet* sequi." Here the changes of pronoun and
tense in the words italicised are prescribed by that
"common-sense" grammar which applies to all languages
alike; the only difference between Latin and English
being that in the former it is easier to express the meaning clearly in reported speech, because English has only
one pronoun, "he," to represent "I" and "you." To
secure perfect clearness, we must either employ a proper
name or substitute a periphrasis for the representative of
"you;" "Caesar said that he would go, if *the other general*
(or *Labienus*) were ready to follow;" whereas Latin, by
employing its "reflexive" pronoun *se* (whose use should
be mastered once for all; see Arnold, rev. ed., 349, 350)
to express in *oratio obliqua* the third personal pronoun
which represents the "*I*" of *oratio recta*, leaves its regular
demonstrative *is, ille*, etc., free to express without ambiguity that which represents the "you" or "he" of *oratio
recta*.

124. Thus far the two languages agree; but there are
two great structural differences between the Latin and
English formulæ as given above, viz. the **infinitive of the
principal clause** (*iturum esse*) and the **subjunctive mood
of the subordinate clause** (*vellet*). In English we connect
the reported speech or thought with the verb of saying or
thinking upon which it depends by the conjunction
"that," the only change necessary in the statements
reported being (in past time) one of tense: "Caesar said,
'I will go;'" "Caesar said that he *would*[1] go;" "I never
see this without admiration;" "He said that he never
saw," etc. And in reports of long speeches the conjunc-

---

[1] It ought to be unnecessary to remind those for whom this book is
intended that "would" in such a phrase is simply the past tense of
"will," not conditional, as in "I would go if I could." But experience shows that even elder students are apt to confuse the two, and
whenever they see the English word "would" to identify it with a
Latin subjunctive. To write *dixit ut iret* here would show equal ignorance of Latin and of English.

tion ' that." is, as a rule, only expressed at the beginning, to indicate at starting the *oratio obliqua*, which, in all sentences subsequent to the first, is expressed simply by a change of first person to third, and of present to past tenses.[1]

In Latin **no conjunction is used** (*that at* ... is al ... wrong), but **the whole structure of the reported statement is altered**, its principal verb passing from the indicative mood to the infinitive, and the subject of that verb passing from the nominative to the accusative case; for *ego ibo* we write (*that*) *se iturum esse*.

125. Secondly, in the subordinate clauses of a reported statement, English makes no change of *mood*, only, where necessary (as in the most frequent usage, after a past tense of narration), a change of tense: " I will go, if you are willing (or *will*) follow." (He said that) he (A) would go, if he (B) was willing (or *would*) follow. But in Latin, the moment that a principal verb passes from the indicative of *oratio recta* to the infinitive of *oratio obliqua*, it carries with it a change in all the verbs that are in any way dependent upon it, the whole sentence alters its structure, so far as the verbs are concerned, and the indicative mood disappears in the adjectival and adverbial sentences to make way for the subjunctive.

126. [Greek, it may be noted, allows greater freedom in the expression of *oratio obliqua* than either Latin or English. In the principal clause of a reported speech it employs either the infinitive construction, which is invariable in Latin, or a conjunction (ὡς, ὅτι), analogous to "that" in English use, either with an optative tense or no change of mood (as English). In the subordinate

---

[1] In translating a reported speech in Livy or Caesar into English *oratio obliqua*, to write (as young scholars sometimes will) ' that ' at the beginning of *every* sentence gives an uncouth appearance to the passage as a whole, and shows ignorance not so much of Latin as of English usage.

clauses it either changes the mood (as Latin always), or,
by a tendency to retain the speaker's words with as little
change as possible, beyond what is necessary to indicate
the fact that they are reported indirectly, retains the
indicative mood, usually without even a change of tense.
Thus, while Latin and English have each only *one* formula
of *oratio obliqua* for reporting the statement, "I will go
if you are willing," Greek can report, *e.g.* the statement
ἐλεύσομαι, εἰ βούλει, in two main ways:

   (i.) εἶπεν αὐτὸς ἐλεύσεσθαι εἰ βούλοιτο ἔκεινος,

   (ii.) εἶπεν ὅτι αὐτὸς ἐλεύσοιτο, εἰ βούλοιτο ἔκεινος—

and can further vary these by the retention in either
subordinate clause of both the mood and tense of *oratio
recta*, with only the necessary change of person, εἰ βού-
λεται; or in the principal clause of (ii.) by the substitution
of the indicative future, or its equivalent optative with
ἄν, for the optative of *oratio obliqua*—εἶπεν ὅτι ἐλεύσεται,
or ἔρχοιτο ἄν. Nothing better illustrates the comparative
elasticity and variety of Greek Syntax than its flexibility
in dealing with reported speech.]

127. The subjunctive takes the place of the indicative
in subordinate clauses, not only where the introduction
of a verb of *saying* or *thinking* followed by the infinitive
clearly shows that the writer is reporting what some one
else states or thinks, but where, in the absence of any such
verb, we have ourselves to supply the idea, "as he said,"
"according to them," or even, "as I then thought."

It is a short mode of distinguishing what the historian
or speaker states *on his own authority*, and what he declines
to make himself responsible for:

> *Queruntur de vobis socii, quod fidem fefelleritis.* The allies
> complain of you because you have (*according to them*)
> broken your word.

Fefellistis would imply that the speaker *himself* thought
they had done so. On this "Virtual *Oratio Obliqua*" see
Arnold, rev. ed., 448.

It is sufficient to call attention here to the tendency (not an invariable usage) of Latin writers to discard the use of the indicative in subordinate clauses where the verb on which they depend is on any ground in any mood other than the indicative; *i e* to introduce the subjunctive mood in relatival and other clauses on no other ground than that they depend on a verb in the subjunctive or infinitive mood.

This tendency does not amount to a rule, but it will often account for the use of a subjunctive which would otherwise be perplexing.

128. A recapitulation of the rules for conversion of verbs from *oratio recta* into *oratio obliqua* may here be given.[1]

I.—Principal Clauses.

The indicative entirely disappears. Statements or *denials* made in the indicative pass into the infinitive; *questions* asked by the speaker in indicative mood pass into the subjunctive (with change of tense from present to past, if the narrative as usual is in past time); *commands, prohibitions,* and *wishes,* expressed by imperative or subjunctive, pass into subjunctive, with the necessary change of tense and person.

Note that—

1. Questions already in the subjunctive remain in the subjunctive, with necessary change of tense and person (*quid faciam ?* becomes *quid faceret ?*)

2 Questions that are merely rhetorical, and expect either no answer at all, or a negative one, inasmuch as they are virtually *denials,* often pass from indicative or subjunctive to infinitive: *e.g. Num haec toleremus ?* (or *toleranda sunt*) becomes *Num haec toleranda esse ?*

---

[1] The substance of this and following sections has already been given in my edition of Arnold, Ex. LXV. : but the great importance of these rules will justify their repetition, for the sake of convenient reference, in the present work.

3. Hypothetical statements in the subjunctive (*e.g.* the "apodosis" of a conditional sentence) are represented by the future infinitive, the present subjunctive by the participle in *-rus* with *esse* or *fore*, the imperfect or pluperfect subjunctive by the same participle with *fuisse; e.g.*

<table>
<tr><td>ORATIO RECTA.</td><td colspan="2">ORATIO OBLIQUA.</td></tr>
<tr><td>*erres (si hoc facias).*</td><td rowspan="3">Dixit eum</td><td>*erraturum fore (si faceret).*</td></tr>
<tr><td>*errares (si hoc faceres).*</td><td>*erraturum fuisse (si adesset).*</td></tr>
<tr><td>*erravisses (si hoc fecisses).*</td><td>*erraturum fuisse (si adfuisset).*</td></tr>
</table>

II.—SUBORDINATE CLAUSES.

The indicative disappears, and all verbs are in the subjunctive mood, the most usual tenses (as reported speech is generally a narrative of *past* events) being the *imperfect* and *pluperfect*, representing respectively, (*a.*) the present or imperfect (and sometimes future i.), (*b.*) the perfect, pluperfect, or future ii. of *oratio recta* :

<table>
<tr><td>(*a*) *qui adsunt (fugiunt).*</td><td rowspan="3">Dixit eos</td><td>*qui adessent (fugere).*</td></tr>
<tr><td>*qui aderant (fugerunt)*</td><td>*qui adessent (fugisse).*</td></tr>
<tr><td>*qui aderunt (fugient).*</td><td>*qui adessent (fugituros esse).*</td></tr>
<tr><td>(*b.*) *qui hoc fecit (errat).*</td><td rowspan="3">Dixit eum</td><td>*qui hoc fecisset (errare).*</td></tr>
<tr><td>*qui hoc fecerat (erraverat).*</td><td>*qui hoc fecisset (erravisse).*</td></tr>
<tr><td>*qui hoc fecerit (errabit).*</td><td>*qui hoc* **fecisset** *(erraturum esse).*</td></tr>
</table>

129. Two apparent exceptions to the universal requirement of the subjunctive in a subordinate clause in *oratio obliqua* are not really so :

1. Where a relative clause in *oratio recta* is really a statement *co-ordinate* with the principal clause (*qui* being =*et is*), it passes into the *infinitive* in *oratio obliqua ; i.e.* it is treated as being what it is in sense, though not in form—a principal clause ; *e g.*

> (Oratio Recta) *Adsunt hostes, instat Catilina, qui brevi scelerum poenas dabit :* (*Dixit*) *adesse hostes, instare Catilinam, quem brevi scelerum poenas daturum esse.*

2. A subordinate clause, which is only an explanatory parenthesis inserted by the writer, remains in the indicative, because it is not really part of the speech which is being reported ; *e.g*

> *Themistocles certiorem eum fecit id agi ut pons, quem ille in Hellesponto fecerat, dissolveretur* Themistocles sent him word that it was intended to break down the bridge which he (Xerxes) had made over the Hellespont.

Here the words *quem .. fecerat* are the historian's own explanation, defining *pons ;* and the mood of such defining relative clauses in a passage of *oratio obliqua* will always show whether they form part of some one else's words being reported, or are a comment inserted by the writer or narrator.

[Note that though, as stated above, the imperfect and pluperfect subjunctive are the regular construction for subordinate clauses of an ordinary *oratio obliqua*, a " rhetorical" use of the *present* and *perfect* subjunctive, analogous to that of the " historic present" in *oratio recta* (57), is not uncommon in the best Latin writers, *e.g.* Livy or Caesar.]

130. The following examples, which illustrate these rules, should be carefully studied and analysed :

1. Oratio Recta.

> *Profecti sunt ; quando redibunt ? vos quantum potestis, ultum ite.* They have gone. When will they return ? Do your best to avenge them.

Oratio Obliqua.

> *(Dixit) profectos esse, quando redituros ? quantum possent, ultum irent.*

Had the question been asked for information, *redituri essent* would have been used.

2. Oratio Recta.

Nonne videtis de libertate nostra hodie agi ?   Maximi refert quid faciatis.   Majorum, quibus orti estis, reminiscimini. Do you not see that our liberty is to-day at stake ? What you do is most important.   Remember the fathers from whom you are sprung.

Oratio Obliqua.

Nonne viderent de libertate ipsorum illo die agi ?   Maximi referre quid facerent.   Majorum, quibus orti essent, reminiscerentur.

Viderent is subjunctive, because a real question is asked.

3. Oratio Recta.

Qui me amatis, me sequemini.   Those of you who love me will follow me.

Oratio Obliqua.

(Dixit) qui se amarent, se esse secuturos.

4. Oratio Recta.

Quantum possum, te ac tua vestigia sequar.   As far as I can, I will follow you and your steps.

Oratio Obliqua.

(Clamavit) se, quantum posset, illum et illius vestigia sequuturum.

5. *Quaerebat : cur paucis centurionibus, paucioribus tribunis, obedirent ?   Quando ausuros exposcere remedia ?*   He asked, "Why do you obey a few centurions, and still fewer tribunes ?   When will you dare to demand redress ? "

Here *obedirent* is subjunctive, because an answer might be looked for; *ausuros (esse)* is the infinitive, because it conveys a taunt rather than a question.

In reported speech the verb or participle on which the infinitive or infinitives depend is often omitted in Latin. The infinitive or subjunctive moods are ample evidence of the meaning:

1. *Legatos ad Caesarem mittunt. "sese paratos esse portas aperire."* They send ambassadors to Caesar : (*saying*), We are ready to open the gates.

2. *Colonis triste responsum redditum est · facesserent propere ex urbe.* The colonists received a severe answer : (*telling them*), Begone at once from the city.

3. *Tribuni primores patrum fatigabant auderentne id postulare?* The tribunes importuned the leaders of the Senate : (*asking them*), Do you venture to make such a demand?

Before attempting an exercise, the learner should convert a few Latin passages from *oratio obliqua* to *oratio recta*, or *vice versa.* Caesar will supply abundant examples, and some excellent ones may be found in Dr. Kennedy's larger *Grammar*, or in Roby, vol. ii. 1788.

See also Exercises XVIII., XIX.

XIII.

Conditional Sentences.

131. By these are meant such compound sentences as consist of a principal or direct clause qualified by a "conditional" clause, *i c.* a clause introduced by *si, si non nisi, si minus, sin, sive,* or *seu.* The following remarks will help to make clear the ordinary construction of such sentences:

First, we must remember that *grammatical* dependence is not to be confused with what we may call *logical* dependence.

In such a sentence as "if you do this you will be sorry," the clause "you will be sorry" is *logically* dependent upon the words "if you do this," for as a matter of *reasoning,* your being sorry or not sorry depends upon your doing or not doing this.

But as a matter of *grammar* "you will be sorry" is the principal clause, and is qualified by a particular kind of subordinate, or *dependent,* clause, which we call a conditional, or *if*-clause. "You will be sorry," not under all circumstances, but *conditionally,* on condition that, or, *if* you do this.

And, *secondly,* we must remember that in Latin **the mood of the principal verb has a great influence on the mood of the verbs that are grammatically dependent on it.** Just as the tense of the principal verb so often gives the time (*i.e.* determines the tense) to all dependent and finite verbs in the whole sentence, so the mood of (or the manner in which a statement is made by) the principal verb will almost always affect the mood of all the dependent verbs to a degree quite unknown in English, where the subjunctive mood is now little used.

And, *thirdly*, we must remember that the indicative mood, in all principal clauses, deals with *facts* and *realities*, which we assert or deny as such, and that the imperative also is, and must be, addressed to actual and real persons, or to things and ideas which we treat as such. The *subjunctive* mood, on the other hand, when used as a principal verb, deals with conceptions and imaginary cases, and, even when it states a fact or gives an order, does so in an indirect or circuitous manner

132. And now, if we bear in mind these three points, (1.) that the *if*-clause, which is called the *protasis*, is, grammatically speaking, the *dependent* clause, while that which is called the *apodosis*, or *then*-clause, is the principal or *ruling* clause ; (2.) that the mood of the principal clause or apodosis generally determines the mood of the whole sentence, and of every clause which it contains; and (3.), that while *amo* means "I love," *amem*, in a principal clause, *means* "I might, *or* would, love," under certain, not real, but conceivable circumstances, we shall readily understand why, as a general rule—

(i.) When the principal verb, *i.e.* the verb in the apodosis, is in the *indicative* (or *imperative* mood), the verb or verbs in the *si*-clause or protasis are also in the indicative.

(ii.) When the verb in the apodosis is in the subjunctive mood, the verb in the protasis is also in the subjunctive.

133. The following **formulæ for the expression of conditional sentences**, with their English equivalents, should be carefully distinguished and remembered:

I. *Si hoc dicis, erras.* If you say this, you are (at this moment, and as a matter of fact) wrong.

> *Si hoc dicebas, errabas, si hoc (dixisti) (erravisti).* If you used to say (or "said") this, you were wrong.

II. *Si hoc dixeris, errabis.* If you say (*lit.* "shall have said," see 65) this, you will (then, as a matter of fact) be wrong.

> *Si hoc dices, errabis.* If you continue saying this (hereafter), you will be wrong.

III. *Si hoc dicas, erres.* If you were to say so, you would (in this imaginary or conceivable case) be wrong.

> *Si hoc diceres, errares.* Had you been saying this (now), you would have been (now) in the wrong, *or* would be now in the wrong.

IV. *Si hoc dixisses, erravisses.* If you had said this, you would have been (in that imaginary, but now impossible case) wrong.

> *Si hoc diceres, errares.* If you had been saying this (during some past time), you would (during that time) have been wrong.

134. It will be observed that the imperfect subjunctive is here referred to two separate heads, supposition in present time (III.), and supposition in past time (IV.): and there is no doubt considerable difficulty in reducing to a fixed law the use of this tense in either clause of a hypothetical sentence. *Si esses,* in the best Latin writers, appears sometimes almost equivalent to *si fuisses,* "if you had been"—a supposition in past time; at other times to differ but little from *si sis*—a supposition in present time. The former of these is no doubt its true and natural use.

The reference of the imperfect tense is to *continued action in past time;* such action being stated as a *fact* by the imperfect indicative, as a *supposition,* etc. (see **82**), by the imperfect subjunctive. In this expression of supposition in past time, the imperfect subjunctive differs from the pluperfect subjunctive much as in Greek the imperfect indicative with ἄν differs from the aorist indicative with ἄν; *e.g.*

> *Si hoc diceres, errares*—εἰ τοῦτο ἔλεγες ἡμάρτανες ἄν Had you been saying this, you would have been wrong (during the time you were saying it).
>
> *Si hoc dixisses, errasses*—εἰ τοῦτο ἔλεξας ἥμαρτες ἄν. Had you said this, you would have been wrong (once for all).

English does not mark (except by periphrasis) this distinction between "aorist" and "imperfect," between momentary and continuous action: and "if you had said this you would have been wrong" is our only natural expression for both these forms of hypothesis. Hence such Latin phrases as *vellem, mallem, crederes, diceres,* in which the imperfect subjunctive retains its proper force of supposition in regard to *past* time, have generally to be translated as if they were pluperfects—"I could have wished," "you might have thought," etc.,[1] and in hypothetical sentences, though we may sometimes express the difference between these Latin tenses in one of the clauses, it is seldom that we can do so in both. In translating *tum si dicerem, non audirer* (CIC.) by "had I been speaking then, I should not have found a hearing," we mark in the *protasis* the difference between this and *tum si dixissem,*

---

[1] Cp. VIRG. *Aen.* iii. 186.

> *Sed quis ad Hesperiae venturos litora Teucros*
> *Crederet, aut quem tum rates Cassandra moveret?*

("Who could have believed . whom would Cassandra have moved?'); or viii. 643 : *At tu dictis, Albane, maneres!* ("You should have stood (or had you but stood) by your word").

non auditus essem, "had I spoken then" (aorist) . . . .: but
in cases where the imperfect is used in one clause and
the pluperfect in another, English will generally fail to
mark the difference. Thus *si vos in co loco essetis, quid
aliud fecissetis?* "had you been *during that time* in that
position, what else could you have done *once for all?*" but
the only direct and natural English equivalent is, "had
you been in that position, what else could you have done?"
a rendering equally suitable for *si . . . fuissetis,* etc. So
in *Quintus fuit mecum dies complures, et si ego cuperem ille
vel plures fuisset, cuperem* and *fuisset* represent the difference between *cupiebam,* a continuous state, and *fuit,* the
simple statement of a fact.

135. Sometimes, however, the supposition expressed
by imperfect subjunctive extends into the present, and
the element of past time seems to disappear; so that *si
hoc diceres, errares* = "if you had been saying this *now*, you
would have been *now* wrong." Yet even here, the English
phrases, "if you had been," "you would have been," retain
a consciousness of *past* time, its extension into the present
being either indicated by the expression "now," or merely
implied. This is still more apparent in such an expression as *si viveret, verba ejus audiretis* (CIC. *Rosc.* 14), used of
one who is dead: cp. HOR. *Epp* ii. 1. 194, *si foret in terris,
rideret Democritus.* And in a large number of cases, or
in nearly all, there is an element of past time which distinguishes the use of the tense from that of the present
subjunctive. It is only occasionally, in fact, that the
time represented by the imperfect subjunctive is entirely present; and it may fairly be said that it is never
future.

Si diceres may occasionally mean "if you were now to
be saying," where the unreality and impossibility of such
a supposition is emphasised; but it never means, as *si dicas*
does, "were you *in the future* to say;" oftenest of all it
means, "had you been saying."

Such expressions, too, as *crederes, diceres* (134), are never
confused with *dicas, credas,* or *credideris* (81, 83).

In short, *si esset* may express either simply *continuous past time*, or the past as reaching to the present; but never the *present as extending* to *the future:*

> *Si sis* = if you were now, or at any conceivable time in the future.
>
> *Si esses* = if you had been (continuous time), or if you *were*, in the past and up to this moment

136. Care must be taken in translating English conditional sentences where the principal clause or apodosis is in future time, while the verb of the protasis or "*if-*"clause is apparently present, but really (see **64**) loosely used to represent a future. Such a sentence as "if you do this you will be punished" should not be translated by *si hoc facis, poenas dabis*, which would more naturally mean, "if you are *now doing* this you will be punished;" still less should it be translated by *si hoc facias, poenas dabis*, which would be as absurd as to say in English, "if you *were to* do this, you *will* be punished." The only correct version would be *si hoc feceris, poenas dabis*. *Feceris* represents the "doing this" as something future as regards the present moment, but as coming before the punishment which will be its result. Hence the exceedingly common use in Latin of this very characteristic tense, which has no corresponding tense in English, though we sometimes approximate to its force by the insertion of "once,"—"if once you do this."

137. On the other hand, the future i. is used in *both* clauses when they express *contemporaneous* time in the future:

> *Veniam, si potero.* I will come if I *can.*
> *Hoc faciant, si salvi esse volent.* Let them do this (in the future) if they *wish* for safety.

[This future is especially common with *possum* and *volo*]

Hence *si* with a future often expresses "so long as:"

> *Naturam si sequemur ducem, nunquam aberrabimus.* We shall never go wrong, *so long as* we follow (*lit.* shall be following) Nature's guidance.

When the future perfect is used in both clauses, *si* may often be translated by "the moment that," "as sure as," etc.:

> *Si hoc feceris, parum urbane feceris.* *As sure as* you act thus, you will act with some want of courtesy (or *by acting* thus you will, etc.).

In the former instances the two sentences cover the *same period*, in the latter they occur *at the same moment*.

138. It is often assumed by young scholars that because the word *si* (or "if") implies supposition, it must therefore be followed by the subjunctive mood. But in two out of the four main heads of conditional sentence (I. and II., see **133**), it is followed by an indicative mood. How can this be, if the indicative states facts, while the very word *si* (or *if*) implies the reverse of a fact, a mere supposition? The answer is that the indicative is itself colourless; it simply predicates, or states, and its mode of stating may be coloured by the word which qualifies it; thus in *fortasse hoc dixit,* "perhaps he said this," and in *si hoc dixit,* the doubt and the condition are expressed by *fortasse* and *si,* and the verb remains un-altered.

139. As a matter of fact, the mood of the verb in the *si*-clause is not affected by the probability or improbability of the supposition, but by the mood of the principal clause, which gives *the tone to the whole sentence.* Thus, when Cicero says, *si es Romae, vix enim puto, sin es,* etc., he uses the indicative, though he expressly says that the supposition is an improbable one, because he goes on to make a practical request. Again, when he says *Excitate eum, si potestis, ab inferis* ("Summon him, your witness, from the dead if you can"), he obviously does not look at the bringing back the dead to life as possible, but he uses the indicative because the imperative mood gives to the whole sentence, including any dependent clause, the colour of reality, as opposed to that of mere conception. Had he used in the principal clause *excitares* in the potential sense, "you *would* call him up from the dead," he would also have written, *si possitis*, "*if you could*."

Hence in such parentheses as *si placet, si videtur, nisi fallor*, the indicative mood is used, unless the whole sentence is in *oratio obliqua*.

So, when *si quando, si quis*, introduce a frequentative clause, the indicative is used, because the apodosis implies that something actually happens or happened on various occasions:

> *Si quem videret, ad se vocabat*   If he saw any one (*or*, whomever he saw) he summoned him.
> *Si quando me videret* . . .   As often as he saw me, he, etc.

[The use of the subjunctive in such sentences, found in Livy and later writers, is an imitation of the Greek optative—ὃν ἴδοι, ἐκάλει.]

140. Exceptions to the ordinary type of conditional sentences will be of two classes: (A.) those which the young composer must adopt as being part of the regular construction of the Latin language, and (B) those which he will occasionally meet with, especially in orators, and still more in poetry, and should account for when he meets them, but use sparingly.

(A) The principal verb is sometimes in the indicative mood, and yet the *si*-clause in the subjunctive.

In these cases it will be found that the indicative is a special kind of indicative, bearing a resemblance in meaning to the *potential* use of the subjunctive.

The indicative is used in combinations of the infinitive mood with *possum, debeo*, the impersonals *licet, oportet*, and the periphrastic tenses formed by the union of the gerund, gerundive, and future participle, with *esse*, and certain phrases, such as *melius fuit*, "it *would have been* better."

The use of these verbs and participial forms should be compared with that of the auxiliary verbs " may," " might," " would," " should," which form the substitute for the subjunctive mood in English :

> *Quid, si hostes ad urbem veniant, facturi estis?*   In case the enemy *should* come to the city, what do you *intend* (*or* are you *likely*) to do?
>
> *Hunc hominem, si ulla in te esset pietas, colere debebas.*   If you had had any natural affection (as you had not), you *ought to have* respected this man.
>
> *Deleri totus exercitus potuit, si fugientes persecuti victores essent.*   The whole army *might have been* destroyed (but was not) if the victors had pursued the fugitives (which they did not).
>
> *Hos nisi manu misisset, tormentis etiam dedendi fuerunt.*   If he had not set these men free, they *must have* been given up to torture (but they were not).
>
> *Si verum respondere velles, haec erant dicenda.*   Had it *at that time* been your wish to make a true answer, this is what you ought to have said.

At the same time the use of the subjunctive mood with *possum* is exceedingly common, unless great stress is laid on the fact of the possibility, as above.

Even with *debeo* and *oportet*, the subjunctive is often used, especially with the imperfect subjunctive, in purely imaginary and improbable cases :

> *Mihi ignoscere non deberetis, si tacerem.*   It *would be* (*or* have been) your duty not to forgive me if I *were* to be silent. But I am and have been speaking.
>
> *Si accusator non adesset, istum condemnari non oporteret.*   If no prosecutor were in court, the defendant ought not to be condemned.   But the prosecutor is here.

So we may say *idem eventurum fuit*, "the result would certainly," *eventurum fuisset* "would probably, have been the same."

141. (B.) More real irregularities (*not* to be imitated by young composers) are those cases where ordinary syntax, *i.e.* grammatical accuracy, is sacrificed for the sake of emphasis. As might be expected, this occurs mainly in poetical or highly oratorical language ; *e.g.*

> *Me truncus illapsus cerebro*
> *Sustulerat, nisi Faunus ictum*
> *Dextra levasset.*—HOR. *Od.* ii. 17.

> *Praeclare viceramus, nisi spoliatum, inermem, fugientem*
> *Lepidus recepisset Antonium.*—CIC. *Fam.* xii 10

> *Omnino supervacua erat doctrina, si natura sufficeret.*
> QUINT. ii. 8 8.

142. Some apparent irregularities are not really such ; *e.g.*

(i.) Where a subjunctive in the apodosis conveys a command, or a modest assertion, or a denial in form of a question, and is practically equivalent to an indicative ; *e.g.*

(*a.*) *Si stare non possunt, corruant* ("let them fall").—CIC. *Cat.* ii. 10.

(*b.*) *Si hoc dicis, nolim dictum.* If you say this, I am sorry that you (*or* "could wish that you had not") said it (*nolim* being the ordinary polite substitute for *nolo*).

(*c.*) *Etenim si nox non adimit vitam beatam, cur dies nocti similis adimat ?* (=*dies n. s. non adimit*, see **150**).

(*d.*) *Si in hoc erravi, quis mihi irascatur ?* (=*nemo mihi irascetur.*)

(ii.) Where the real protasis to a subjunctive apodosis is not the condition expressed in the indicative mood, but another not expressed, which would be in the subjunctive ; *e g.*

> *Si unquam tibi visus sum in republica fortis, certe me in illa*
> *causa admiratus esses* (i.e. *si affuisses*).

(iii.) Where, similarly, the apodosis to a subjunctive
si-clause is not that which appears in the indicative mood,
but a suppressed apodosis which would either be in the
infinitive of *oratio obliqua* or in the subjunctive mood; *e.g.*

> *Mortem tibi denuntiavit, nisi paruisses.*   He threatened you
> with death unless you obeyed him.

Here the real apodosis to *nisi paruisses* lies in *mortem*
=*fore ut morereris,* and *nisi paruisses* is really a subordinate
clause in *oratio obliqua.*

(iv.) Where *si* has a semi-*final* sense="to provide for
the case that," etc.; *e.g.*

> *Denos vobis sestertios misi, si forte pecuniâ opus fuisset.*   I
> sent you each 10 sesterces, in case you had required
> money.

Here the *si*-clause does not qualify the *misi.*   The
speaker had *certainly* sent the money; but the *si* is
equivalent to "to *provide for* the *case that*," etc., and this
final sense, as with *qui, dum,* etc., involves the use of the
subjunctive in the *si*-clause.   We might supply the
apodosis, *ut iis* or *quibus uteremini,* "for you to use."   The
subjunctive, therefore, of *fuisset* is not irregular, but in
accordance with all the usage of Latin.

(v.) Finally, there is a use of *si* which approaches very
nearly to that of an interrogative particle.   It is used
after such verbs as *expecto, experior,* in the sense of "in
the hope that," and, as expressing *the feeling under which*
the subject of the verb waited, or made the experiment,
is in the subjunctive mood of *oratio obliqua :*

> *Caesar expectabat, si hostem castris elicere posset.*   Caesar
> was waiting *in the hope of* enticing the enemy to leave
> his camp.

The *si*-clause does not qualify conditionally *expectabat,*
but it explains *his feeling* in waiting; there is no *apodosis*
at all; we may supply "that he might attack them," or

something of the kind, but none is expressed. This will explain passages in Caesar and Cicero where *si* appears to be used (like the Greek εἰ and our own *if*) as a purely interrogative particle.

143. Formulæ for the conversion of conditional sentences into ordinary *oratio obliqua* (cp 128):

ORATIO RECTA	ORATIO OBLIQUA.
I. *Si hoc dicis, erras,* *Si hoc dicebas, errabas,*	(*Dixit*) eum *si hoc dicat, errare.*
Si hoc dixisti, errasti,	„ „ *si hoc dixisset, errasse.*
II. *Si hoc dixeris, errabis,*	„ „ *si hoc dixisset, erraturum esse* (or *fore ut erraret*).
Si hoc dices, errabis,	
III. *Si hoc dicas, erres,* *Si hoc diceres, erraret,* (of present time)	„ „ *si hoc diceret, erraturum esse.*
IV. *Si hoc dixisset, errasset,*	„ „ *si hoc dixisset, erraturum fuisse* (or *futurum fuisse ut erraret*).

XIV.

Concessive Clauses.

144. By concessive clauses we mean such subordinate and adverbial clauses as are introduced in English by " although," in Latin by *etsi, etiamsi, quamquam, quamvis, licet;* and also by *quum* and the relative *qui*.

They are called *concessive* because they *concede*, or grant, something, *in spite of* which the statement of the main clause is true They are therefore nearly allied to conditional clauses, which suppose something on *condition of which* the truth of the main clause rests. Hence the use, for "although," of *etsi, etiamsi*, "even if," "even supposing that."

Their peculiarity is that the concession made *heightens by contrast* the statement made in the principal clause.

145. *Etsi, etiamsi*, and *tametsi* (=*tamen, etsi*) are used with the indicative when they introduce an actual *fact* which is contrasted with another *fact*. The particle *tamen*, "yet," "still," will often be inserted in the principal clause, and marks an opposition to the *concession* involved in *etsi*, or *etiamsi*:

> *Caesar, etsi nondum eorum consilia cognoverat, tamen fore id, quod accidit, suspicabatur.* Though Caesar had not yet learnt their plans, he began to suspect the result which actually occurred.

Tamen therefore answers to *etsi, quamquam, quamvis*, etc., exactly as *idcirco, ideo*, etc., to *quod, quia*, etc.; or as *eo consilio, idcirco*, to final *ut, ne;* or as *adeo, sic*, etc., to *ut, ut non*.

The subjunctive will be used (precisely as with *si*) only when the conjunction introduces an *imaginary* concession, contrasted generally with a statement which is not real, but only *imaginary:*

> *Equidem, etiamsi mors oppetenda sit, domi malim mortem oppetere.* For myself, even though I had to face death, I would prefer to face it at home.

146. *Quamquam* (a reduplicated *quam*, signifying "however much ") is used to introduce a *fact* represented as such, and contrasted with another *fact*. It therefore, unless for some special reason, is invariably followed by the indicative mood :

> *Quamquam abest a culpa, suspicione tamen non caret.* Though not actually to blame, yet he is not free from suspicion.

In classical Latin a subjunctive mood with *quamquam* is exceedingly rare unless the clause is in *oratio obliqua.*

But *quamvis*, when followed by a finite verb, **requires a subjunctive :**

> *Quamvis sit magna hominum expectatio, tamen eam vinces.* Although men's expectations are great, you will surpass them, or, *however* great *may* be, etc. . . . as *quamvis* suggests rather than states the clause conceded.

Quamvis=quam vis, "as you will," must have a subjunctive from the nature of the case, as the above sentence would originally be, "*Let* expectations *be* as great as you please, you will surpass them."

The verb, therefore, introduced by *quamvis* is, properly speaking, not *subordinate,* but a principal verb in a *co-ordinate* clause, and the subjunctive is used in its jussive sense, while the word *quam vis* is properly a short *modal clause,* "as you choose."

Indeed, *quamvis* is occasionally inflected ; *quam volet cunctetur, tamen peribit,* "however much he may delay, yet he shall perish," would be Ciceronian Latin.[1] It is sometimes used simply with an adjective, *quamvis audax,* " however bold ;" *quamvis nocens,* " however guilty."

---

[1] Cp. Cic. *Div.* i. 26 : *Caius Gracchus dixit sibi in somnis quaesturam petenti Tib. fratrem visum esse dicere, Quam vellet cunctaretur, tamen eodem sibi leto, quo ipse interisset, esse pereundum.*

147. *Licet*, "although," is properly the impersonal verb "it is allowed," or "granted," and therefore properly introduces a co-ordinate clause. It is, of course, always used in classical Latin with the *subjunctive*, never with the indicative:

> *Fremant omnes licet, tamen quod sentio dicam.* Though all murmur (all may murmur), yet what I think I will speak.

In later Latin the origin of these words became quite obliterated and the indicative was used freely with *quamvis*, and even with *licet*. Such constructions should not be imitated. As is natural from their original meaning, *licet* is **never,** *quamvis* **rarely, used with a verb in past time.**

Quamquam (rarely *etsi*) is frequently used in a manner recalling the connecting and co-ordinating use of *qui* (109), and of temporal *quum* (116). It answers to our English use of "although," equivalent to "and yet," and introduces a *fresh clause*, or even a long sentence corrective of something which has just been said. It is frequently used so in Cicero, and opens in this sense one of the finest passages in Virgil, *Georgic* 1. 469 *seq.*:

> *Tempore quamquam illo tellus quoque*, etc.

148. The conjunction *quum* of attendant circumstances is frequently used in a concessive sense, practically equivalent to "although." In classical writers the subjunctive is used:

> *Cum moenibus hostem propulsare posset, in aciem copias eduxit.* Though he might have kept back the enemy from the fortifications he led out his troops and formed them in line of battle.

Or, as we should say, "instead of remaining on the defensive behind his walls he offered battle."

As the use of *pro* with the gerundive is almost unknown, this is a frequent mode of expressing the English "*instead of doing so and so.*" (Cp. **117, 175.**)

Ut is often used in the concessive sense of "granted that." The clause to which it belongs stands before the principal clause:

> *Ut enim quaeras . . . non reperies.* Though you make inquiries, you will not find it.

The subjunctive is the only mood admissible in this usage. The negative of *ut* in this sense is usually *non* ·

> *Ut ego non dicam, apparere vobis puto.* Though I were not to speak, I think it is plain to you.

149. (*a.*) In Livy (and sometimes in Cicero) *sicut* and *ita* are often used to express a *contrast* The two clauses are placed side by side as though to show correspondence, really to emphasise the contrast between them.

The transition to this very common idiom will be made clear by a similar use of *ut* .

> *Ut nihil boni est in morte, sic certe nihil mali.* Just as (almost=although) there is no advantage in death, so (=yet) there is at all events no evil.

(*b.*) As with causal clauses, so with concessive, the corresponding English idiom will often be, not a subordinate clause, but a preposition or prepositional phrase, followed by a substantive ; *e.g.*

> Notwithstanding (*or* in spite of) his fears. *Quamquam timebat,* or *quum timeret,* or *qui timeret.*

(*c.*) It is also even more common in Latin than in English to put two contrasted clauses side by side, and to leave the "although" or "while" to be supplied by the reader:

> *Laetari se quod sibi gratulati essent, quod collegae nomen praetermisissent aegre ferre.* (He replied that) *while,* or *though,* he rejoiced at their congratulations, he was distressed at their having passed by his colleague's name.

"While" in this sense should never be translated by *dum.*

(*d.*) A concession is often made by two co-ordinate clauses, in one of which *ille quidem* (*tu quidem,* etc) is used, in the other an adversative particle such as *sed, tamen :*

> *Fuit ille quidem vir optimus, sed mediocris ingenii.* Though an excellent man, he was one of moderate abilities.

XV.

Note on Rhetorical Questions.

150. Questions that do not require an answer, but are only put in the form of a question in order to produce a greater effect on those to whom they are addressed, are called *rhetorical* questions, *i e.* such questions as a speaker would use to impress his audience. Thus, *ubi quemquam ejusmodi invenias* or *inveneris?* "where *could you* find any one of the sort?" is equivalent to "you could (*or* would) find no one," but the form of the question assumes that those addressed have the answer "nowhere" ready. So *quis crederet?* implies "no one *would have* believed."

When a matter of fact is denied, the rhetorical question will be in the indicative: *quis nescit?* "every one knows;" *quis ingemuit?* "not a soul uttered a groan." A very large number of questions introduced by *num, nonne,* and even *ne,* are purely rhetorical.

An when used to introduce a single question is invariably rhetorical, *i.e.* it takes for granted a certain answer by suggesting what is manifestly untenable, so that it is often equivalent to "you will hardly say," and follows often another question:

> *Quis neget omnes leves, omnes cupidos, omnes denique impro-*
> *bos esse servos? an ille mihi liber, cui mulier imperat?*
> Am I to count him a freeman who is ruled by a
> woman?

144

151. Similarly, the **subjunctive** in questions of surprise or indignation implies denial of the *possibility* or *probability* of the question suggested :

> *Egone tibi rationem reddam ?* And am I to give an account to you ?=Surely it is inconceivable that I am to be responsible
> *Egone pro patria non pugnarem ?* Was I not to fight for my native land ?=It is not likely that I should not (at that time) have fought, etc.

Sometimes (by an ellipsis of such a phrase as *potest fieri*) an *ut* is prefixed to the verb :

> *Egone ut haec furium, facerem ?* Is it possible that I should act, *or* have acted, so ?

And by the ellipsis [1] of some verb of believing or thinking a still more exclamatory form is used by the employment of the infinitive :

> *Quemquam,* or *quemquamne, tam furiosum esse,* or *fuisse ?* Could any one be, *or* have been, so insane ?

152. The rhetorical question is often used in such phrases as :

> *Quid plura de hac re loquar ? unde rectius ordiri possum quam a . . . ?* I need say no more on this question. I cannot begin better than with . . .

So *quin taces ?* " why are you not silent ?" *i.e.* " be silent."
It will be remembered that while the indicative may be used in either a true or a rhetorical question, the subjunctive and infinitive (in *oratio recta*) are always used *rhetorically*

---

[1] It is however equally probable that this idiom is a purely exclamatory use of the infinitive, analogous to the " *accusativus exclamantis* " (*Me miserum!* etc): cp. VIRG. *Aen.* I. 37.

Quid? Quid enim? are constantly introduced in Latin in a manner which no literal translation can render.

The former is often used to introduce a fresh argument, put in the form of a question (rhetorical), and may be translated by "again," "to go on," sometimes by "tell me." Its use in infinitive clauses (*oratio obliqua*) is curious, as it is used within the clause, but quite independently, after a verb of thinking:

> *Quid enim me quo tum animo fuisse censetis?* For as to myself, what do you think were my feelings then?

Quid enim? may often be turned by " for consider this point;" *quid ergo?* "what conclusion follows?" So *quid tum? quid postea? Quid quod . . .?* (sometimes printed *Quid? Quod . . .?*), "what are we to say to the fact that . . .?"

XVI.

Specimen Lecture on Latin Prose Composition.

NARRATIVE STYLE.

153. In this chapter an attempt is made to illustrate practically the teaching of Latin prose composition by taking certain passages of English, and explaining in detail (as a teacher might to his class) the process of translation into Latin. The first instance will be a narrative or historical passage:

"Meantime a flag of truce arrived from the enemy, inviting us to a conference outside the fort, and professing that they had a communication to make which they hoped would put an end to hostilities. On one of our field-officers being ordered out, the Rajah assured him that, in attacking our cantonments, he had not acted on his own will or judgment, but under compulsion from his people; that, though nominally commander, his authority over his soldiers was hardly equal to that which they exercised over himself. He was not, he added, so ignorant of the world as to believe that his forces could defy the power of England; but he had found resistance to the general rising of his nation quite impossible. Now that he had satisfied the claims of patriotism, he earnestly warned the general to save himself and his soldiers. He offered his solemn oath to guide them in safety through his own territory to the next cantonments. In doing this he should, he said, both serve his own countrymen and show substantial gratitude for many past favours to his English friends. Only let there be no delay or hesitation. Before three days were over the insurgents would be largely reinforced, and all hope of safety would have absolutely disappeared."

154. How are the first few words to be turned ? "A flag of truce" will at once present difficulties. The words *vexillum* and *indutiae* may be thought of, and it might occur that *vexillum indutiarum signum* would be an adequate rendering. Possibly so in some cases, but obviously not here; for all that follows **(and no passage should be attempted till it has been carefully read through)** shows that no truce or armistice is spoken of, but that the word "flag" is used, somewhat loosely, for the person or persons whom it covers or protects on a message from combatants to combatants, in this case from besiegers to besieged. This is made more clear by the words "inviting" and "professing," which are placed in apposition with "flag of truce." As no such recognised custom of protecting messengers during actual hostilities or battle by a white flag or other conspicuous sign is recorded, we must think of something equivalent, and use the word *legatus* or *legati*, remembering the sacred and inviolable character that was attached to such persons. Write, therefore, for the first line, **adsunt interea hostium legati.**

The tense of **adsunt** will give liveliness to the picture; this will be increased by placing the verb in this unusual position (see Order of Words, **10**), thus emphasising the sudden appearance of "the flag of truce." The subject of the sentence will accordingly be placed last; the **hostium,** which marks that the visitors come from no friendly nation, but from foes in arms, and thus completes the idea of "a flag of truce," will of course come before it, while the **interea** will take the central position. We are thus breaking up the English sentence, which is not a period (**21**), but a loosely constructed sentence, into two or three short Latin co-ordinate sentences, the descriptive effect of which is heightened by placing the verb in each as the opening word (**10**). For "inviting," therefore, after carefully avoiding the present participle (**98**), and instinctively shrinking from the word *invitare* (**34**), [though there is no special objection to its use here, and *ad colloquium extra arcem* or *castellum invitant*

would do very well], we write **postulant ut aliqui e nostris
ad colloquium prodirent.** If you look out *prodire* you will
find it often used for coming forth from the walls of a
city into the open country. But what of the *tense* of
prodirent? Surely after *postulant* we should expect *pro-
deant.* The answer is simple: *postulant* is merely the
praesens historicum (**57**), far more common in Latin than
in English, and often followed in subordinate clauses
by tenses which remind the reader that, though in form
it is a present tense (**57**), it is describing a past event.
For "and professing" we might begin a third co-ordinate
sentence with *profitentur*, or *simulant*, or *dictitant*, a
word often used in the sense of an insincere assertion.
But there is, in fact, no occasion for any such word: the
transition to the infinitive mood will be quite sufficient
in Latin to mark that the sentence which follows is in
oratio obliqua, and expresses, no longer the sentiments of
the historian, but the words of some one else as reported
by him (**123**). Write therefore simply **habere se,** equivalent to "they had, they said," and notice the necessity of inserting *se*, the two words answering to the *habe-
mus, inquiunt* of *oratio recta*   How are we to turn "communication"? It would be quite useless to look it out
in an English-Latin Dictionary. It is one of those
innumerable abstract nouns, so common in modern language, which are so rare in Latin (**33, 40**), and which
you cannot possibly render literally. We must at once
go behind the word to look at its meaning, which is
very simple, and write, **habere se quae dicere vellent,**
"they had something which they wished to say." The
mood of **vellent** is, of course, accounted for by its being
part of a reported speech in which the indicative is absolutely inadmissible; the tense might be present, *velint ·*
but the past time is preferred, as above in **prodirent.**
For the rest of the sentence we might again start with
the verb, and write *sperare se*, but the effect would be
monotonous, and it is therefore better to go on with a
relatival sentence, using the relative however in its co-
ordinating sense, and write *quibus dictis*, or, as *quibus* by
itself would be somewhat ambiguous, introducing the

word *rebus*, **quibus rebus,** and add **pugnandi finem fieri
posse sperarent.** The whole sentence thus winds up with
a verb, the principal verb of the last clause, the normal
ending of a Latin sentence (7). The mood and tense
of the verb have been already explained. The in-
strumental ablative of **quibus rebus** and the use of **fieri**
should be noticed: *haec res finem pugnandi fecit* would
be good Latin, but such a quasi-personification of a yet
unmade communication as would be involved in the use of
the active voice would be alien to Latin (32); a passive
construction is therefore adopted. Notice also the use of
posse with **sperarent.** Verbs of hoping almost uniformly
take a future infinitive (*sperat se diu victurum*), but the
present of the verb *possum* is constantly used, and here
dispenses with the awkward form *factum iri*. The use
of the simple and concrete form **pugnandi** for the English
abstract term " hostilities " should also be noticed. The
first sentence, then, stands thus :

**Adsunt interea hostium legati ; postulant ut aliqui e
nostris ad colloquium prodirent ; habere se quae dicere
vellent, quibus rebus pugnandi finem fieri posse sperarent.**

155. The next sentence begins with the phrase " on
. . . being ordered out." These combinations of " on,"
" after," with an apparent participle, may generally be
turned either by a *quum*-clause (116), or, if merely short
phrases, such as " on hearing this," by the ablative
absolute (99). Here, however, the more graphic style already adopted of co-ordinate sentences may be maintained:
Mittitur ad eos colloquendi causa unus e tribunis nostris.
This is equivalent to *Ad quos quum colloquendi causa unus
e tribunis nostris missus esset* (or *prodire jussus esset*). Notice
in this clause the unemphatic use of **unus** and the word
tribuni as answering best to our " superior officers " (*cen-
turiones* would be a lower grade, *legati* a higher: *duces*
would be " guides "). We may then, by the aid of the
relative used co-ordinately, link on the next clause, and
introduce the long passage in *oratio obliqua* which follows

to the end of the passage: **apud quem** ("in whose presence") **regulus** ("the petty king") **hunc in modum locutus est.** These last words will express that the general drift of his conversation (not a set speech, which would be *hujusmodi orationem habuit*) is what is given.

Mitittur adeos colloquendi causa unus e tribunis nostris, apud quem regulus hunc in modum locutus est.

156. This expression of the Rajah's views and offers is continued, it will be remembered, to the end of the Exercise, the whole of which is in *oratio obliqua* **It is of the utmost importance to notice this, as otherwise the whole passage will be hopelessly mistranslated.** It must be remembered that, in English historians, long passages of *oratio obliqua*, that is of the views and sentiments, not of the historian, but of some of the persons mentioned in his narrative, are often introduced with no mark but that of past instead of present tenses, and the third person instead of the first; and a careless reader will forget that in Latin such passages require other changes, such as, above all, the substitution of the infinitive mood for the indicative in some verbs, of the subjunctive in others **(124).**

157. To proceed: "in attacking our cantonments" we may either write simply, **quod castra nostra oppugnasset** or **oppugnaverit**, or (as Caesar writes) **quod fecerit** (or **fecisset**) **de oppugnatione castrorum**, using in the former **quod** for "in that," "as to his having." The word *oppugnare* is the only word suitable, being the one regular word in use for an attack on a city or camp (any use, therefore, of *invado, ingredior, adorior*, etc., will be wrong); the tense may be either perfect or pluperfect. The latter would, of course, be more logical, but the former is also very common in Roman historians, and answers precisely to the use of the historic present " as to the fact that he *had* or *has* attacked." Of the mood, of course, there can be no doubt. *The indicative must be absolutely banished from*

any passage in oratio obliqua. " He had not acted," etc.:
" acted" must of course be in the infinitive; the use of
the indicative would be fatal to any hope of rendering
the passage correctly. Avoid also the word *ago*, which is
constantly misused owing to the resemblance of sound
(34) (e.g. *hacc mecum egit* is not " he *acted* thus with
me," but " he *spoke* thus with me"), and write **id se non
voluntate sua aut judicio fecisse**; where for once the two
substantives closely resemble the English, but are placed
in a different part of the clause, leaving the final place
for the verb. " But under compulsion," etc ,—here again
avoid all attempts at reproducing so abstract a noun, and
beware of the jingle of sound suggesting the use of *com-
pellere*, " to drive;" write, **sed coactum a suis**, and note
both the special sense of *sui*, and its emphatic place.

" That, though nominally," etc. This sentence is somewhat difficult. *Verbo* or *nomine* are sometimes opposed to
re, re ipsa, but the real difficulty lies in " though." All
attempts to express it by *quamvis* or *quanquam* should be
avoided. It may be rendered in two ways: **verbo se imperare,
re ipsa non minus in se juris habere exercitum quam ipse
in exercitum**, or by a very common use of *ita* in a restrictive
sense, **ita se imperare**, " so far, *and so far only*, did he
exercise command (*imperium*), that," etc (105). Notice
carefully *in te jus habeo*, " for I have *authority* over you,"
and beware especially of using *auctoritas* in any place
where "authority" represents, as it generally does, "power,"
(" authority deserts a dying king "); *auctoritas* is " moral
influence," not " jurisdiction" or military or regal " power."
The Rajah's speech thus far stands :

**Quod fecerit (or fecisset) de oppugnatione castrorum, id se
non voluntate sua aut judicio fecisse, sed coactum a suis; ita
se illis imperare, ut non minus in se juris haberet exercitus
quam ipse in exercitum.**

158. " He was not, he added," etc. Of course "he
added" must not be turned by *adjecit*, etc., in a parenthesis; but " he was not" should be in the infinitive of

oratio obliqua, and "he added" expressed (if at all, for in the English it is mainly inserted to mark the *oratio obliqua*) by *praeterea*, or simply *neque;* and we shall thus write **praeterea non adeo** (or, **neque adeo**), **se esse imperitum rerum** : *rerum imperitus* exactly answers to our "ignorant of life," or "of the world;" **rerum** being placed in an unusual position to give it emphasis (**3**), *i.e.* "the real world" (it is hardly necessary to warn against *mundi, vitae,* etc , see **28**). "As to believe," etc ; the word "defy" comes to us from the feudal customs of the middle ages, and can rarely be adequately turned in Latin; avoid any attempt to introduce *provocare ad bellum*, which would be far too rhetorical, and use simply **superari**. "Power of England ." avoid carefully such a word as *Anglia, Britannia;* these personifications of a geographical term are most unusual in Latin prose authors. Write **populus noster**, or **populus Anglicanus** (or, in this case, *populus Romanus*[1]): **ut suis copiis populum nostrum superari posse confidat** or **confideret** (immaterial which). "But that he had found it," etc : the words "impossible," "resistance," and even "rising," may present difficulties. Of course there are no such words as *possibilis, impossibilis*, in Latin; but the infinitive *resisti* will readily (**41**) supply the abstract substantive, and its impersonal use in combination with *possum* and a dative will meet the difficulty. For "rising" avoid *rebellio*, which is a "renewal of war:" *defectio*, a revolt of subjects or subject allies, will be better: and note for "general" (adjective) the very common combination of *tantus* with *tam* and another adjective: **sed tantae tamque communi suorum defectioni resisti non potuisse.** The sentence will now run:

Praeterea non adeo se esse imperitum rerum, ut suis copiis populum nostrum superari posse confideret, sed tantae tamque communi suorum conjurationi resisti non potuisse.

---

[1] The substitution of *ancient* names of nations or individuals in the translation of a *modern* historical passage sometimes involves inadmissible, or even absurd, historical parallels. It should therefore be used with caution · and, as a general rule, it is best to Latinise the modern name, if in any way capable of a Latin form.

159. "Now that he had satisfied," etc. You may find this hard. "Patriot" is usually *bonus civis, homo reipublicae studiosus*, etc.; and you might begin *boni civis se officio functum esse:* but Caesar writes **quibus quoniam pro pietate satisfecerit** (or **satisfecisset**), "and as he has done all that is due to these (his countrymen), in accordance with the dictates of natural affection" "He earnestly warned:" "earnestly" need not be turned by an adverb; *vehementer* would do, but the combination of two verbs is better: **hortari monere (54, 104)**; note the infinitive, and make sure that you thoroughly understand it, as well as what it is that here makes a subjunctive necessary after *quoniam* **(114)**. "The general" may be *consulem*, or a proper name may be adopted; "general," as a word expressing rank in the army, does not exist in Latin; *illum* might be used between the two verbs, as *ille* in *oratio obliqua* often expresses "the other party" to the speaker. "To save himself," etc.: the English infinitive will, of course, be expressed by **ut**, not merely because fresh infinitives would cause great ambiguity, but because verbs of the character of *hortari* and *monere* require this construction (distinguish between *Caesarem hoc facere moneo* and *Caesarem ut hoc faciat moneo*). For the word "save," *conservare*, however literal, would be too rhetorical for Latin; *conservare velit* might do, but the general context is in favour of a less exaggerated expression; write, therefore, **ut suae ac militum saluti consulat.** Note the tense of *consulat* as more picturesque than *consuleret*, which would be equally good Latin, and the genitive **militum** exactly corresponding to the adjective **suae.** We read then:

Quibus quoniam pro pietate satisfecerit, hortari, monere, ut suae ac militum saluti consulat.

160. "He offered his," etc. It would not be impossible to treat this as *oratio recta*, but it is better to regard it as part of his language ("I offer you," etc.). How to turn such a word as "solemn"? Use two verbs as above, and

write **illud se polliceri, ac jurejurando confirmare velle,** and
notice how often *illud* is put forward at the beginning of
a sentence to mark something of importance (sometimes
a well-known quotation) that is to follow. "To guide them
in safety:" of course the regular construction after verbs of
promising, *i.e.* the *future*, not the present, infinitive must be
used (74). "In safety" will of course be the adjective *tutus*
(or *incolumis*); why would *securus* or *sine injuria* be entirely
wrong? **tutos per fines suos ad proxima castra ducturum:**
why would *acturum* be wrong? Notice that the usual *se*
with the infinitive future is often omitted when it has
preceded an infinitive *oratio obliqua* of the verb of promising.

161. "In doing this," etc. "This" will, as so often at
the beginning of a fresh clause, be turned by the relative.
Quod quum faciat; the subjunctive is used, *not* on account
of *quum*, but because the indicative is throughout inadmissible: "he said" is only inserted in the English to
mark that it is the Rajah, not the author, who is speaking;
this is made quite clear in the Latin by the moods used,
and the insertion of *dixit* would be worse than needless.
"He would both serve," etc.: avoid *servire*, "to be a slave,"
which would be absurd here; *inservire* is used no doubt
as a metaphor "for to devote one's-self to," but this is not
the meaning required; write **et suis (or civibus suis) profuturum.** "And show substantial gratitude," etc: dismiss
at once all idea of using *ostendere* or *monstrare*, but note
that the verb, whatever it is, should here close and wind
up the sentence. For "English friends" it will be quite
sufficient to put *nostri*, "the author's countrymen" (or to
substitute *Romani*); write therefore **et nostris pro meritis
multis.** Notice the word *merita* used substantively for
"past good services:" *favor* would be quite absurd: *bene-
ficium*, which is "an act of kindness," would do. *Prae-
teritis* would be most unclassical: the word "past" is
implied in **merita**: with *beneficiis*, an *acceptis* might be
inserted. "To show gratitude" is almost invariably to be
turned by *gratiam referre,* just as "to express gratitude"

is *gratias agere*, " to feel it " *gratiam habere;* write, therefore, simply **gratiam relaturum** (the *esse* is constantly omitted in the future infinitive). This sentence now stands ·

Illud se polliceri et jurejurando confirmare velle, tutos se per fines suos ad proxima castra ducturum, quod quum faciat, et suis profuturum, et nostris pro meritis multis gratiam relaturum.

162. " Only let there," etc. Here in *oratio recta* the imperative of *cavere* would be used ; probably with an emphatic *tu : tu igitur cave,* or *cave modo ne ;* in *oratio obliqua,* **modo ne** will be sufficient with the imperfect, or even, for the sake of *vividness,* the present subjunctive : **Modo ne ille cunctaretur aut dubitaret.** The **ille** marks the transition from the speaker to the person addressed, just as *tu* might have done in *oratio recta.* " Before three days," etc. (here of course the mood must again be the infinitive, as the language passes from that of entreaty to that of statement (**intra triduum**) : notice this common use of the preposition *intra* to express time) ; " insurgents" belongs to a whole class of substantives which hardly exist in Latin (**33**), and *insurgentes* would be absurd: write therefore simply **hostibus** (*eis qui defecissent* would be needless circumlocution) **magna adfore subsidia,** and notice this meaning of *subsidia,* and the impossibility of turning " I am largely reinforced " · literally into Latin. " And all hope," etc. Do not for a moment think of Latin words answering to " disappear " (which is obviously, when we examine it, a pure metaphor), but write **salutis spem relictum iri nullam,** and notice both the curious use of the supine with the impersonal infinitive of *itur* for the future infinitive passive, and also the emphatic position of *nullam,* which sufficiently expresses the intensive English adverb " absolutely."

The whole passage therefore runs thus :

Adsunt interea hostium legati ; postulant ut aliqui e nostris ad colloquium prodirent: habere se quae dicere vellent, quibus rebus pugnandi finem fieri posse sperarent. Mittitur ad eos colloquendi

*causa unus e tribunis nostris, apud quem regulus hunc in modum
locutus est. Quod fecerit (or fecisset) de oppugnatione castrorum,
id se non voluntate sua aut judicio fecisse, sed coactum a suis, ita
se illis imperare ut non minus juris haberet in se exercitus quam
ipse in exercitum. Praeterea non adeo se esse imperitum rerum
(or non quo adeo ipse esset imperitus rerum) ut suis copiis populum
nostrum superari posse confideret, sed tantae tamque communi
suorum conjurationi resisti non potuisse. Quibus quoniam pro
pietate satisfecerit, hortari, monere, ut suae ac militum saluti
consulat. Illud se polliceri, et jurejurando confirmare velle, tutos
se per fines suos ad proxima castra ducturum: quod cum faciat, et
suis profuturum, et nostris pro meritis multis gratiam relaturum.
Modo ne ille cunctaretur aut dubitaret. Intra triduum magna
adfore hostibus subsidia: salutis spem relictum iri nullam.*

Metaphorical and Abstract Expressions.

163. Let us now take some sentences illustrative
of the treatment of Metaphorical Expressions (27-31).

Such a sentence as, " He was ready, he said, to sacrifice
all private animosities, all private friendship, on the altar
of patriotism," might easily occur in a modern author.
But the metaphor would be quite alien to the genius of
Latin. We should write simply **omnes se simultates,
amicitias omnes, rei publicae posthabere velle.**

Notice here—(1.) the omission of the parenthetic " he
said," and the substitution of its Latin equivalent, the
infinitive of *velle;* (2.) the plural of the abstract term
amicitia: friendship with many persons (**44**).

164. " It seemed as though in the darkest hour of
national gloom, a gleam of light had illuminated the
cheerless horizon."

Such a passage is obviously highly figurative; yet it
would not strike us as unduly or absurdly so, but to turn

it literally into Latin would be impossible, for reasons
given above (**30, 31**).

The following would represent it in the style of Cicero:

**Itaque in tristissimo reipublicae tempore lux quaedam
afflictae civitati oblata videbatur.**

Note first the position and use of **videbatur**: its *position*
as the verb at the close of the sentence (**7**); its *use*,
in that it is used (as always) not impersonally, as in
English ("it seemed that"), nor parenthetically, but *personally*, and as a principal verb, partaking in some degree of
a modal or qualifying nature, like *possum, volo*, etc. etc.:
"They are, it seems, wrong in this matter," is in Latin *hac*
or *qua in re errare videntur*. This, however, is a question
of syntax: no knowledge of syntax will suffice for a guide
through the rest of the sentence. We should begin with
some connecting particle; **itaque** would perhaps suit the
unknown context as referring to the probable circumstances. "In an hour:" any use of *hora* is out of the
question; for Latin is far too literal and unpoetical a
language to use *hora*, a subdivision of day and night, for
a political crisis. But it so happens that *tempus* is used
in this secondary sense; see such phrases as *tempori inservire*, etc. May we therefore write *in* (note the use of the
preposition, Arn., rev. ed., 273) *tempore obscurissimo?* No:
this would be meaningless in Latin; for the Romans, though,
like all human beings, they preferred sunlight to darkness,
had no words which connected unconsciously the ideas of
darkness and depression. We are therefore obliged to be
more matter of fact, and to write **in tristissimo rei publicae
tempore**; and we can hardly express the English words
more nearly than this. For the adjective "national" we
must substitute, as often, the genitive of *respublica*.

165. But are we to turn aside entirely from the figure
of *light in darkness* which the English sentence conveys?
Not entirely, but we must introduce the figure *as a figure*,
and not mix up the figurative language, and that which
it signifies, with the boldness natural to an English writer

handling a familiar figure. We may write *lux quaedam,* using *quidam* in a very common sense, "light, so to speak;"[1] but what about "the cheerless horizon"? For reasons given above (**30, 31**), omit the phrase, or rather substitute what *it means* for what *it says,* and write **afflictae civitati,** "the nation in its humiliation," adding **oblata esse,** a Ciceronian expression in a similar passage—or, if you wish to keep up the metaphor as nearly as possible, use the verb *offulgere,* and, not forgetting perhaps to insert *tanquam* to remind an unimaginative Roman that you are not talking nonsense, write **tanquam offulsisse videbatur.**

This sentence, which should be carefully re-read, will give a good instance of the enormous difference between the two languages, in their capacity for absorbing into common use figures of speech drawn from the remotest sources.

166. " The politician, the student, the votary of science, the mere sensualist, while they differ on all other points, are, I incline to think, entirely unanimous on this."

Not one of these substantives or phrases, expressing different classes, can be turned into Latin by any closely corresponding word.

There is no such word as *politicus* in genuine Latin ; *studere* and *studium* have no essential connection with our word " study" in its modern sense (**34, 35**). It is therefore necessary in each case to use a paraphrase and substitute a *qui-* clause :

Qui ad rempublicam se contulerunt, qui vel literarum vel naturae cognitione delectantur, qui totos se dederunt voluptatibus, ceteris de rebus inter se dissentiunt, de hac re haud scio an omnes uno ore consentiant.

Note the invariable force of *haud scio an,* equivalent to " perhaps," " I incline to think." And remember that *respublica* (in the singular, never used in this sense in the plural) is the Latin for " politics " (**36,** A).

---

[1] See Arnold, rev. ed., 361, *Obs.* 1.

167. Again, we might easily meet in English, and pass over without notice, such a sentence as " And the sequel of his life was in entire correspondence with this its opening chapter."

We see that the metaphor is drawn from a biography or novel, but such a figure of speech would be impossible in Latin, where printed books were unknown. If we use any metaphor at all, we must take one drawn from the acts of a play, and say,

Et qualis ille in primo vitae tanquam actu exstitit talem se ad finem or ad exitum gessit ;

or drop the metaphor entirely, and write with Cicero,

Atque his vitae ejus principiis reliqua consentiebant omnia.

168. So, again, take such a sentence as, " It is quite within possibility that a man's political views may be admirable, but that he may be denied the faculty of expressing his thoughts in finished or graceful language."

In attempting to turn such a sentence we must first grasp the obvious meaning of the English, and discard all endeavour to reproduce its form. If once we try to think what is the Latin of " quite," of " possibility," of " political," we start on a wrong track, and are sure to go wrong. We may begin **Quid enim facilius fieri potest**, inserting an *enim* almost at guess, in order to connect the sentence with an imaginary context, for we remember how rarely a Latin sentence, unless for a rhetorical purpose, begins without some connecting word (5), and we notice also how much simpler and more concrete is the Latin than the English form which the question assumes.

We continue with **quam ut**, the ut introducing a substantival sentence in close connection with *fieri possit*. How are we to turn "political views"? There is no Latin adjective answering to " political," and if the word *sententiae* occurs for a moment, it is better to remember that the ordinary Latin for " these are my views " is not *haec mea est sententia*, which would have a quasi-technical sense of a speech in the Senate, but *haec sentio* · we accordingly write **quam ut optime** (dismissing all thought of *admirabiliter*, etc, and going to the meaning rather than the sound of "admirable") **quis** (for the use of this indefinite *quis* see Arnold, rev. ed, 357) **de republica sentiat.**

"But that he may be denied the faculty," etc. Here, again, the moment we think of how to use *argui, facultas*, or *exprimere*, and so to construct the sentence on English lines, we are lost; our Latin must be much simpler and more direct. Write **sed ea quae sentit polite atque eleganter eloqui non possit.**

As a rule we must be on our guard in the use of adverbs (52-54), but the two used here have abundant authority. *Eleganter* will often express our " with good taste."

POLITICAL TERMS.

169. A few examples will now be given of the manner in which passages dealing mainly with political terms and ideas should be translated.[1]

Take first such a passage as

I. "Political harmony, he added, was only attainable in countries where the interests of all classes were really or apparently identical. It was to the conflict of selfish aims, springing from the incompatibility of divergent interests, that the demons of faction and discord owed their birth."

It is not necessary to say that " he added " must not be literally translated. It is merely a sign that the passage is taken from a *reported speech,* and is therefore in *oratio obliqua ;* and any such verb as *addidit, praeterea dixit*, etc., would show that the translator was unfamiliar with the style of Latin authors.

---

[1] For a list of some such terms see **36,** A.

The passage looks like the conclusion of some remarks. We may therefore connect it with what is supposed to have come before by the co-ordinating conjunction *denique.* Write for the first sentence: **In ea denique civitate gigni posse concordiam.**

Notice, as often, the absence of any Latin adjective for " political;" its place is taken by the word **civitas,** for which, however, *populus* (an organised and civilised people) might be substituted; notice also the use of **gigni,** a metaphor not uncommon in Cicero and the best writers, "to come into being."

But the next clause, " in which the interest," etc , seems much harder; yet it is really easy, if once we shake off its English dress, and. instead of hunting for the Latin of " interest," " classes," " identical," " really," " apparently," go at once to the root of the matter, *i e* to the real and simple meaning of the words, and write **in qua idem omnibus vel conducat vel conducere videatur.**

Notice that " classes " need not here be expressed at all; that the adverbs " really " and " apparently," though sometimes they may be turned by *re* and *specie,* may appear in quite another shape in the Latin. Notice also the present tense of the impersonal **conducat.** The reason of the mood is obvious (*oratio obliqua*), but though the imperfect tense would seem natural, and would be good Latin, the present is better, as the maxim is a general one, extending over all time.

170. The next sentence will seem at first sight to defy translation, and is difficult to any one unaccustomed to read Cicero. We may begin it thus: **Ex utilitatum diversitate,** or even **diversitatibus.**

Utilitas is constantly used by Cicero as an abstract term for " interest," " self-interest," as opposed to *honestas,* " duty." Its plural, when applied to the interest of more parties than one, is entirely in accordance with the tendency of Latin to treat even an abstract noun as something concrete, *e.g. multorum amicitiae* (**44**).

Diversitas, it is to be remembered, means not "variety," but actual "divergence," "opposition" [*diversi abeunt*, "they depart in opposite (*not* "various") directions"] The plural is more than admissible here; but the singular would be equally good Latin.

"Springing from," etc Here again we must set the English form entirely on one side, and be content with something so simple, yet so completely answering to the idea which we wish to express, as **quum aliis aliud expediat**; the idea being that mere *variety* of interests causes *divergence*

"That the demons," etc. It need hardly be said that the expression "demons" is a metaphor drawn from sources to which the language of the Romans had no access. How shall we turn it? Obviously by some strong expression. *Res perniciosissimas* might do, but we might find even a stronger: **pessimas rerum publicarum clades** is a Ciceronian phrase, and will remind us of the meaning of *respublica* in the plural, *i.e.* not "public affairs," in which sense it is always used in the singular, but "commonwealths," or "states" This phrase will, of course, be in apposition with what follows, gaining emphasis by standing first, just as *rem pretiosissimam, libertatem*, would translate "the priceless jewel of freedom."

"Faction and discord:" even here we must be on our guard. *Factio* is good Latin, but in what sense?—"*a* faction," not the abstract idea of "factiousness." We must therefore use the plural, and it will be better, though not necessary, to do the same with *discordia*, and write **factiones ac discordias nasci solere**; *nasci* and *gigni* (see above) being common metaphors in Latin authors.

The whole passage therefore will run:

In ea denique civitate gigni posse concordiam, in qua idem omnibus vel conducat vel conducere videatur: ex utilitatum diversitate, quum aliis aliud expediat, pessimas rerum publicarum clades, factiones et discordias, nasci solere.

171. Again, take such a passage as:

II. "In the history, sir, of this country, the aspirants to political life and to political eminence have always fallen into two classes. Of these the one has practised and professed the principles of a popular, the other those of an aristocratic, party. Those who aimed at gratifying the masses by their measures and their language were classed among the former; to the latter were assigned those who so shaped their conduct as to win for their policy the approval of the best members of the State."

Here we must at once set aside the word "history," which is not emphatic enough to call for such a phrase as *si antiquitatis memoriam replicare vis;* but it is well to remark that when we wish to express "history" we should avoid such phrases as *annales, fasti,* and even *historia,* and use *rerum scriptores,* or *antiquitatis memoria,* as the context requires (**36, B**); in the present passage *semper* is all that is needed.

"Sir," it need hardly be said, is merely the mark of the words being taken in *oratio recta* from a parliamentary speech. If turned at all it should be by *patres conscripti;* it is hardly needed here:

Duo genera semper P. C. in hac civitate fuerunt eorum qui versari in republica atque in ea excellentius se gerere voluerunt.

Note that the words which close the English sentence, "two classes," are so emphatic that they come first of all in the Latin; "fall into two classes" *may* be turned by *in duo genera dividi possunt,* but such a phrase would be needlessly cumbrous here. For "country," as in passage I, use *civitas;* nothing could be more absurd than to write *terra,* though it is a degree better than *rure* (see **28**). Notice how "aspirants" is turned; how large the number of English nouns which have nothing to correspond to them in Latin (**33**). "Political life," *versari in r. p.* is the regular expression for "to take part in politics;"

compare also the phrases, *ad r. p. accedere ; r. p. attingere ; r. p capessere.* Notice too the mode of turning "political eminence," and the real force of *atque,* and of the comparative *excellentius,* "with some degree of eminence."

172. In the next sentence we must be careful. It will be best to write it down at once in Latin:

Quibus ex generibus, alteri se populares alteri optimates et haberi et esse voluerunt.

It is hardly necessary to notice the connecting use of the co-ordinating *qui,* if it were not for the temptation to overlook the tendency of Latin to unite one sentence with another, and not, as in English, to leave the reader or hearer to do this (see **5**).

Of course, as the *genera* or "classes" are two, *alteri,* not *alii,* is used, and the use of a gender explains itself. If the singular were used it would of course be *alterum.* Observe how "professing and practising" are turned; this antithesis between *esse* and *videre* or *haberi* is very common. Above all, notice the right words for a "popular" or "liberal" and an "aristocratic" party. The words *patres* or *patricii* would be absurd in Cicero's time; and though *nobiles* is often used, it is somewhat different in sense, and suggests a less favourable meaning than *optimates* (cp. **36**, A).

173. "Those who aimed at," etc We must be careful here as to the use of words. "Aimed at," "measures," "language," may greatly mislead us, especially the two latter; they mean nothing more than "acts and speeches;" but such words as *acta* (proceedings of the Senate), *res gestae,* "exploits," *sermones,* "conversations," will be quite inadmissible. We might begin *Qui facta sua atque dicta,* but had better follow the guidance of Cicero, and write:

Qui ea quae faciebant (note the tense) **quaeque dicebant multitudini jucunda esse volebant, populares (habebantur).**

forensic speech, **creditote, judices**; *judices* answering to our "gentlemen of the jury," as *Patres Conscripti* to "Sir," or "Mr. Speaker." But the main difficulties are obviously in the words "principle," "duty," "expediency," "interests." They will be quite insuperable to those who have used some portion of Cicero's philosophical works, such as the *De Officiis*; to those who are familiar with his style it will be perfectly easy; and the first part of the sentence may run thus:

Hoc autem creditote, P. C., neminem posse iis quae utilia sint non recta et honesta (or virtutem et honestatem) posthabere.

Note mood *sint*. The subjunctive is right if expressed as part of their belief, *i.e.* as strictly subordinate (though by *posthabere* to *creditote*); but the indicative would suit if looked on as coming from the speaker's lips, as more definition of *iis* (cp. 114 (2), 127).

Notice the absolute impossibility of reproducing the better metaphor in "sacrifice."

Sect. 1. is fairly easy; but how are we to turn the preposition "without" followed by the verbal noun "injuring"? The whole passage will illustrate the means of doing this; and it is enough to say that any use of the English preposition *sine* will lead us far astray into every conceivable absurdity.

Quin iis rebus (or utilitatibus, plural of abstract noun) quibus servire (or prodesse) velit, noceat. Observe the mood *velit* as part of the belief which he wishes to impress on his hearers, and thus *virtual oratio obliqua* (127).

176. "That the three estates of this realm," etc. We are here in the very midst of English modern political phraseology, familiar to us from childhood, but wholly

Notice that *qui*, in the sense of "whoever," "all who,"
is joined, not, as you might imagine from the analogy of
Greek, with a subjunctive, but with an indicative; *vellent*
would be a mark of later Latin (72, 139). "The former"
is expressed by repeating the term **populares**.

174. The next clause may be shortened in the Latin
by keeping the two clauses in close connexion, and turning "classed among" and "were assigned to" by the
single word *habebantur*. We may turn it thus:

**Qui autem ita se gerebant ut sua consilia optimo cuique
probarent, optimates habebantur.**

Note at once the disappearance in the Latin of such
nouns as "conduct," "approval," though "policy" is represented by **consilia** The phrase *optimus quisque* is very
common in Cicero, and is, like *boni omnes*, used for "the
well affected." Notice also the very common use of *pro-
bare* with the dative: *hoc tibi probo*, "I win your approval
for this."

175. A third instance will embrace at once an oratorical
and a political passage:

III. "This at least I would have you believe, that no one can
sacrifice principle and duty to expediency without injuring
the very interests which he would fain promote; that the
three estates of this realm, the sovereign, the aristocracy, and
the commons, are so closely bound together that you cannot
infringe on popular rights, or on equality before the law,
without shaking the foundations of the throne; you cannot
impair the position of the peer without overturning the pillars
of the whole edifice. So in private life, any one of experience
will tell you that it is impossible for ruin to overtake any
circle of individuals without numbers of other persons being
involved in the same calamity."

"I would have you believe," if addressed to a single
person, would be **credas velim**; if to judges, as in a

forensic speech, **creditote, judices**; *judices* answering to
our "gentlemen of the jury," as *Patres Conscripti* to "Sir,"
or "Mr. Speaker." But the main difficulties are obviously
in the words "principle," "duty," "expediency," "interests." They will be quite insuperable to those who
have not read some portion of Cicero's philosophical works,
such as the *De Officiis ;* to those who are familiar with his
style they will be perfectly easy, and the first part of the
sentence will run thus :

**Hoc saltem creditote, P. C , neminem posse iis quae utilia
sint (or sunt) recta et honesta (or virtutem et honestatem)
posthabere . . .**

Note the mood *sint.* The subjunctive is right if expressed as part of their belief, *i.e.* as strictly subordinate
through *posse posthabere* to *creditote ;* but the indicative
would stand, if looked on as coming from the speaker's
lips, as a mere definition of *us* (cp. 114 (2.), 127)

Note also the absolute impossibility of reproducing the
latent metaphor in "sacrifice."

So far is fairly easy ; but how are we to turn the preposition "without" followed by the verbal noun "injuring"? The whole passage will illustrate the means of
doing this ; and it is enough to say that any use of the
English preposition *sine* will lead us far astray into every
conceivable absurdity.

**Quin iis rebus (or utilitatibus, plural of abstract noun)
quibus inservire (or prodesse) velit, noceat.** Observe the
mood of **velit** as part of the belief which he wishes to
impress on his hearers, and thus *virtual oratio obliqua*
(127).

176. "That the three estates of this realm," etc. We
are here in the very midst of English modern political
phraseology, familiar to us from childhood, but wholly

alien, it might seem, to the Roman world. Those who
have studied all that remains of Cicero's treatise *De
Republica* will demur to the latter statement, and will
find the difficulty far less than appears. We may write:

Tria esse in hac republica tanquam elementa [or **tribus
tanquam elementis contineri** (bound together) **hanc nostram
rempublicam**].

Notice the deliberate setting aside of the word *regnum*,
which means properly "regal power;" the avoidance also
of the word *ordo*, which is mainly confined to the sena-
torial and equestrian "orders." Taking, if we like, the
first, as the simplest, of these two renderings, we may go
on to enumerate these *elementa*: **regem, optimates, populum
ipsum**. *Plebs* is too narrow in meaning, and often in
Cicero used in a depreciatory sense.

177. We may now proceed :

Haec (or **quae elementa**) **tam arcto vinculo** (a common
metaphor) **conjungi inter se ac cohaerere** (venturing for
once on a certain Ciceronian amplification), **ut neque jura
populi et juris aequabilitas** (a Ciceronian rendering of the
Greek ἰσονομία), **salvo regali imperio imminui possint** . . .
Observe the aid given us by this common use of the
ablative of *salvus* (*salva fide*, "without breach of faith"),
and beware of trying to reproduce the English, or rather
Asiatic, metaphor of "throne," or the stronger figure of
"shaking the foundations." .We continue: **Nec possis**
(notice the common use in Latin, as in English, of
"you," corresponding to German *man*, French *on*) **ita
nobilitatis** or **nobilium** (*nobilis* in the singular would
mean *a* noble) **statum labefactare, ut non corruant ea quibus
tota civitas innitatur.** We thus approach as nearly as we
can with safety the English metaphor of "the pillars."

We have thus far turned the difficult English "without," neither by such barbarisms as *sine* or *nisi*, nor in a
single and uniform manner.

178. The last sentence, which appears easier, has difficulties of its own. We may turn it thus :

Ita in re domestica scit quivis rerum paulo peritior non posse multos privatos homines rem suam ac fortunas amittere ut non plures secum in eandem calamitatem trahant.

Notice how to turn "any one of experience;" *quivis* is used in its usual rather depreciatory sense, "any one living," and the comparative (with *paulo*) in its idiomatic sense; for "ruin," it is hardly necessary to say that any approach to the word *ruina* would be disastrous. Note also the combination of *multos* with *privatos homines*, which is treated as one word, so that an *et* is not needed. The English metaphor of "ruin overtaking" and of being "involved in" calamity must of course be set aside

179. Let us now take an oratorical passage .

IV. "The honourable and learned member, himself not without some tincture of historical knowledge, asks me for a definition of this British constitution, which I am in the habit, he says, of praising so extravagantly. For himself, he cannot fix its date or origin, or ascertain its limits, or refer to its authors. I remember, Sir, hearing an illustrious relative of the honourable member say within these walls, that we English had this advantage over other nations, that our forefathers had never been favoured with a Solon or a Lycurgus, or even, let me add, with one like a person of whom we hear in a neighbouring nation, who boasts that, give him pen and ink, he will frame a constitution every day of his life; that the English constitution (to quote his own impressive words) was the offspring, not of a single brain, but of many ; was settled, not in the lifetime of an individual, but by the slow growth of centuries and generations "

The opening words are of course a purely conventional parliamentary mode of designating a member of the English House of Commons. In the Roman senate a member would be simply named, or even addressed by his name.

It will be best, therefore, here to introduce a proper name
and begin with a somewhat emphatic word : **Quaerit** (or
quaeris) ex me Metellus (or **Metelle**) ; still, as the *two* adjectives seem here by what follows to be somewhat empha-
sised, the words **vir doctissimus amplissimusque** may in this
case be added.   But beware of *iste*, which would never be
used by one senator of another, but only by a prosecutor
of the defendant at the bar, who sat near the *judices*.

" Himself," etc.   Here we must be on our guard against
all the barbarous modes of expressing " history," " study,"
etc. (see **36,** B ; 171), and write simply, **nec ipse antiquitatis
memoriae plane imperitus.**

" For a definition," etc.   If we attempt to introduce such
a verb as would represent " asks me to tell him," we must
beware of the infinitive mood, *demonstrare,* etc., and use *ut;*
but it is far better to pass at once to the dependent interrogative and express the term "definition" by **quid sit ac quale.**

"This British constitution," etc.   The word "British" need
not be expressed literally : **haec nostra respublica;** observe
the various meanings of this last word, which will represent, according to the context, a great variety of English
words : " constitution," " realm," " politics," " political life,"
" nation," " country," etc. (**35, 36,** A).   " Which I am in the
habit," etc.   The parenthetic "he says" is here, as elsewhere, to be discarded in Latin : the subjunctive of
virtual oratio obliqua will take its place : **quam ego** (the
pronoun is obviously needed) **nimiis laudibus ferre** (note
the phrase) **sim solitus** (the **sim** might be placed between
nimiis and **laudibus** ; see **9**).

180. " For himself," etc.   There is no necessity for any
periphrasis, such as *quod ad se attinet.*   The right pronoun in a prominent position is all that is needed, just as
a sentence beginning with " for myself " would commence
in Latin by *ego.*   But the whole sentence will need care.
" Date," " origin," etc., will lead us far astray if we go in
search of Latin substantives, just as above we might

have blundered over "tincture," "definition," "habit." So again, as the speaker is clearly quoting a statement from his opponent's speech, the use of the indicative would be destructive to any attempt at Latinity. Write **nescire se** (se emphasised by being out of its usual place; see 11) **quando** (*quum* is inadmissible in interrogative clauses) **et unde orta** (or **nata**) **sit, quemadmodum et a quibus definita sit ac constituta.** You will see that the whole difficulty of turning these English nouns is overcome by the use of interrogative forms with the proper verbs (cp. 42). If it is worth while expressing the English "ascertain" by a fresh verb instead of covering the whole ground by an emphasised *nescire*, we may insert **nec** before *quemadmodum*, and end with **reperire atque enumerare,** but this is scarcely necessary.

181. "I remember." The orator here comes back to himself; we should therefore mark this, and begin with an *ego*, or **equidem.** How to turn "Sir"? Of course *princeps*, *domine*, would be mere absurdities; here, instead of the ordinary *Patres Conscripti*, it may be well, according to a usage frequent in Cicero and Livy, to address his opponent by name, and begin, **Equidem, Metelle, memini.** Remember the idiom by which *memini* is used with the present indicative to express, "I remember hearing some one say;" remember also the place for the adjective "illustrious," and the right word for "relative," avoiding the too definite *consanguineus* or *affinis*, or the too remote *familiaris*, *necessarius*, and go on thus · **propinquum tuum, virum fortissimum** (or **praeclarissimum;** it is only with such strong laudatory superlatives that *vir* takes the place of **homo** in these appositional constructions) **in hac Curia** (or **apud hunc ordinem**) **dicere.**

182. "That we English," etc. Avoid *nos Anglos*, and be very careful not to write a sentence which will be ambiguous, such as *nos ceteros ... superare;* but turn "we English" thus: **ob hanc** (or even **illam,** in the sense of "the follow-

ing") **causam praestare nostrae civitatis statum ceteris, civitatibus**; beware of *alienus,* which is not "alien," "foreign," but "another man's," and still more avoid *natio,* which would be a term of insult if applied to a civilised nation (**35**).

" That our forefathers had never," etc. Avoid *avi, patres,* and other fatal mistakes, and use the only word permissible in ordinary prose; and beware of blundering over "favoured," which merely gives a slight touch of irony to the passage: **Quod nemo unquam apud** ("in the time of") **majores nostros extitisset qui id faceret quod vel apud Athenienses Solon ille vel apud Lacedaemonios Lycurgus;**[1] the introduction of the *apud Ath., apud L.,* gives point to the comparison; and notice the *ille,* answering here to our indefinite article.

183. " Or even with one like a person," etc.: **Nec vero quisquam** (or, more emphatically, **ne unus quidem**) **qui id jactet** (not *quite* equivalent to "boast," but the nearest available word) **quod nescio quis hodie** (a certain touch of contempt) **apud finitimam gentem** (or **populum**).

Note that the interposition of "let me add," and the present "we hear" shows that the sentence about the Abbé Sieyès is introduced by the speaker himself, and is no longer a quotation; this will be sufficiently marked by the tense of **jactet,** and below by the mood and tense of *aiunt* and tense of *adsint* [though we might insert **ut ego aliquid de meo adjiciam**].

" Who boasts that," etc.: **Quem profiteri aiunt se, modo habeat quae ad scribendum opus sint**; note the reason of the mood of *sint,* and also of the case of **quae** rather than *quibus* (Arn, rev. ed., 286, *Obs*), and the substitution of a general phrase for any literal rendering of our familiar "pen and ink."

---

[1] **Quod nemo unquam apud majores nostros vel Solonis, ut ita dicam, partes vel Lycurgi egisset,** would be an alternative rendering.

[T. L. P.]

"He will frame a constitution," etc.: **Posse singulas respublicas in singulos dies describere.** If you look out *describere* you will see that to "write down," to "lay out," "sketch," or "frame on paper," *not* "to describe," is its true meaning; the distributive use of **singuli** should be carefully noticed, and the fact that it is never used in the singular.

184. "That the English constitution, to quote his own impressive words," etc.. **Sed quod nostra haec respublica;** it is as well to avoid, where it can easily be done, the use of modern proper names and adjectives [1] **Ut gravissimis ipsius verbis utar ·** avoid such an error as the use of the Latin infinitive for the English infinitive "to use" (86, 101; cp. Arnold, rev. ed., 100), and note the place of the adjective.

"Was the offspring," etc Here we are in the midst of English and rhetorical metaphors; to turn "brain" literally would be merely absurd in Latin, and the whole passage can be made sufficiently rhetorical by paying careful attention to the order of the words and the rhythm of the passage:

Non unius ingenio sed multorum, non unius vita sed paulatim et quasi gradatim permultis saeculis et aetatibus esset constituta.

We might even insert, for the sake of antithesis, **ingeniis** after *multorum:* remembering that it is only thus that *ingenium* can be used in the plural; cp. *multorum amici-tiae* (44)

The whole passage then runs thus ·—

Quaerit ex me Metellus, tu doctissimus amplissimusque, nec ipse antiquitatis memoriae plane imperitus, quid sit de quale haec nostra respublica, quam ego nimiis laudibus ferre sim

---

[1] See however note to **158** (above, p. 153).

solitus: nescire se quando et unde orta sit, quemadmodum et a quibus definita sit ac constituta. Equidem, Metelle, memini propinquum tuum, rarum praeclarissimum, apud hunc ordinem (in hac Curia) dicere, ob hanc causam praestare nostrae civitatis statum ceteris civitatibus, *quod nemo umquam apud majores nostros exstitisset qui id faceret quod vel apud Athenienses Solon ille vel apud Lacedaemonios Lycurgus, nec vero quisquam qui id jactet* quod nescio quis hodie apud finitimam gentem, quem profiteri aiunt se, modo habeat quae ad scribendum opus sint, posse singulas respublicas in singulos dies describere; sed quod nostra haec respublica, ut gravissimis ipsius verbis utar, non unius ingenio sed multorum, non unius vita sed paulatim et quasi gradatim permultis saeculis et aetatibus esset constituta.

---

* — * *Or, quod nemo umquam apud majores nostros vel Solonis, ut ita dicam, partes vel Lycurgi egisset, nec vero quisquam id jactasset . . .*

[T. L. P.]

EXERCISES.

[*Part I., Short Sentences; Part II., Historical and Narrative Passages; Part III., Oratorical; Part IV., Miscellaneous.*]

THE Exercises in Part I., illustrative more or less directly of various sections of the Introduction, may be found useful either in preparation for, or in connection with practice in, the longer continuous passages. The latter, no doubt, come more particularly within the scope of the present work, the preliminary training by means of disconnected sentences being provided for in the revised edition of *Arnold's Latin Prose Composition*. But long experience has shown that an occasional recourse to short testing passages is so good, so almost indispensable a means of trying the strength or exposing the weakness, not merely of beginners, but even of more advanced scholars, that no excuse seems needed for including in such a work as the present a certain number of such Exercises

The references at the foot of the Exercises are to *sections* of the Introduction, which should in each case be carefully read through; the object of the reference generally being not so much to supply a direct rendering for the English, as to help the student in thinking it out for himself.

PART I.

Short Sentences.

EXERCISE I.

(*Latin Period.*)

1. Napoleon saw that the enemies' forces were increasing and their courage rising. His own troops, exhausted by heat and fatigue, were pressed hard by a fresh and unwearied host, and were struggling in vain against superior numbers. He accordingly advanced [1] from the rising ground where he had long been watching [2] the issue of the fight, called round him the Old Guard, which it was his habit to reserve for the last crisis of the battle, and addressed them thus. . . .

2. Both sides had exhausted their ammunition. The fight had raged at close quarters for three hours without any result. The carnage was horrible. The soldiers were suffocated with the heat and dust, and could scarcely keep their feet on the bloody and slippery soil ; but no one could say that he had seen the back of a single foe, or heard a single voice asking for quarter. It seemed as though the gods of Mexico had inspired the nation with superhuman strength, and a courage proof against wounds and death.

3. When the news of this defeat was brought [3] to Venice panic and grief prevailed for some days. The shops were closed,[3] and a solitude as of midnight reigned [4] throughout the city. The Council sent officials from house to house to urge the opening of shops and the removal of every sign of national mourning. The Doge himself at last addressed the people assembled in the great Piazza, and begged them,

---

[1] *Advanced . . . called . . . addressed,* **97.**
[2] *Had long been watching,* **58.**   [3] **99.**   [4] **31.**

as the sons of men who had faced worse disaster, not to be overpowered by a single and retrievable calamity.

Consult Introd. **21-26.** Each of the three passages should be fused into a single sentence by the aid of participles, relatives, and conjunctions.

EXERCISE II.

(*Use of English Derivatives from Latin.*)

1. It is a great consolation to me to have lived to[1] see the nation secure against the vile arts of these persons. 2. Nothing is more fatal to a nation than for all public offices to be in the hands of the rich. 3. It is unwise to provoke the world[2] by a needless display either in acts or words. 4. When dying from a mortal wound in the hour of triumph, he foretold the ruin of his country. 5. Two centuries ago our fathers gave freedom to this nation, oppressed by the barbarous tyranny of an alien and savage race. 6. I call heaven to witness that he has inflicted on me a deadly injury ; but I am bound to pardon him, for[3] I believe that he did it not designedly but by pure accident. 7. This plain has been the scene of many a furious fight. 8. It is a common thing for men to acquire alike riches and rank by the vilest arts. 9. He urged me with tears not to[4] leave him, nor expose him to the fury and indignation of his brother. 10. He promised never to[5] cease to watch over my children's interests : by these promises he obtained what he desired. 11. He was a man of a kindly heart, and incapable of a crime like this. 12. At last he held his peace ; I was astonished at his doing so, for I[6] knew that he was a famous orator. 13. It is not easy to write a short history of the mode by which Rome became mistress of the world.[2] 14. They say that God made the country, than the town. 15. All the world knows that the country is most indebted to you. 16. It was foretold to

---

[1] **101-104.**   [2] **28.**   [3] *For*, causal conjunction ; see **114.**
[4] **104.**   [5] **74.**   [6] *For I*, relative ; see **111.**

A. W. L. P.   M

him in his boyhood that he would attain to the highest offices
in the nation.   17. It is difficult to say to which class of his
countrymen he was most obnoxious.

Consult Introd. II , especially **34, 35.**

Exercise III.

(*Political Terms.*)

1. At the moment when I first entered public life, the
whole government was in the hands of a powerful oligarchy.
2. I can scarcely say which is the greater evil, the tyranny
of an ignorant mob, or of a single despot. 3. Though[1] he
held the sceptre[1] for more than thirty years, he was never guilty
of a single unconstitutional word or act. 4. Early in life he
joined the ranks of the aristocratic party, and relying on
their aid conceived the hope of holding the reins[2] of government. 5. In monarchical states there is often, I suspect,
larger scope for individual energy and ability than in those
which are under the iron rule of a narrow oligarchy. 6. For
my own part, I prefer a mixed and balanced form of government to all others, one in which the people exercise the suf-
frage, confer office, and are admitted through their representatives to a voice in legislation and national policy, but in
which a monarch holds the reins,[2] without[3] the power of
either abrogating or enacting law, or of violating in any way
the constitution. 7. For myself, when I first took in hand
the government of the nation, I made it my first object to
put a check on demagogic licence, and to reconcile the leaders
of the democratic party with the aristocracy, who were at
that time most unpopular with the masses. 8. The constitutional monarchy was finally sacrificed rather to the faults of
the ruler than to the anti-monarchical tendencies of the
nation. 9. The statesman who has long presided over the
national interests will look beyond the passing hour; he

---

[1] **148.**   [2] **31.**   [3] *Without*, etc. : avoid *sine*, and see **105.**

knows that when once constitutional freedom has begun its
downward course the pace to ruin soon becomes fast and
furious; the state [1] of his country after he is laid in his grave
will cause him as much concern as its present condition, [1]
but he knows too well that it is easier to foresee the causes [1]
and course of national decay than to prescribe the treatment [1]
that will arrest the mischief.

Read carefully Introd II. **36, A**, and cp **169-184**

EXERCISE IV.

(*Metaphorical and Abstract Expressions.*)

1. Such, in fact, was the force of his genius and character,
that the nation,[2] no longer in the swaddling-clothes of infancy,
but on the very verge of manhood, cheerfully submitted its
highest interests to his undisputed judgment and control.

2. It would appear that at this date the national culture
and learning had, owing to an inoculation with external influences, taken a great start forwards.   The Continental [3]
revival of study and literature was followed on English soil,
not by the mere trickling of a slender rill, but by the influx
of a mighty stream of arts and sciences whose source lay
outside our borders.

3. It is the presence [4] of these conditions that constitutes
happiness; in their absence happiness is impossible.

4. In this noisy and crowded life of ours, filled to the full
with vanity and display, with puffing and pushing, with fever
and fury, calmness and repose are nowhere to be found; high
thinking and plain living have passed away.

5. In spite of all these clear intimations of the bent,[4] tendencies, aim, and law of Nature we contrive to close our ears
to her daily warnings.

---

[1] See **33, 41, 42.**   [2] **35.**
[3] *Continental:* render by "elsewhere."   [4] **41.**

him in his boyhood that he would attain to the highest
in the nation. 17. Its difficult to say to which class
countrymen he was most obnoxious.

Consult Introd. II., especially **34, 35**.

Exercise III.

Political Terms.)

1. At the moment when I first entered public life,
whole government was in the hands of a powerful oligarc[hy]
2. I can scarcely say which is the greater evil, the tyra[nny]
of an ignorant mob, or of a single despot. 3. Though
held the sceptre[1] for more than thirty years, he was never gu[ilty]
of a single unconstitutional word or act. 4. Early in life
joined the ranks of the aristocratic party, and relying
their aid conceived the hope of holding the reins[2] of gover[n]-
ment. 5. In monarchical states there is often, I suspe[ct]
larger scope for individual energy and ability than in tho[se]
which are under the iron rule of a narrow oligarchy. 6. F[or]
my own part, I prefer a mixed and balanced form of gover[n]-
ment to all others, one in which the people exercise the su[f]-
frage, confer office, and are admitted through their represen[ta]-
tatives to a voice in legislation and national policy, but i[n]
which a monarch holds the reins,[2] without[3] the power o[f]
either abrogating or enacting law, or of violating in any wa[y]
the constitution. 7. For myself, when I first took in hand
the government of the nation, I made it my first object to
put a check on demagogic licence, and to reconcile the leaders
of the democratic party with the aristocracy, who were at
that time most unpopular with the masses. 8. The constitutional monarchy was finally sacrificed rather to the faults of
the ruler than to the anti-monarchical tendencies of the
nation. 9. The statesman who has long presided over the
national interests will look beyond the passing hour; he

---

[1] 148.　　　[2] 31.　　　*Without*, etc. : avoid *sine*, and see **105**.

knows that when once constitutional ....
downward course the past is too ....
furious; the state of his country after ....
will cause him as much concern as ....
but he knows too well that it is vain to ....
and course of national things than to ....
that will arrest the mischief.

6. In proportion to [1] a man's wealth, resources, position, influence, interests, and independence, should be his sense of responsibility for such gifts.

7. A man's readiness to suspect evil in others is often in inverse proportion [1] to his own advance in goodness.

8. Let us persevere in the path which all true heroes [2] have trodden before us, and close our eyes to every signal of recall.

Before attempting this or Exercise V., these sections of the Introduction which deal with the handling of metaphorical expressions (28-33) should be carefully read. Beware throughout of *literal* renderings into Latin, and think what every English expression *means*.

Exercise V.

(*Metaphorical and Abstract Expressions.*)

1. It is exactly the man of tainted reputation who will be most eager to clear his damaged character by a rigorous severity in passing sentence on others.

2. Indeed, I incline to think [3] that the real and earnest student [4] may sometimes be a loser from the influence exercised by professed teachers. He ceases to exercise his own judgment, and accepts as final that of his favourite authority.

3. Great crises in history [5] are often determined by trifles light as air.

4. All evil is easily nipped in the bud; time almost invariably brings it vitality. [6]

5. For myself, I do not profess to have arrived at any final or entire solution [7] of so difficult a problem; I do claim to have aimed at doing so.

---

[1] *In proportion to,* etc. · "as each one . . . so."   [2] **36, B.**
[3] **166.**   [4] **33, 166.**   [5] **36, B.**   [6] **97.**   [7] **41, 42.**

6. I am amazed that so keen-sighted an observer should have failed to see the wide gulf[1] between the school that distinguishes duty[2] from self-interest, not by a verbal, but by a real and generic difference, and that which so far blends the two ideas as to leave no distinction in kind, but only one of amount and degree.

7. He who has tasted the delights[1] of a pure and unselfish friendship will make it his first prayer to be allowed to reach the end of his journey side by side with those in whose company he started on the pilgrimage of life.[3] What greater happiness can he desire than that the sun of friendship whose morning radiance shone upon his early path may still shed its beams on his failing steps? But not the less, considering all the frailty and uncertainty of this mortal life, he will be ever on the watch for those who will accept and return his affection, remembering that life without affection is robbed of all its sweetness.

Consult Introd. II **28-33**, and see note to Ex. IV.

Exercise VI

(*Use of Substantives.*)

1 It happens occasionally that duty and expediency are really or apparently in conflict. 2. He refused to listen to my warnings, yet he wore an air of alarm rather than of confidence. 3. The voices of warning were now lost in the shouts of applause and admiration. 4. A great disagreement arose between the despisers and the admirers of Greek literature. 5. It is no easy task to recount the number, nature, and magnitude of his services to the country. 6 None of his predecessors on the throne[4] had been so beloved by his subjects, none of his successors, not even the most eminent of all, eclipsed the memory of his virtues. 7. I have not

---

[1] **41, 42.**　　　　　[2] *Duty, self-interest* see **33, 40.**
[3] Use metaphors from the racecourse.　　　[4] **31.**

forgotten who is my client, and who his prosecutor, nor when
I act[1] as his advocate will I fail in my duty.   8. You have
brought forward many arguments in proof of the existence of
a God, you have stated no justification for the denial of the
proposition.   9. You are apparently forgetful of the character
and magnitude and probable duration of this war which you
are acting so unwisely as to stir up.   10. The scene and the
manner of his murder are still uncertain ; some assert that he
was cut off by poison, others by violence; there is a general
agreement among them that his murderers were unpunished.
11. As a boy I cultivated the friendship of many illustrious
men, whose genius and character I equally admired.   12. The
soldiers' spirits were shaken by the absence of the general,
the report of his death, and the almost total consumption
of their ammunition.   13. In spite of their holding their
peace, their mere silence is a sufficient explanation of their
refusal to do this.   14. It seems as though you were the one
person to whom Heaven has vouchsafed the realisation of
every hope, every prayer, every aim.   15. The being of use
to the largest possible number of one's countrymen is in itself
a source both of advantage and of credit: it tends not only
to the gaining of friends and the increase of resources, but the
securing of popularity, interest, position, and influence.

Consult Introd III. **37-48.**   The English substantives in this
Exercise are for the most part *not* to be represented by substantives
in Latin.

Exercise VII.

(*Adverbs.*)

1. He was apparently a man of ideally perfect character
and really heroic courage, yet on this occasion he, beyond all
doubt, unaccountably allowed himself[2] to swerve from the
path of duty, and to sacrifice to his own personal safety the
dearest interests of the nation.[3]   2. I earnestly[4] implore you

---

[1] **64.**   [2] **104.**   [3] **35.**   [4] **54.**

never to do anything which you cannot do with a good conscience and honourably, and to take the most earnest pains [1]
to avoid the appearance [2] of acting in anything with a view
to your own advancement or gratification. 3 It is with
reluctance that I say anything that [3] can apparently serve the
interests [2] merely of my enemies, but the nation [1] is obviously
in such a critical state that we must think only of the public
safety. 4. While still quite young I observed the fact [5] that
self-made [6] men were not often popular in Parliament : they
are now not only popular out of doors, but are constantly
elected to this House, and occasionally attain to the highest
consideration within its walls. But it was not till the present
year that any one of their number has actually taken a part
in the administration.[7] 5. At last, whether of his own free
choice, or in the hope of saving his imperial crown,[8] or at the
suggestion of his surrounders, he suddenly returned to take
the aggressive Too soon he found that it was not a question
merely of a frontier or a river, but of his own crown and the
existence of his nation.[4] 6. For many years he attempted in
vain to reach by sea the western side of the continent of Asia.
He never accomplished the object of his earnest desires,
though he refused to despair of its ultimate realisation.[2] But
it is obvious that he did not spend such exertions and courage
to no purpose , nay rather that few have conferred greater
benefits on humanity [9] than one who, as is often the case, was
while he yet lived treated with ingratitude and indifference,
adored, and reverenced after death.

Consult Introd. IV. 49-54.

---

[1] **104.**   [2] **41.**   [3] **113.**   [4] **35.**   [5] **160.**
[6] *Self-made men, Parliament, this House* think of corresponding
Roman phrases, and see **30, 35**   [7] **36, A.**   [8] **31.**
[9] *Humanity*. abstract for concrete, **40.**

Exercise VIII.

(*Use of Tenses.*)

1. My speech is over, gentlemen, and I have sat down , do you decide on this question ; for myself, I hope, and have long been [1] hoping, that I shall be acquitted by your unanimous verdict. 2. But the defendant, while he was [2] accusing me, had forgotten that it was he who was on his trial, that no one is taxing or has taxed me with this crime. I will therefore bear his insults and taunts calmly, for it is clear to me, and you too seem to agree with me, that he is either unable to control his temper, or else that he has simply lost his senses. 3. But in a moment everything was changed. It seemed as though the war in which we had so long been engaged with a powerful and gallant neighbouring nation [3] was drawing to a close, but while we were all sighing for peace, and hoping that an end would be put to such a melancholy strife, suddenly and unexpectedly a storm arose from a quarter whence we least looked for it 4. That marvellous genius learned to speak so difficult a language as Greek in his old age ; he had long studied and mastered ancient history, [4] and to the latest period of his life learned daily something new. 5. We read in Caesar that neither the beech nor fir grew in England in his day ; he tells us also that the Britons used a copper coinage, and that by far the most civilised were the inhabitants of Kent. 6. When you arrive [5] at Rome, you will find the same state of things as you found at the beginning of the spring ; but if you keep [5] your promises, my father will protect you.

Consult Introd. V. **55-80.**

---

[1] **58.**   [2] **120.**   [3] **35.**   [4] **36,** ʙ ; **166, 179.**   [5] **65.**

Exercise IX.

(*Substantival Infinitive.*)

1. Expressing gratitude is one thing, feeling it another, showing it another still. 2. Self-satisfaction is easy, the satisfaction of others by no means so easy. 3. Such language is a sign of good sense, such conduct, of courage, but the union of speech and action is a sign of perfect and entire goodness. 4. For such a man to mention religion, or piety, or patriotism,[1] or honour, is the same as for a bandit to enlarge on honesty or a savage to discourse on philosophy. 5. Putting confidence in liars, was not, he said,[2] the same as inspiring it in men of truth ; the former he did not care to do ; success in the latter seemed to him worth any man's while. 6. Speaking much and knowing much are, as you all know, quite different. 7. For a poor man, in spite of the extreme of poverty, to have kept his word is most honourable, and is rightly praised ; for a rich man, in the possession of every kind of affluence, to break his word, is, in my opinion, neither honourable nor praiseworthy. 8 Delay, procrastination, indecision, half-measures, were never to his mind , he followed all his aims by the shortest road, employing the utmost zeal and energy. 9. Happiness[1] is nothing else than obedience to the laws of virtue. 10. You, it seems, place the whole idea of happiness at one time in pleasure , at another in wealth ; I look on pleasure and wealth alike as inferior to goodness ; but I do not care to refute your arguments, nor is it my practice to enlarge on this and similar questions in the presence (of those who are) so inexperienced in life. 11. It is time for all good men to devote themselves to public affairs,[3] nor will it be at all difficult at such a crisis to divert our attention from our private concerns. 12 There will be no difficulty in overwhelming the enemy by a sudden charge, while wearied with forced marches, and entangled in a wooded district.

In all these sentences the abstract noun is to be rendered by the Latin infinitive. See especially Introd. VI. 89.

---

[1] 33.   [2] 94.   [3] 36, A

EXERCISE IX.

(Substantive Infinitive.)

1. Expressing gratitude is one thing, feeling it another, showing it another still. Self-satisfaction is easy, the satisfaction of others by no means easy. 3. Such language is a sign of good sense, and modesty, of courage, but the union of speech and action is a sign of perfect and entire goodness. 4. For such a man to mention religion, or piety, or patriotism,[1] or honour, is the same as for a bandit to enlarge on honesty or a satirist to discourse on philosophy. 5. Putting confidence in liars is not, he said, the same as inspiring it in men of truth: whatever he did not care to do, success in the latter seemed to him worth any man's while. 6. Speaking much and knowing much are, as you all know, quite different. 7. For a poor man, in spite of the extreme of poverty, to have kept his word is most honourable, and is rightly praised; for a rich man in the possession of every kind of affluence, to break his word is in my opinion, neither honourable nor praiseworthy. 8. Delay, procrastination, indecision, half-measures, were not to his mind; he followed all his aims by the shortest way, employing the utmost zeal and energy. 9. Happiness is nothing else than obedience to the laws of virtue. 10. Yet, if some place the whole idea of happiness at one time in power, at another in wealth; I look on pleasure and wealth as far inferior to goodness; but I do not care to relate your arguments, nor is it my practice to enlarge on this and similar matters in the presence [of those who are] so inexperienced a life. 11. It is time for all good men to devote themselves to public affairs,[2] nor will it be at all difficult at such a crisis to divert our attention from our private concerns. 12. There will be no difficulty in overwhelming the enemy by a sudden change ... ... with forced marches, and entangled ...

In all these sentences ... ... the Latin infin...

Exercise X.

(Use of Infinitive; chiefly with Impersonal Verbs.)

1. I shall be allowed to seem a good man, (but) I shall prefer being one.   2. Those philosophers of whom you speak are ashamed alike of compassion and of envy; they take no pleasure either in love or hatred; the whole of the human race may, as far as they are concerned, live or perish; whichever happens[1] they will be undisturbed.   3. He ought to have[2] obeyed the laws of his country, but he preferred being a king to being the member of a constitutional state.   4. Contentment was your duty, but you had resolved to grow rich, and tempted by this hope you ventured on things which you ought not even to have[2] thought of.   5. You might, as far as I was concerned, have[2] had as much weight in the Senate as you desired to have; and you might with my aid have attained to the highest honours; but all this you threw away, and now you feel regret and remorse at having done so.   6. This is the course that should then have been taken; but your unprincipled friend wished his own interests consulted. He might have[2] shown himself an honest man, he preferred becoming a rich one.   7. You do not care to hear the details of my sufferings, and I do not wish to be tedious, but I am bound to put before you the main point, and I needs must fulfil the commission I have received from your father.   8. He resolved on returning at once to the city, and becoming once more a private person; but an uproar and rush[3] to arms began in the camp, and he therefore reluctantly resumed the command which he had wished to abandon.   9. About noonday the fighting ceased; for some time past the heat had been unprecedented in our experience of the present campaign, and the soldiers from exhaustion could scarcely stand in the ranks with their armour on.   10. I do not wish to be

---

[1] 65.   [2] 73.   [3] 41.

troublesome to you, for to be troublesome to one to whom I acknowledge myself to be under such an obligation as binds me to you, would be most shameless.

See Introd. VII. 89.

EXERCISE XI.

(*Indirect Predication.*)

1. He obtained, they say, the crown[1] by fraud and treachery, there is a general belief[2] that he will one day pay the penalty of so many heinous crimes. 2. The king, tradition[2] says, fell in this battle, but there is sufficient evidence that he survived the defeat of his friends and the ruin of his country, and reached in safety the mountains, valleys, and solitudes in which he was born and reared. 3. We have heard that you were the first to enter that contest, the only one who survives to-day, and we all believe that you are a true patriot, and have both sacrificed much and would have[3] sacrificed everything to the national welfare. 4. The soldiers said that they had not taken and would not take up arms against their country and their countrymen, but were gathering together and arming in the interest of all good patriots 5. Word[2] is brought that the enemy are flying in different directions, and are nowhere (facing) even the first charge of our troops 6. Word was brought to Napoleon that the day was for the second time doubtful, that the battle was quite undecided, and that the bravest (soldiers) were exhausted with fighting and wounds. 7. History[4] tells us that he was the first king of Spain to make a treaty with us. 8. It is a false doctrine that friendship should be cultivated (part. in -*dus*) for the sake of our own advantage only, and that a wise man will not make much of affection and love. 9. It is a false belief that you and I are changing with our changing fortune.

---

[1] 31.   [2] 41   [3] 67, 74.   [4] 36, B.

10. For myself, I hope that I have acted rightly, and I am glad that I have shown you my gratitude for your many great acts of kindness. 11. I see in imagination the nation [1] disunited from the Parliament, and the most important matters being settled by the fiat of the ignorant mob. 12. At daybreak Columbus imagined himself to see land and to hear the voices of men and the song of birds.

Consult Introd. VI. 92-96.

EXERCISE XII.

(*Use of Participles.*)

1. I am quite aware that if I dissent from your policy I shall be taunted with sluggishness and cowardice. 2. Returning[2] from Italy, he died at his own house; his friends and relations stood round his deathbed, the whole house echoed with cries of sorrow.[3] 3. Thereupon an order was issued to give quarter to those who laid down their arms, that the rest should be treated with the utmost severity of war. 4. Throwing[2] themselves at his feet, they appealed to him not to[4] give over to certain death men who were not injuring the nation[1] thus far, and were likely to be of great value to it one day. 5. While sailing from Africa, he was taken seriously ill, and died on reaching London. 6. Turning[2] to the Ambassador, who stood near him, he asked him with assumed indignation, whether he wished to ask for peace or to declare war; he replied that he had come with the intention and hope of putting[4] an end to every disagreement between him and his master. Then he overwhelmed him with every kind of abuse; and, as he attempted to speak more, bade him be silent, and left him, to the consternation of the bystanders, without a word of greeting. 7. His words were almost drowned in cries of disapproval and expressions of remonstrance and

---

[1] 35, 182.   [2] 98.   [3] 43.   [4] 102.

indignation.[1] 8. While sitting in the Senate-house, we heard a centurion say that that place where he was standing was the best. 9 I heard him with my own ears ask if your proposal had not been the more taking at first sight, his the more serviceable in practice. Distrusting[2] my own sense of hearing, and seeing my brother stand near, I asked whether I had heard correctly. He answered my question in the affirmative. 10. The landing[1] of the troops in Normandy, the advance towards the city, caused the utmost panic in France ; but not even this was so prejudicial to the national cause as the extinction[1] of military discipline, and the scattering[1] in distant garrisons of the French forces, so that they were incapable of aiding each other, or learning the lesson of obedience to a single leader.

In this Exercise Participles are to be used wherever admissible in Latin as a substitute for dependent clauses or substantives See Introd. VII. **97-100.**

Exercise XIII.

(*Ut-* or *Ne-clause after Verbs.*)

1. He warned Caesar not to put confidence in any of the Gauls, but to return to his province with the greatest possible speed.
2. He determined first to have an interview with Pompey on the earliest possible opportunity, and to make it his first object to let slip no chance of peace that should offer. 3. He succeeded at length by urgent entreaties[3] in persuading the barbarians not to break their promise, and not to be induced to supply the enemy with provisions. 4. His aim was to let[4] the enemy lose breath and become exhausted by running over[5] a double distance ; and he therefore[6] forewarned his men to receive the enemy's charge without moving, and thus

---

[1] **43.**   [2] **98.**   [3] **54.**
[4] *To let :* say merely, " for the enemy to . . ."
[5] *By running over*, etc. : i.e " by doubling their course."
[6] *Therefore*, " to produce which result " (*fio*).

the line of attack would[1] lose its formation, and the soldiers' physical strength be impaired. 5. I allow that you have served the nation[2] right well, I refuse to allow the national interests to be sacrificed to your reputation or your prospects. 6. I have acted against my will in persuading, as I have sometimes done, a jury to acquit the guilty; I have never been able to persuade myself that I was[3] acting rightly. 7. At last by his earnest entreaties[4] he prevailed on the conqueror to issue an order for quarter to be given to all who laid down their arms, and for no further severities to be exercised on the townsmen. 8. The Spaniards could not be persuaded to remain longer, and not to lose, by a premature departure, all the results of their brilliant success. 9. I could not possibly avoid your speaking thus of me, but I think I have deserved that you should take a different view of my character; consider whether you have not treated me with the greatest unfairness. 10. Do you not grant that you have already been adequately answered ? 11. Will you not grant us to cross[5] the ocean and return home ? 12. The reformation and improvement of the national character was always his object.

Consult Introd. VIII. **101-105.**

Exercise XIV.

(Substantial **Ut-** *or* **Quod-***clause with Impersonal Verbs.)*

1. The fact of the city having been betrayed in my absence[5] is most unfortunate; it remains for me to retake it in the same manner as that by which I lost it. 2. It has never happened to me, in spite of the greatest political difference, to alienate a friend ; I trust it will never be my lot; but if it ever befall me through no fault of mine, I will try and bear[6] it with resignation. 3. I happened at that time to be

---

[1] **74.**   [2] **35, 182.**   [3] **68.**   [4] **54.**
[5] **99.**   [6] *Try and bear* · "take care to bear," **104.**

giving no more time to my own affairs than was absolutely
necessary, but to be almost entirely absorbed in the administration of the country [1] 4. Besides this, he had never
entered political life,[1] but had made it his very first object to
live wholly in the country, and devote himself to farming [2] and
rural life. 5. So far from being at a loss what to say, I
might have spent a separate day on each separate point,
but I was unwilling to be tedious, and moreover I aimed
at [3] speaking with modesty and self-respect. 6. It remains
for me to ask how it could have been possible for him to
be present at the moment when the murder was committed,
for it is no longer possible for you to try and prove that
he could have been [4] at the same moment in two such different places as Rome and Naples. 7. Moreover he speaks
about my administration [1] as though it had been an open
question whether I should undertake the government [1] or no.
8. Your candidature, instead of [5] being disliked, is favoured [6]
by all. 9. The resistance [7] ceased after midnight, but for
some hours the city was one scene [8] of slaughter, at daybreak
a tardy order was issued to spare the women, children, and
non-military inhabitants. 10. For me to endure calmly such
wrongs and ignominy is neither right, nor honourable, nor
possible

Consult Introd. VIII, especially **106-108**.

EXERCISE XV

(*Qui Causal, Concessive, Consecutive, and Final.*)

1. Disappointed in this [9] hope, the Moors, seeing that the
enemy whom they had lately despised was not one [10] to be
conquered either in fair fight or by a *coup-de-main*, suddenly
despaired of the day, and retired with the confusion of a beaten

---

[1] **36, A.**   [2] *Farming* "cultivation of land," sec **43.**
[3] **104**   [4] **73**   [5] **107.**   [6] **39.**   [7] **41.**
[8] Avoid *scena* (**36, B**), and render the *meaning* of the expression.
[9] **4, 109.**   [10] **113.**

army to the stronghold from which they had issued. 2. Then he orders the Indian chiefs to be brought into his presence; the unhappy men, entertaining no suspicion or dread of his intentions, hurry in joyfully. 3. The Indians being incapable of defending any longer either their persons or their property from injury, wrong, and violence, surrender the remnant of their land to the Spaniards, and are formally received as subjects of the Spanish crown. 4. Thereupon my client, though anxious to be cleared of so revolting a suspicion, yet being unwilling to plead his own cause, resolved to wait till I, who had undertaken his advocacy, returned into court. 5. All who knew by experience the vast difference[1] between freedom and slavery crowded to meet him as he entered city after city, it seemed that he had attained a height of glory that was too great for man to retain or preserve entire. 6. There are other things which I fear still more; in his absence,[2] his brother, inasmuch as his influence with that faction is unrivalled, will be still more formidable; as long as he lives,[3] can you imagine that the party of disorder will ever lack a standard[4] round which to rally? 7. There is no one living[5] who believes it possible for such a man to command his reason either by day or night, seeing that by night he must be incessantly aroused from sleep by fears of a guilty conscience, and haunted in his waking hours by the phantom and memories of his cruelties and enormities. 8. Who is there who does not cherish and value the memory of the heroes[6] of the past though he has never seen them? 9. The sentiment which you avow is not of a kind either to win friends or get rid of foes. 10. Religion is the only power that can pluck so profound and deeply-rooted a melancholy from our heads. 11. These are persons whose influence with their countrymen alike from their ability and character is such that as private individuals they have more power than any

---

[1] **41, 42.**   [2] **99.**   [3] **64.**
[4] *A standard:* metaphor from military life; may be translated literally.   [5] **28.**   [6] **36, B.**

magistrates. 12. Caesar[1] saw that the tide of battle was turning, and that the decisive moment had come; he instantly sent forward all his cavalry, which he had hitherto held in hand with that very object, to at once check the rear of the retiring enemy, and charge the horse who were intended to cover his retreat. 13. Yet in spite of all these entreaties and tears there was not a single state in the whole province which refused to send a deputation to accuse him.

Consult Introd. IX. 109 *seq*

EXERCISE XVI.

(*Temporal Clauses*. ubi, postquam, simul ac, quum.)

1. No sooner was he made aware by the hoisting of[2] a flag on the summit of the citadel that the advanced guard of the enemy was at hand, than he caused the gate to be thrown open, and dashed gallantly into their midst. 2. The first moment that this story reached me, I saw the great importance[3] of conveying it to headquarters, and though from the serious nature of my wounds I could scarcely bear the motion of a horse, I pushed on without stopping that day, or the following night, through a district beset with enemies, to the nearest outpost of our forces. 3. As soon as I found that all slave-owners[4] shunned my society and conversation because[5] I had given freedom to my fellow-creatures, I made up my mind to live there no longer, feeling[6] sure that the moment I reached England I should be better. 4. The moment that he heard of the enemies' landing, instead of remaining at home, as a man of his advanced years might have[7] done without incurring disgrace, he determined to take up arms, and do all that an old man could to repel the invasion. 5. But your

---

[1] Fuse the two sentences into one; see **25**, and cp Ex. I.
[2] **99.**   [3] **42.**   [4] *Slave-owners*. "who kept slaves at home."
[5] **114, 2.**   [6] **98.**   [7] **73**

friend had no sooner heard that the fleet was crossing[1] the channel than his heart suddenly failed him, and instead of[2] volunteering, as a young man of his years should have done, to enter the ranks, he was at his wits' end for a resource[3]; he pleaded at one moment a legal exemption, at the next ill health. The enemy might, for all he did, have[4] planted his standard at St. Paul's. 6. In spite of[5] this heavy blow, instead of[6] quailing under it, he not only bore it calmly, but so demeaned himself as to win the admiration even of envy and malice. 7. Though he might have[4] been greatly honoured by the sovereign in his own country, and lived in the highest favour with the nobility, he preferred living in exile here to seeing his countrymen at the mercy of a despot's will. 8. Accordingly, though he could scarcely refrain from tears of indignation,[7] he assumed a cheerful countenance and dissembled his resentment. 9. When your city was being stripped of the spoils of war, when your countrymen were disarmed, your nation dishonoured, not one of you so much as heaved a groan; you gave your applause and cheers to the conqueror; when worse things befall,[8] you will wail, I fear, in vain. 10. Whenever he heard[9] anything of this kind he would[10] instantly say that some neighbour or townsman must have invented the story. 11. When he saw[9] any young man of an ardent and enthusiastic temperament, instead of blaming him as old men often do, he would pay him all possible attention and respect. 12. Whenever I see men of this stamp expressing their gratitude in return for some trifling civility, and paying honour to some inexperienced youth of rural habits and tastes, I know that they are so acting for their own gain and advantage, and encouraging[11] their victim in false hopes of fame or success.

Consult Introd. XI. **115-122.**

---

[1] **95.**   [2] **117.**
[3] *At his wits' end*, etc. : " did not know what to do."   [4] **73.**
[5] **99.**   [6] **107.**   [7] Avoid *lacrimae indignationis*, and see **43.**
[8] **65.**   [9] **72.**   [10] **68.**
[11] *Encouraging in :* render " holding out to."

EXERCISE XVII.

(*Temporal Clauses·* dum, quoad, quamdiu, donec,
priusquam.)

1. I would have you then undertake this trust provided
you are not likely [1] either to neglect it or turn it to your own
gain. 2. I am ready to pay you the greatest possible honour
on condition of your consenting to pledge your word to
estimate all the detraction of my rivals at its proper value.
3. So long as I believed you to be collecting such stores of
plate, of pictures, of statues, and all objects of art as a matter
of taste, I honoured you highly, as soon as I perceived that
you were amassing all these treasures with a view to sell them
at an enhanced price, I paid you, I confess, less attention
and deference, and, without [2] despising you, I rated you at
your true value. 4. The launching [3] of this small body of
cavalry against the enemy's left caused such disorder in the
whole army that while the general was asking the staff what
was happening, one or two regiments had broken and fled.
5. As long as those who are to be at the head of our armies
are [4] chosen either by chance or by interest, it will be quite
impossible for success [5] to be obtained. 6. He sends word to
his colleague at Nola that while [6] the siege of Casilinum is
going on a second army is needed to make head against the
Campanians. 7. I continued to do this as long as [7] my physical
strength permitted; I will do it always to the utmost of my
power. 8. Or are you waiting silently until the enemy
marches at the head of his invading army into the heart of
your city in the hope that [8] you may then lay aside [9] your
feuds and carry on the government [10] in unity of temper and
policy ? 9. To the last moment of his life he so governed the
country that it is now for the first time that we recognise the

---

[1] 67.   [2] *Without despising* beware of *sine*, and see **105, 177**

[3] 43.   [4] 64.   [5] 42.   [6] 120.

[7] 124.   [5] **101, 102.**   [9] 99.   [10] 36, A.

enormous influence which may be exercised by individual genius and character. 10. Before they could [1] reap the fruits of their hard-won victory, a second army came on the scene, and the battle had to be begun anew. 11. I refuse to go till I have [2] had an interview with the General and tried the amount [3] of my influence with him in procuring not my own but another's safety (also, in usual *oratio obliqua,* " He refused to go," etc.). 12. Those who dream that they have secured happiness [4] without [5] attending to those conditions often do not find out their mistake till some severe affliction forces on them the teaching of experience.

Consult Introd. XI. 115-122.

Exercise XVIII.

(*Oratio Obliqua.*)

1. They say (said) that he who does (did) not till his land will (would) look in vain for a harvest. 2. You said that we all knew that he would never enjoy the harvest which he looked for. 3. History [6] tells us that even his deadly enemies, such was his gentleness of spirit, he cheerfully forgave. 4. They say that politicians [7] are apt to make light of students; our friend would often say that the mere student sometimes looked down unduly on the politicians. 5. He would [8] often say that the nation [9] had, as all his hearers knew well, long been the slave of the vilest of its members, and that the masters of the world had long obeyed a single unprincipled despot. 6. He brought word that she for whom you were seeking was present. 7. He reminded us that he now saw in old age the scenes [10] which he had left so unwillingly in boyhood, and for which he had so often sighed in mature life.

---

[1] **122.**   [2] **65.**   [3] **33, 42.**   [4] **33.**
[5] *Without attending:* beware of *sine,* and see **99, 177.**
[6] **36, D.**   [7] *Politicians, students,* **33 ; 36, B.**   [8] **68.**
[9] **35, 182.**   [10] **35.**

8. He promised to give me all the books which his brother
had left. 9. They tell him that the hill whose seizure [1] by his
own troops he had ordered is in possession of the enemy.
10. They bring word that his successor would [2] soon be on the
spot and would relate to him all that had happened at Rome.
11. The king pretended to have frequent interviews with a
goddess who prescribed for him all the laws, institutions, and
customs which the nation was to observe. 12. He expressed
a hope that a nation [3] which had always been so hostile to
the people and name of Rome would speedily be punished for
such long-standing animosity.

Consult Introd. XII. **123-130** , and cp. EXX. XXIII., XXXVII., XLVI ,
XLVIII., LV., LVII., LXV., LXVIII.

EXERCISE XIX.

(*Oratio Obliqua*)

1 He said that it was quite impossible for habit and
education to hold their own for any length of time against
instinct. 2. It seems that he thought it made little difference
whether he was pardoned [4] unheard, or acquitted after due
and legal trial. 3 " Alas," he said,[5] " that things should have
come to such a pass that no man could any longer trust his
neighbour. It seemed as though truth and honour and
innocence and chivalry [6] had died out of the world [7] ; and
freedom of conscience [8] and of speech had died with them."
4. Those, he maintained,[5] should be the first objects [8] of charity
whom poverty [9] allows to feel and to express gratitude,[10]
but debars from any active display of it. 5. Others take
a lower and a coarser view. Friendship, they tell us, should
be cultivated not from motives of affection or regard, but
with a view to gain aid and protection ; and the desire to

---

[1] 41   [2] 74, 124 (note).   [3] 35, 182.   [4] 39.
[5] 12 (*d*), 163, 169   [6] *Chivalry :* think of what this term means.
[7] 28, 35.   [8] 41, 42.   [9] 32.   [10] 33.

make friends should bear an exact proportion to the sense of
weakness and dependence.   6. Who is there, he asked,[1] who
would care to roll in wealth,[2] and be surrounded with every-
comfort, at the price[3] of loving none, and being loved by
none ?   7. There is, perhaps, some truth in the saying, "The
world is apt to take a man at his own estimate."[4]   8. He
would often say that he knew no sentiment more fatal to true
friendship than the maxim, "men should love as though they
would one day hate"; which he characterised[5] as the shallow
utterance of an utterly corrupt and selfish spirit.[6]

See Introd. XII., and references to Ex. xviii.

Exercise XX.

(*Conditional.*)

1. If I speak truly, believe me.   2. If ever any one was in
love with literature and culture I may say so of my client.
3. If we could not touch your heart separately, yet we ought
to have[7] done so by our united prayers.   4. If such a list of
precedents has no effect on you nothing ever will.   5. If of
this money you appropriate[8] ever so little to your own use I
shall at once order you to be taken to prison.   6. You must
love me therefore for my own sake if ever we are to be friends.
7. If ever any one was indifferent to the bubble reputation it
was I.   8. The moment that you say[8] that anything besides
what is right is to be aimed at, or that you count anything
else as good, you put an end to duty, and annihilate the whole
idea of goodness.[9]   9. As sure as you take[8] anything from a
fellow-creature to serve your own purposes, so surely do you
cease to act as a human being and violate the law of nature.
10. When once hostilities have commenced, we shall find

---

[1] 12 (*d*), 163, 169.
[2] *To roll in wealth* · beware of a literal translation.   [3] 105.
[4] 41, 42.   [5] 28, 35.
[6] *Utterance* beware of *verbum*, and note the real meaning of *spirit.*
[7] 73.   [8] 65, 136-138.   [9] *Duty, goodness :* see 40.

that if we abandon [1] the war we must also abandon the hopes
of peace.　11. If ever any enemy ought not to have been
slain, why am I (who am) a friend not to be spared ?
12. Whenever [2] they began to despair of success they would [3]
bring down all their property to the sea-side, and embarking [4]
in their galleys, retreat to the neighbouring islands.

Consult Introd. XIII., especially **138**.

Exercise XXI.

(*Conditional*)

1 If your country were to use this language [5] to you, would
she not have a claim to obtain her request even if she could
not employ force ?　2. Time would fail me, were I to wish
to reckon up the kings and commanders who have rashly
crossed the sea as invaders to the equal ruin of themselves
and their armies.　3. Had I been present during the whole of
that interview I would never have calmly endured that expression of yours.　4. Had the enemy been able to carry the war
into the most distant part of our territory, what consternation
and panic would have threatened [6] the whole country !　5. It
is rapid action that is needed ; had we employed it earlier we
should have had [6] no war to-day.　6. Even if virtue were de-
prived of this reward she would be satisfied with her own self.
7. What a life would have been mine had I foreseen, as a boy,
the series and the amount of troubles that I was [7] to endure in
age !　8. These men, had you permitted it, would have been [6]
alive to this day, and instead of expiring in tortures at the
stake would have been maintaining sword in hand the national
cause.　9. If patriots objected to any member of the community resembling themselves, the loss would extend not only
to the nation [8] but to the whole human race.

Consult Introd. XIII.

---

[1] 65, 136-138.　　　[2] 72.　　　[3] 69.　　　[4] 98.　　　[5] 41.
[6] Continuous result, see 82.　　　　　[7] 67.　　　[8] 35, 182.

Exercise XXII.

(Conditional.)

1. Even had he obeyed your warnings[1] and postponed his journey for one, two, or even more days, the result would certainly have been the same. 2. Had he known the character of his audience[1] he might possibly have[2] treated so difficult a question with more care and caution. 3. These men ought not to assist you if they had the power; they could not do so had they the will. 4. Such a man, so distinguished, so noble, so able, you could not have dismissed with insult and ignominy had there been in you a spark of honour, or sense of duty, or even human feeling. 5. Had all your hopes,[3] all your aims been crowned[4] with success you ought not even then to have been so elated with prosperity. 6. Were you to live as long as Nestor, were you to outlive all your contemporaries, all your seniors, all your juniors, yet you must die one day. 7. This is the course which, had I been born in the same position as you, I should have had to take. 8. He threatened him with death and every kind of penalty unless he remained loyal himself and kept his countrymen in their allegiance. 9. He arrived with so rapid a march, and at so well-timed a moment, that he found the enemy still off their guard and unprepared, and had not some accident betrayed his approach just before his appearance, would not only have surprised, as he did two-thirds of the army, but have taken the king asleep in his bed. 10. The German cavalry pushed on at full gallop in hopes of dashing into the camp before his arrival could be discovered; such was their speed that had not a single soldier who had been disabled by a recent wound from leaving the camp, seen the pressing nature of the danger and closed the gate, that day would have witnessed a terrible disaster. 11. So pressed by want were the French forces,

---

[1] *Warnings, audience* see **40**.   [2] **73**.   [3] *Hopes, aims,* **41**.
[4] *Crowned:* avoid *coronare* (**31**), and think of the real meaning.

that, had not the General dreaded the alarming effect of the
semblance of flight, he would have at once led them back to
their own country. 12. Such in fact was the force of his
genius and character that had he not refused to accept the
responsibility, the nation [1] would have gladly submitted its
entire control to his undisputed will and judgment.

Consult Introd. XIII. In this Exercise, the moods in the two
clauses of each conditional sentence will, as a rule, be different.

---

[1] 35, 182

PART II.

Historical and Narrative Passages.

EXERCISE XXIII.

A council of war was summoned,[1] and the momentous discussion began. The difference of opinion was great, and a hot discussion[2] was maintained till midnight. Many were in favour of at once taking the initiative in hostilities, and an immediate attack was warmly advocated on the ground of the effect of an offensive operation in raising the spirits of the soldiers. On the other hand it was urged[3] that any rash step was to be deprecated, still more the evacuation of the fort without orders from headquarters. Reinforcements might be counted on within a week's time. Meanwhile their stores were abundant, and they might defy behind their walls and guns any conceivable number of native troops. What,[4] indeed, could be more scandalously foolish than to take so critical a step on the suggestion of so worthless a character, in whom no confidence could be placed ? At last the General rose and gave his decision. "The time," he said,[3] "for deliberation was short. Everything depended on instant action. It would[5] be too late to act when the enemies' forces had been swollen to double their present number. The fort must be abandoned, and the Rajah trusted." The officers acceded to these and similar arguments, and the Council broke up with the determination to start at daybreak, all arrangements being made for an immediate march.

Consult Introd. I. **25, 26,** and (for *oratio obliqua*) XII. **123** *seq.*
The Historic Present (see **57**) may be employed in this passage.

---

[1] **99.**   [2] **39.**   [3] **88, 158.**   [4] **130.**   [5] **124, note.**

EXERCISE XXIV.

A king, while [1] walking on the road to his capital with a
single nobleman, happened to [2] meet a boy who was collecting
a few sticks from the trees which grew here and there at long
intervals on the road-side.   The king asked him why he
hesitated to go into the neighbouring forest where he would
be sure to find [3] abundance of wood.   The boy replied that it
was the king's forest, and that a proclamation had been made
by the king that no one was to enter either to collect fuel or
for any other purpose.   It is even said that he added that
he was sure that the speaker was a bad man, or else he could
not possibly have [4] advised him to break the law, and incur
the danger of death or some severe punishment.   For the
king was not the kind of man to [5] forgive those who neglected
his commands ; but rather it was his habit to deny to his
subjects what God had given them.   The good-natured
monarch was so far [6] from angry at the boy's impertinence
that he sent for him the next day, and, instead of [6] blaming,
sent him home with a present of considerable value.   "Your
speaking as you felt was so far," [6] he said, "from displeasing
to me, that I am and always shall be grateful to you for
your boyish frankness."

This Exercise illustrates certain uses of the Substantival *Ut* (*ne-*)
Clauses ; see Introd. **106-108**, and cp. Ex. XIV.

EXERCISE XXV.

Accordingly a resolution was unanimously adopted for one
of the few remaining ships to be despatched to Spain, and
that the gold and jewels and other valuables should be conveyed directly to the king by two envoys in whom Cortes

---

[1] **98, 120.**   [2] **106.**   [3] **67, 74.**
[4] Use *fieri posse*, and see **73, 106.**   [5] **113.**   [6] **107.**

could place special reliance.   They were strictly[1] enjoined to sail past the island of Cuba, and on no pretext to touch there even for a single hour.   But unfortunately one of the envoys was anxious to visit a farm which he had long owned in Cuba, and persuaded his companions to cast anchor and remain for a short time on the northern side of the island.   The result was the speedy publication of the whole matter, to the great danger of all concerned.

In his absence a sailor found an opportunity of swimming to shore to pay a short visit to his family, and whether through some want of care, or purposely, caused the news of the arrival[2] of the ship, and of its destination,[2] to reach the ears of the Governor.   He resolved at once to make it his first aim to detain the envoys, and to take measures to prevent the arrival in Spain of any messenger from Cortes. Seeing that there was no time to lose, he despatched the two fastest sailing-vessels he had to Cape Marienum, and ordered those whom he placed on board to take every precaution to prevent the possibility of escape on the part of the emissaries of Cortes.

But, whether providentially, or by a happy chance, they arrived too late.   Some Cuban had warned the captain, who was already chafing under the delay and ashamed of his own weakness, not to linger.   Accordingly, on hearing of the intentions of the Governor, he weighed anchor and put off to sea with his whole crew the day before the ships whose commander was prepared to[3] detain him, by fair means or foul, reached the spot.

This Exercise also illustrates the use of *Ut*, *Ne*, introducing a Substantival Clause after "verba imperandi[4] et efficiendi," impersonal verbs, and *velim*, *nolim*.[5]   See Introd. VIII. **101-107**; and cp. Arnold, rev. ed., Ex. XVI.

---

[1] **54.**   [2] *Arrival, destination*, **42.**   [3] **67.**
[4] Except *jubeo*, which requires accus. and infin., a construction also usual (though not invariable) with *volo, cupio, prohibeo, conor, sino, patior*.
[5] After these phrases, and *licet, oportet, necesse est*, the *ut* is frequently omitted.

EXERCISE XXVI.

At length a Rajah of tried fidelity, having[1] with difficulty reached our camp, warned us that all the neighbouring tribes were clamouring for war; that our troops had sustained a defeat across the river, and that his own people were[2] daily flocking together and demanding arms He himself was, had been, and ever would be, grateful to the English for their many great services towards him, but it was impossible for the enthusiasm of his people and the confederacy of so many warlike nations to be any longer resisted [3]

The General, they say, thanked him for his good-will, but put little confidence in his words. I know for certain that he replied that he should take no step for the present, but wait for a letter from the commander-in-chief, that he was in no distress for provisions, and, protected by his fortifications and artillery, could defy any blockade or assault on the part of the Indians.

Your brother and I think differently. We have ascertained that the Rajah spoke the truth, that the whole of India is in a ferment, that many states have either already rebelled, or are thinking of rebelling, and the rest are being tempted to rebellion; that few will resist the invitation of their countrymen; that their soldiers cannot be trusted, that a very serious mutiny is threatening.

Consult Introd. **92-96** (Indirect Predication).

EXERCISE XXVII.

At a much later period, when the star[4] of Cortes seemed on the wane, a great terror seized on the soldiers. Some[5] of them had long repented of their daring enterprise, and were

---

[1] **97, 116.**   [2] **95.**   [3] **39.**
[4] *Star* · not a Roman metaphor. see **29-31.**
[5] Render, " There were some who . . . "

weary of their long absence from home and country. It seemed as though their present toils would never come to an end ; they were distressed by the loss [1] of so many gallant comrades, and, disappointed in all their hopes of gain, were ashamed of their excessive confidence in the promises of their sanguine leader. For they could not hide from one another that they had found in Mexico, not the gold or wealth or fame which most of them had looked for, but in some cases wounds, in others an early grave,[2] in all want and sufferings. Such was the purport of their murmurs and complaints.

In the midst of this deep and general disaffection, an officer who had formerly served under Narvaez is said to have spoken as follows : [3]—" It is plain enough, soldiers, that we must start at once, and no longer obey this mere madman, Cortes. If we remain here, it is clear that we must needs be either butchered like sheep, or reserved for a fate more horrible than even death. Yonder altars are even now smoking in our sight and demanding fresh victims. We might, not many days ago, have [1] returned home unharmed and laden with booty, a step which would then have been both possible and sensible. But for these many months we have been too ready to consult the interests, not of ourselves or those for whom we ought to have [1] considered, but of one rapacious and ambitious man. Let none of us therefore blush to avow that he repents his folly, and will no longer pay the penalty of another man's want of sense."

This Exercise illustrates the use of Impersonal Verbs.

---

[1] 42. [2] *Grave:* think of the meaning.
[3] *It is plain,* etc. . . . To be rendered in the first instance in *oratio recta,* but afterwards the construction may be changed to that of *oratio obliqua;* see 128 *seq.* [4] 73.

Exercise XXVIII.

1. At the commencement of summer, when, owing to the excessive heat of the year, the corn outside the enemies' lines was now beginning to ripen unusually early, and the wells and tanks in the city were becoming dry, the inhabitants of Genoa, who, dating from the first assault on their walls, were now in the second year of a rigorous blockade, and for full eleven months had as yet received no supplies, either of men or provisions, which had been promised, began to be seriously dissatisfied with their condition and prospects. Nearly three months had passed from the time when the Duke had pledged himself by letter to come to their aid within thirty days; they had taken it for granted that he would appear at the appointed moment. Disappointed in these hopes, and feeling the daily pressure of want of food, water, and all necessaries, the stoutest hearts began to fail, and to have fears for the issue of the siege.

2. The daily and nightly sallies, which at first had been events of constant and almost daily occurrence, had later on been partially discontinued, and carried on at longer intervals, were now rendered impossible by the superiority of the enemies' numbers and the failure of their own strength. The visitation of disease which, as is usual in times of famine, beginning with the lower classes, had now become general, was daily becoming more serious, and it was evident that either their allies had given over all hope of raising [1] the blockade or hesitated to risk their lives and fortunes in behalf of others. Besides this, desertions to the enemy were becoming numerous, members of the lower orders, in despair of safety, were leaving the city after nightfall, no longer singly, but in crowds, and imploring the enemy to allow them to take refuge in their own farms, or in neighbouring towns.

---

[1] *Of raising*, **43.** Think of a Latin equivalent for the technical term, "raising a blockade."

EXERCISE XXIX.

As the political horizon[1] became brighter and more cheering, many of the towns which had revolted to the Carthaginians returned to their allegiance. But the defection of Tarentum, long hoped for by Hannibal, and suspected by Rome, was hastened by an accidental circumstance. A Tarentine, long resident[2] at Rome, under the pretext of a public commission had tampered in repeated interviews with the hostages of his nation to whom he had contrived to obtain access, and persuaded them to join him in a secret flight from Rome. All were arrested near Terracina and brought back to Rome, and with[3] the approval of the people flung from the Tarpeian Rock. This terrible punishment so exasperated not only the natural spirit of the most distinguished of the Greek settlements in Italy, but the feelings of individuals who were connected by ties of blood or friendship to the victims of so terrible a death, that it removed in an instant all hesitation on the part of Tarentum as to abandoning the alliance of Rome,[4] and throwing themselves into the arms of her deadliest enemy.

EXERCISE XXX.

At length, in accordance with my own view and that of my whole staff, it was agreed to send and open negotiations with the Governor for the surrender of the fort. Nothing could be[5] more monstrous than for an obscure town to stand over a month's investment and assault on the part of the royal army; and for one who had been trained in all the arts of war under so illustrious a leader as yourself, and gained victories over great generals and strong armies, to endanger the success of the whole campaign in a conflict with a handful of sailors and raw troops raised at a moment's notice. But

---

[1] 31.
[2] *Long resident.* "who had long been" (continuous plup., see 58).
[3] 99.   [4] What does *Rome* here mean? See 158.   [5] 150

as[1] the Governor kept putting off day after day, and at one moment tried to dupe us by demanding time to think, and the next returned defiant and self-confident answers, I saw that the time for temporising and wasting time was past, and that I must either carry the fort sword in hand, or abandon the attempt to the utter disgrace of myself and my men.

Exercise XXXI.

At length the father and son were ferried across the stream by an old man who kept asserting that he acted with reluctance, and demanded of them no slight payment for his trouble. On their landing[2] they were surrounded by a vast multitude of persons, who asked each of them whence they came and the reason[3] for their venturing to visit that country. They, wishing[2] to keep them in the dark as to the motive[3] of their arrival, made fictitious answers, and begged them all, and especially importuned the one who seemed their chief, to conduct them to their king. For a long while their request[4] was met by a flat refusal; at last the people informed them that their real fear was that, having once been informed as to the dwelling-place of the king, the strangers would shortly return thither with a Spanish army.

Exercise XXXII.

At these words the envoys threw themselves at his feet. They earnestly[5] implored him not to abandon them in their hour of need. To whom could they have recourse, if repulsed[6] by the Spaniards? They had no allies, no other hope in the whole world![7] They might have[8] avoided the present peril if they had consented to fall off from their allegiance, and join the general confederacy. They had been proof against all threats and terrors in the hope that they would find abundant

---

[1] 117.	[2] 98.	[3] 42.	[4] 40.
[5] 54.	[6] 97.	[7] 28	[8] 73.

resources and succour in the Spaniards. If doomed to disappointment, they were resolved, reluctantly and under compulsion, to abandon the alliance. They would rather perish with the rest of their countrymen than die, solitary and unaided, by their hands.

For the present the audience closed without their receiving a reply. The following night was passed by the general in harrowing perplexity. He was loath to betray his allies. He was equally loath to diminish his forces, a step which might involve delay in accepting an engagement, or else make an engagement hazardous.

Consult Intiod. XII. **123** *seq.* (on *Oratio Obliqua*).

Exercise XXXIII.

1. Day was now dawning, and the king rode along the ranks of his soldiers, with head uncovered and cheerful countenance. His approach[1] was everywhere received with cheers, and never before had the soldiers been so enthusiastic and full of confidence. As the sun grew[2] warm the mist which had settled on the plain dispersed, and the new clear daylight revealed the army of the enemy in possession of the somewhat rising ground to which they had retreated : their arms and shields and standard were glittering in the sunlight which streamed upon them. For a time he enjoyed in silence the fair prospect, then, turning to his staff, " Yesterday," he said, " we achieved something; to-day let us finish the rest of our work." At the same moment he gave the word for a general advance.

2. The summit of the mountain range was now reached, the fury of the wind had sunk, and the noonday heat was relieving the weary and frozen limbs of those who were mounting it. The prince was the first to reach the top, and to look down silently and mournfully on the wide fertile plains spread beneath his eye. The very scenes which he

---

[1] **40.**   [2] **99.**

had left so unwillingly in boyhood, and had so often sighed
for in adult life, he now saw in old age. Then turning [1]
to his companions, who could scarcely stir for fatigue and
exhaustion, he pointed out and enumerated to them the
streams, the towns, the churches, the citadels, all known to
him, all most dear. Too late, it seemed, had Fortune
changed.

3. The ill-starred old man was bound to the stake, the
fagots lighted. As his limbs were consumed by the fire,
physical torture was overpowered by inward serenity, and
undoubting hopes of a happier life beyond the grave.[2] First
of all stretching out his right hand (*abl. abs.*), "Too late," he
said, "I have done my duty; with this hand I sinned. let
this part of my body be the first to suffer" A dense
crowd stood round him as he died [1] and watched the cruel
end of one once powerful and honoured; at last as the flames
died out, they stole away home silently and sadly.[3]

EXERCISE XXXIV.

Every stage of their march [4] was made through roads lined
by orderly crowds of both sexes, who poured in from the
country districts, and to the constant sound of vows and
prayers and blessings. They were hailed as the hope and
defence of the country,[5] the champions of the nation [6] and of
the empire. "Our lives and liberties, ours and our little ones,"
men cried, "hang on you and on your swords. May all the
blessed saints [7] vouchsafe you a happy march, a successful encounter, a speedy triumph over the enemy! May we have to
discharge the vows which we have offered for you! As to-
day we follow your march with beating hearts, so, ere the
week is over, may we hail with joy your triumphant and
victorious columns!"

In this Exercise no *oratio recta* should be used.

---

[1] 98.   [2] *Beyond the grave* · think of the meaning.
[3] 54.   [4] 41.   [5] 28   [6] 35, 182
[7] *Saints* · beware a literal translation, and think of an equivalent idea.

Exercise XXXV.

1. Having heard[1] that the siege of Paris had begun, the king determined to set out at once with the few forces which remained after his recent defeat. He sent accordingly for the regimental officers and hastened to lay before them his plan. "All of you know," he said, "that the whole of the neighbourhood is swarming with the foe; that they have twice attempted to storm our camp; but have been unable to obtain any success. I have resolved nevertheless to delay no longer, but to march this very night through the midst of the enemy. Fortune, it is said, favours the brave; let us dare to be brave men, and not unworthy alike of those who have fallen in the fight, and of those we have left at home; I myself, who have often led vast armies to battle, am ready to be your guide, and the sharer of every danger. I will cease to be your emperor and learn anew to be a soldier. I would rather be a good soldier than a bad and cowardly king."

2. The officers on hearing this language were differently affected, but all were struck by the courage and resolution of their king, and scarce ventured to open their lips. Then, looking at each other, they seemed at once desirous and unwilling to express their opinions. The first to reply was an old officer of undoubted valour, who had served many campaigns under the king's own command with the greatest distinction. "I am loath," he said, "either to seem or to be a coward; I am ready to dare anything which a man can do; but I cannot speak otherwise than I think. I venture therefore, as indeed I ought, to speak for my neighbours. To be brave and to be rash are very different things; those who begin in haste sometimes are also the first to leave off. Fortune, it is true, favours, as you say, the bold; but it is not a sign of wisdom to tempt Fortune unduly. If one of our two armies is crushed[2], it will be all over with the other. If

---

[1] 116. [2] 65, 136.

you consent to wait for the favourable moment they will help each other." His language was vague, but at the same time sufficiently clear. After he had ceased to speak, the rest gave various advice ; some wished to start at once and avail them-selves of the darkness of night and the unsuspecting mood of the enemy ; others agreed with the old officer, at the same time blaming his excessive outspokenness. The king heard them all in silence ;[1] he resolved to do precisely what he had determined on.

This Exercise illustrates certain uses of the Infinitive ; see **85-91**
Oratio recta may be used.

EXERCISE XXXVI.

1. Having lost his father in the war with the Saracens, and succeeding to the throne [2] almost in infancy, Henry soon found the scanty influence [3] of the name of king upon the aris-tocracy [1] of Castile. Coming [5] at last to man's estate, and see-ing how his resources had been impoverished by the fraud and rapacity of the nobles, he recovered in the following manner, if we may believe the traditions of Spain, much of his losses :—Returning[5] home one evening somewhat late from the chase, he was chagrined, as was natural in a young man unusually fatigued and famished, to find no meal in preparation   In answer to his indignant remonstrance [3] his steward declared that he had neither money nor credit left, and knew no longer whence to obtain the bare necessaries of life. Meantime, having heard that a great banquet was being held at a noble-man's house hard by, and that those seated at the table allowed their neighbours to enjoy the sight of the splendid entertainment, the king, having satisfied the cravings of his appetite on the results of the day's sport, succeeded in suppressing for the moment his indignation, and resolved to imitate the far-famed Caliph of Arabian fiction.

---

[1] 54.   [L][2] 31.   [3] 41, 54.   [4] 36, A.   [5] 98.

2. Accordingly, changing his dress, and adopting to the utmost of his power the appearance and demeanour of a villager or servant, he entered the house, and, mingling with the crowd of those enjoying the spectacle, realised the contrast between his own scanty means and the wealth and luxury of men who, instead of acting as the guardians and protectors of their monarch's defenceless minority, had left no stone unturned to appropriate to themselves the wealth which his gallant forefathers had won by their swords from the Moorish conquerors. Having watched the sight for an hour or two, and witnessed a display of gold and silver plate and other adornments of banquets of the kind beyond what he had thought possible to be found in a private mansion, he returned home, and after earnestly enforcing on his faithful steward the importance to his safety of nothing that he had done being disclosed, he departed next day before daybreak for the capital.

Consult Introd. VII. **97-100** (Use of Participles). For a continuation of this passage see Exercise LX.

EXERCISE XXXVII.

He repeated and enforced the same arguments which he had used with Maitland. He warned him of the danger to which he must expose himself by the public accusation of his sovereign. Mary would never forgive a man who had endeavoured to fix such a brand of infamy on her character. If she ever recovered [1] any degree of power, his destruction would [2] be inevitable, and he would justly merit it at her hands. Nor would Elizabeth screen him from this by a public approbation of his conduct. For whatever evidence of Mary's guilt he might produce, she was resolved to give no definite sentence in the cause. Let him only demand that the matter should be brought to a decision immediately after hearing the proofs, and he would be fully convinced how

---

[1] **84, 4; cp. 136, 143.**　　　　　　[2] **124,** note.

false and insidious her intentions were, and by consequence
how improper it would be for him to appear as the accuser
of his own sovereign.

Consult Introd XII. 123-130 (*Oratio Obliqua*).

EXERCISE XXXVIII.

He warned Cortes that the number of the enemy was quite
unprecedented, that the position of their camp was such as [1]
he had never seen before, that they had availed themselves
with the greatest skill of the stream and of the hills; had
abandoned the former after breaking down the bridges, and
were holding the latter with strong detachments. Nor was
this the end of the danger: the spirit and courage of their own
men was not what [1] it had been the day before; it seemed as
though they scarcely hoped any longer for victory, or thought
themselves capable of overcoming, in the face of so unfavourable a position, such a swarm of enemies as were now challenging them to battle with cries and insults. The undaunted
leader replied that he promised that day should [2] turn out
differently to what the other expected.

This Exercise illustrates the use of *is, tantus*, etc.

EXERCISE XXXIX.

In order to prevent the loss [3] of all the results of his past
sufferings [3] and achievements, Cortes now resolved to put in
execution a plan which he had [4] long been silently meditating.
Being [5] aware that his enemies would try every means to
prejudice the Emperor against himself and his friends, he
resolved to [6] despatch a vessel at once to Spain with the
intention of addressing a letter to the monarch personally,

---

[1] 113.   [2] 74

[3] *Loss*. in rendering this and the other substantives to which this
note refers, consult Introd. 40-42.

[4] 58.   [5] 98, 116.   [6] 102.

and announcing to him the nature and extent [1] of his successes, and the hopes of gain and empire which he had formed for the future. He hoped thus to [2] secure the confirmation [1] by the Emperor of his past proceedings, and conciliate alike his good-will and the favour of his ministers.[3] To prevent the soldiers from refusing to part with so large a portion of their booty, and to secure their submission [1] to the step which he proposed to [4] take, he put before them the greatness of the rewards which they might fairly look for, and the number and amount [1] of obstacles over which they had already triumphed.

This Exercise illustrates the use of *ut, ne, quo* with Final Clauses.

EXERCISE XL.

In the reduction [5] of the enemy to submission, the Admiral had to deal with a difficulty unknown to those who [6] had been the first to enter Peru. His predecessors had found allies in the natives from their disaffection to their Spanish conquerors, while he was in the position of one who had to enforce servitude upon men who had tasted the sweets of freedom. But he was a man of such natural and constitutional energy that he entered into and discharged every detail of duty, down to the minutest; and, not content with [7] laying his plans, and giving orders for the steps necessary to their execution, there were few which he did not carry out in person. Severe and rigorous as was his discipline, he enforced it on no one more sternly than on himself: in hard living, in scanty sleep, in exposure to fatigue, he put himself on a level with the humblest of his soldiers, nor in the ranks of his army did he claim a single distinction beyond that of his office [8] and authority.

The first two sentences should be fused into one; the remainder of the passage into another. See Introd. **25, 26.**

---

[1] *Loss:* in rendering this and the other substantives to which this note refers, consult Introd. **40-42.**
[2] **74.**   [3] **34.**   [4] **67.**   [5] **43.**   [6] **113.**
[7] *Not content with:* beware of a literal translation, and see **107.**
[8] **34, 35.**

Exercise XLI.

In the camp of Crassus was a member of his staff, C. Cassius Longinus, who had acted in the same capacity with Caesar, and served with the highest distinction in the campaigns of Gaul. Though a dashing soldier, he was no mean student[1] of the science and practice of war, and in spite of the unbounded hopes held out by Ariamnes, who had contrived to worm himself into the good graces and confidence of Crassus, he saw that there was no room to doubt that the one was uttering nothing but falsehoods, the other preparing to[2] embark in a perilous or fatal enterprise. Accordingly, though at all times a zealous upholder of soldierly subordination and discipline, he made it his object[3] to warn his commander against putting any trust in the fair promises of the barbarian. [4]"Though I know," he said, "the difference between the duties of my own office and of yours, yet I hope that you will pardon my language,[5] however frank, if only I speak the truth. Indeed, you will forgive me for saying that though you, my general, rebuke your officer, though all count me impertinent, I must needs state my views. However eager you may be to carry the standards of Rome beyond the walls of Seleucia to the heart[6] of Bactria, and to reach, like another Alexander, the ocean that washes the shores of India, yet a wise commander will consider the terrible loss of brave men's lives that even the first step of such a series of achievements must entail. For even though we should conquer by repeated conflicts the enemy, who now, under the pretence of flight, is enticing us to hot pursuit over these dry and barren plains, yet I incline to think[7] that such a victory is scarcely preferable to an immediate and remediable defeat. Though[8] a brave soldier will face any foe, a good general will never despise an untried enemy. These Parthians, though[9] armed with bows and arrows, are quite different from the

---

[1] 33, 41.   [2] 67.   [3] 104.   [4] *Oratio recta* may be used.
[5] 40.   [6] 30.   [7] 166.   [8] 149   [9] 145.

archers who have swarmed elsewhere around our legions without[1] daring to face the charge of a single maniple. The mounted archer, clad in a panoply which[2] is proof against the Roman pikes, and who from a safe distance can at full speed launch his arrow through the heart of a Roman soldier, is not a foe whom even a Roman legionary soldier can count cheap. Do not let us imagine that it was men like these whose countless hordes Alexander drove like sheep before him when he shattered with steel the throne[3] of Persia, and penetrated with a mere handful to the confines of the world." In the midst of these words he received a formal order for silence from his general, and in spite of the vehemence and earnestness with which he subsequently put before him the arguments which he had intended to use, Crassus fancied himself bound to persevere or, to speak more accurately, resolved to do so.

Consult Introd. XIV. 144 *seq.* (on Concessive Clauses).

Exercise XLII.

It is certain the consternation was very great at London, and in the two Houses, from the time that they heard that the King marched from Shrewsbury with a formed army, and that he was resolved to fight as soon as he could[4] meet with their army. However, they endeavoured confidently to keep up the ridiculous opinion amongst the common people, that the King did not command, but was carried about in that army of the Cavaliers, and was desirous to escape from them; which they hoped the Earl of Essex would give him opportunity to do. The first news they heard of the army's being engaged was by those who fled upon the first charge; who made marvellous haste from the place of danger, and thought not themselves safe till they were gotten out of any possible distance of being pursued. It is certain, though it was past

---

[1] 105.   [2] 113.   [3] 31.   [4] 85, 4.

two of the clock before the battle began, many of the soldiers, and some commanders of no mean name, were at St. Albans, which was near thirty miles from the field, before it was dark. These men, as all runaways do for their own excuse, reported all for lost, and the King's army to be so terrible that it could not be encountered.

Exercise XLIII

It is here that tradition places the scene[1] of Hannibal's famous vision. He saw in his sleep, says the story, a youth of angelic beauty, who announced himself as commissioned by Jupiter to lead him on his way to Italy. He had[2] but to fix his eyes on his guide and to follow him steadfastly. At first a great awe, the story went on to say, fell on him, and he followed, looking neither behind, nor to the right, nor to the left. But after a while, as he began to ask within himself what it was on which he was forbidden to look back, he could no longer control his eyes, so he looked, and saw behind him a monstrous serpent moving forwards, while trees and houses fell crashing before it. Storm and a peal of thunder followed. Then, as he asked in wonder what the monstrous form portended, he heard a voice say,[3] "Thou seest the desolation of Italy, go[2] onwards on thy way; cast no look behind, nor question further, nor try to draw the fates from their obscurity."

Consult Introd. VI. 92-96 (Indirect Predication), and XII. 123 *seq* (*Oratio Obliqua*).

Exercise XLIV.

It was a common saying of the great Napoleon, whom no one would look on as a mean authority on the art of war, that nothing is more ruinous to an invader than an undue contempt for the enemy. And in truth the careful choice of

---

[1] 35.   [2] 130, 162.   [3] *Oratio obliqua* to be used.

ground, alike for encampment and for fighting, the taking adequate precautions for the safety of baggage, wounded, and sick, the providing for supplies and everything necessary for troops on a campaign on an enemy's soil, are matters of an importance which no one at all inexperienced in offensive warfare would readily believe. The neglect of such points, and of a hundred others of the same kind, has repeatedly, as every student[1] of history knows, ruined famous commanders and gallant armies; the former have paid with their lives or their reputation the penalty of their ignorance and foolhardiness, the latter have fallen victims, as often happens, to the blunders of their generals.

This Exercise illustrates the use of the Substantival Infinitive
(Introd. **42-89**).

Exercise XLV.

1. It was now pretty clear that our troops were drawing near and that the term of our many sufferings was at hand. About noon word[2] was brought to the beleaguered (troops) that there was agitation[3] in the whole of the enemies' quarters; that at daybreak there had been a rush[2] to arms; then an important debate was going on, that some were in favour of awaiting Sertorius' arrival, others of setting out to meet him. Smoke, too, had been seen, it was said, at some distance, which was, men hoped, a signal of the march of the army. It seemed that Fortune was at last changing, and taking sides with us.

2. To our men, exhausted with hunger, thirst, sleeplessness, toil, and fighting, it seemed that the day would never come to an end. A letter, it was believed, had been brought in by a spy from Caesar (to the purport) that he hoped to[4] arrive before sunset. But evening was now coming on,[3] and some (began) to express indignation at our forces' delay,

---

[1] **36, 166.**   [2] **41.**   [3] **39.**   [4] **74.**

others to lay aside all hope of safety, others to complain of being deceived and abandoned. Suddenly a rumour ran through the town, and soon reached the citadel, that the enemy were silently[1] stealing and flying in all directions, and that there was nowhere any resistance or fighting.

Consult Introd. 90 *seq.* (Infinitive of Indirect Predications).

Exercise XLVI.

[To be rendered into *Oratio Obliqua.*]

"Let us," he said, "do nothing hastily, of what use at such a crisis can either rashness or flurry be to us?[2] If any serious disaster occurs,[3] I, not you, shall have to give account to the nation,[4] and I do not wish to detain any of you here against his will. If, therefore, any one is terrified by this report, let him leave the camp, as he can, without difficulty or danger, if he does not waste time by delay.

"It is in vain, therefore, that you appeal to England.[5] You should have done this when your king was successful in retaining you, however reluctantly, in your allegiance, before you had taken upon yourselves to[6] rebel against his rule and abandon our alliance. What do you think your envoys will gain from the English parliament or monarch, if, in spite of the obligations of their religion and of their unfamiliarity with that element, I send them across the ocean? Will any one believe[2] that you, who by the blackest treason murdered the best of kings, were justified in attacking the camp of the staunchest of allies? Had you complained of your king's maladministration[7] or of any act of oppression towards your people on our part, I would at once have listened to your remonstrances,[8] and have cheerfully, if your demands were

---

[1] 53.   [2] 128, I 2   [3] 65, cp with 84, 4.
[4] 35, 182.   [5] *England* see 158.
[6] *Taken upon yourselves to* use a suitable adverb or a phrase with an *ut*-clause (104).   [7] 36, A; cp with 41   [8] 40

reasonable, have satisfied them. Now these appeals to heaven and to the absent are too late."

N B.—Before turning this or any other passage of English *direct* speech into Latin *oratio obliqua*, it is well to think how the words would stand if reported *indirectly* in English, *e g.* in the Parliamentary report of a newspaper. See Introd. XII. **123** *seq.*

Exercise XLVII.

Many sad memories[1] rose before him as he gazed on the ocean that bathed the shore beneath his feet; the almost entire destruction of his magnificent armies; the death and capture, or, more painful still, the alienation of so many generals; the annihilation of his fleets after years of lavish outlay and preparation; the change in popular opinion, the loss of all his allies, the divorce of the bride of his youth, the disappointment of his dreams[1] of empire and dominion. The thought too came home to him, that after[2] all his splendid achievements, after subduing Europe by his arms, defeating army after army, receiving the submission of so many crowned heads, and pushing forward year after year the frontiers of his country, he was now sitting as exile on a paltry island, while France was smarting under the loss of the flower and prime of her children, applauding the restoration of her king, and forgetting his own exile and despair.

In this Exercise abstract nouns are to be expressed by a combination of substantive and participle. See Introd. III. **40** *seq.*

Exercise XLVIII.

Night surprised us while still in anxiety and suspense. But in the third watch, while we were[3] waiting sleeplessly for the dawn and for our doom, word was brought to your father that a spy who had made his way safely through the

---

[1] *Memories, dreams:* beware of apparent Latin equivalents.
[2] **99.**   [3] **120.**

remissly guarded camp of the enemy had brought a letter,
which he eagerly, as you may well believe,[1] snatched and[2]
read with joy and thankfulness to Heaven. The General
wrote that it was against his will and under compulsion that
he had broken the pledge which he had given; that he had
done all he could; that the few cavalry whom he had with
him were worn out with fighting and foraging; that all the
country which they had traversed was beset with armed foes;
that there had been fighting daily, almost hourly, that he
was bringing up a sufficient supply of provisions, which in
the last three days they had taken from the enemy, a task
which was by no means easy, with such a small number
of baggage animals; that before morning he would[3] send
forward the best troops he had into the enemies' camp, and do
his utmost to force his way into the city and end our miseries.

> Consult Introd. XII **123** *seq* (*Oratio Obliqua*), and **92** *sq*.
> (Indirect Predication)

EXERCISE XLIX.

[Bear in mind what has been said (Introduction, p. 7 , II. **27** *sq*,
and throughout the Lecture on Latin Prose Composition, **153** *sq*)
on the more direct and less figurative and metaphorical tendency
of Latin expression as compared with English.]

1. No sooner had he thus won the crown[1] than he
endeavoured to consolidate on a fresh basis of law, justice,
and morality, a throne[4] which owed its origin to violent and
bloody usurpation. Being[5] aware that a state of warfare
with its inevitably brutalising tendencies was fatal to the
assimilation of these better principles,[6] he made it his first
object[7] to humanise his subjects by weaning them from the
soldier's life, and by familiarising them with peaceful pursuits.
After[8] gaining the goodwill of the neighbouring governments

---

[1] **83, 2.**　　　[2] **97.**　　　[3] **124,** and note　　　[4] **31.**　　　[5] **98.**
[6] *These better principles* : *i.e.* "law, justice, and morality"
[7] **104**　　　　　　　　　　　　　　　　　　　　[8] **116.**

by treaties of alliance, he felt that the rude spirits of his nation needed some restraining influence to compensate for the withdrawal of foreign foes and of military discipline. He recognised the necessity of a state religion, as the most effective of all checks that could be brought to bear on masses of men, in the low level of culture and civilisation to which his countrymen had then attained.

✓ 2. Such were the abilities, and such the virtues of this prince, that his subjects adored him in his lifetime, and lamented his decease with tears [1] of genuine grief and veneration. Yet there is good historical [2] evidence to show that he was so far from being one of those in whose favour fortune forgets her fickleness, that in his youth he was repeatedly unsuccessful in the field; and that it was not till [3] he had passed the extreme term of middle life that he finally crushed the haughty and habitual invaders of his kingdom, and secured his own throne [4] and his nation's [5] independence by a signal and decisive victory. The impression [6] produced by this success was unexampled. He reigned from that day no longer by a disputed title, or by the hazardous tenure of the sword, but in the heart and affections of an undivided nation.

Exercise L.

On news being [7] brought (on perceiving) that the soldiers were not so anxious about their own lives as that of their general, and that there was a danger of their slackening in the assault in order to preserve his safety, he reluctantly allowed himself to be persuaded not to accompany in person the escalading party; then as the spirits of the Roman soldier rose, and the ladders were raised and planted against the walls, a desperate contest followed. At last, in spite of the long and fierce resistance of the besieged, the citadel was car-

---

[1] 43. [2] Avoid *historicus*, and see **36, 178.**
[3] 122. [4] 31. [5] **35, 182.** [6] **10, 41.**
[7] Two possible constructions: see **98, 116**; and **99.**

ried, and without a moment's interval the victors streamed down with a cheer at full speed into the city, where, under the eyes, and cheered by the voice of their sovereign, the flower of Mexico was maintaining the fight And indeed both parties might well strain every nerve for victory, for to each alike success and life hung on the issue of the fight.

This Exercise illustrates the use of " Ablative Absolute ; " see Introd 99, 100

EXERCISE LI.

So he departed into his own tent, where, after some time spent in agony, he called unto him a servant of his that had the custody of his poison, and tempering [1] a potion for the queen sent it unto her with this message, that gladly he would [2] have had her to live with him as his wife, but, since they who had power to hinder him of his desire, would not yield thereto, he sent her a cup that should preserve her from falling alive into the hands of the Romans, willing her to [3] remember her birth and estate, and accordingly to take order for herself. At the receipt [4] of this message and present, she only said that if her husband had no better token to send unto his wife, she might have [2] died more honourably if she had not wedded so lately before her funeral. And herewithal she boldly drank off the poison.

Consult Introd. IV. (use of Adverbs), and XII. (*Oratio Obliqua*).

EXERCISE LII.

Sounds borne on the night air, followed by the reports of spies, soon betrayed to the natives the movement of our troops and the evacuation of the cantonments. They at once placed a strong detachment in ambush on a suitable position,

---

[1] 97, 98.   [2] 74.   [3] 130 *ad fin.*   [4] 99.

and awaited the arrival of their intended victims. No sooner had the column disappeared in the deep valley through which the march lay, than they suddenly displayed themselves on both our flanks, and began at once to press fiercely on the rear, and attempt to cut off the leading files from the higher ground in front. The General, taken entirely by surprise, flew in hot haste this way and that, and strove to make the necessary dispositions called for by the emergency. But even here he showed a want of decision not unusual in men who have to form their plans in the heat of action. He gave the order to abandon the baggage. The step was in itself excusable, considering the emergency; but its results were deplorable. Interpreted as a sure symptom of alarm and despair, it disheartened the soldiers, and inspired the enemy with fresh spirit. A member of his staff who had foreseen the possibility of the present misadventure, and had declined to concur in the movement of the troops, upheld in every way the honour of his country.

EXERCISE LIII.

Such was the effect of his words upon the bold spirits of his soldiers, that they not only listened to these suggestions [1] with patience, but surrendered, at his pleasure, the very treasures for the sake of which they had crossed [2] a perilous ocean and penetrated unknown regions And indeed nothing can be a greater proof of the universal influence [3] of Cortes' abilities and strength of mind, than the fact of [4] his having obtained this request from his comrades, who were by no means of a temper likely to [5] abandon easily spoil won by such novel and daring enterprises. But, though [6] covetous and rapacious, the Spaniards were yet capable of perceiving that they must use every effort to prevent any one from so

---

[1] 40   127
[3] *Universal influence :* neither word to be translated literally, see 41.
[4] 108   [5] 67.   [6] 105.

thwarting their leader's policy, as to rob men alike of the moderate prizes they had already, and of the vast wealth which they hoped soon to realise. So powerful with them was this consideration that, as often happens, no one scrupled to sacrifice the possessions[1] of the moment to the dreams and hopes of the future.

This Exercise illustrates the construction of *Consecutive* Clauses.

Exercise LIV.

The Count having first[2] ordered his few remaining cavalry to disperse in aid of those who required assistance, formed his infantry in close column and advanced to meet the enemy. Of the horse, some lost their way through ignorance of the country, or misled by cries for succour that met them from every point of the compass; some were suffocated with their horses in the bottomless morass, those who followed the causeway that led through the impassable swamp, came into sudden collision with the whole array of the Spaniards, and were slain or taken to a man

The main battle was fiercely contested. Numbers and discipline were arrayed against patriotism and despair. At last the Hollanders were overwhelmed by numbers. Many perished in close fight, some were cut down in flight, few asked for quarter, none received it. The Count himself was in the utmost danger. His horse was shot under him, and fell heavily with his rider, who narrowly escaped destruction as he lay helpless on the ground He was saved by an orderly, who dismounted on the instant, and placed his master, whose nerves had given way under[3] the immediate prospect of death, on his own saddle, conjuring him to ply the spur and save himself. The faithful soldier fell a victim to his loyalty; incapable of keeping up with the mounted

---

[1] *Possessions, dreams, hopes* see **41.**   [2] **118, 119.**   [3] **99.**

fugitives, he fell under the weapons of a host of foes drawn
to the spot by his leader's fall. The Count himself, after a
desperate ride round the edge of the fatal marsh, reached the
citadel, at the moment when all hope of his safety had been
abandoned

Exercise LV.

The General now saw that, thanks to overweening self-
confidence, he had been deceived and outwitted by his
untaught and uncivilised foe. To what was he to have[1]
recourse? how was he to carry on the war? His soldiers
had no rations, their strength was failing, and he dared not
send out the few mounted men that remained to forage;
the mere numbers of the enemy who were roaming close
beneath his entrenchment precluded all hope of the arrival
of a relieving force. It was clear that within three days
his soldiers would either perish of hunger or be taken
prisoners by a ruthless enemy. He repented sorely of his
rashness and want of foresight, and felt that all would
rightly attribute to him the present sufferings and the
coming disaster. With one hope alone he consoled himself,
that the enemy would also on their part be straitened for
want of provisions, and depart without effecting their object,
or else, from their leaders giving different advice, would at
last fight with one another.

Two legions were drawn up in line of battle, but, as a
stream with steep banks flowed between them, they could
not assist each other; each accordingly fought for itself, and
each did its utmost to maintain its ground, and drive back the
immense swarms of the enemy.

This Exercise illustrates the use of Reflexive and Reciprocal
Pronouns.

---

[1] 82.

Exercise LVI.

The General received the soldiers' demands in silence, and with unmoved countenance and undaunted spirit. When they had finished, he expressed his wonder at their having so lost heart as to give up the game in despair, and be ready to make shipwreck [1] of their honour and their career, because in one or two battles the day had gone against them. He reminded them that the dangers on which they had enlarged could not possibly be diminished by the flight, to characterise by its right name the march they urged, which they were design-ing. He bade them ask each other whether the allies, who up to that moment had with such enthusiasm and loyalty braved in their company alike the smiles and frowns [2] of fortune, had deserved to be abandoned to the merciless barbarity [3] of the Mexicans.

He assured them that he had no doubt that he would yet fulfil all that he had promised them; and that he had the fullest confidence that the reinforcements which he had summoned would soon reach them. As regarded himself, he had determined to persevere in the work which he had begun; as he had been the first to hope for victory, so he would be the last to despair; but he had no wish to have around him men who,[4] either through weakness or cowardice, were content to depart with their object unachieved: he would therefore in no way interfere with the departure of all who, forgetful of their former victories, so resented their late defeat as to turn their back to the foe, ready to a step which brave men account as the last disgrace. In his own view, the boldest policy was at once the most honourable and the safest.

Consult Introd. XII. (*Oratio Obliqua*).

---

[1] *Give up the game, make shipwreck of* has Latin any equivalent metaphors?   [2] 30, 32.
[3] *Merciless barbarity* : use two substantives.   [4] 113.

Exercise LVII.

The next day he summoned [1] a council and did his utmost [2] to soothe and cheer them; he begged them not to be too dispirited or unduly disconcerted by a single check, reminding them that any who expected unbroken success in war were out of their reckoning,[3] and that it was neither by valour nor military science, but by the merest accident, that the enemy had won the day. What,[4] he asked, would those who were in such consternation and despair, on account of a momentary reverse, have said,[5] if the reserves had failed to appear on the scene before nightfall, and if they had had to sustain a terrible defeat instead of merely retreating with no considerable loss, to their quarters? He bade them, therefore, instead of wailing over the past, return thanks to Fortune, whose power in war they all knew, that the enemy had abandoned the attack which they had commenced upon their camp, had quitted the field of battle without [6] obtaining their object, and had reaped no result whatever from their apparent success.

See Introd. XII. (*Oratio Obliqua*).

Exercise LVIII.

The protector [7] published a manifesto, in which he enforced all the arguments for that measure. He said,[8] that Nature seemed originally to have intended this island for one empire; and having cut it off from all communication with foreign states, and guarded it by the ocean, she had pointed out to the inhabitants the road to happiness [9] and security. The education, too, and customs of the people concurred with

---

[1] 99.   [2] 104.   [3] 30.   [4] 128, I. 2.
[5] *Would have said*, 74.   [6] 99.
[7] *Protector:* avoid *tutor, protector*, etc., and think of a Roman term implying extraordinary rule.   [8] 130 end, 169.   [9] 33.

Nature; and by giving them the same language, and laws, and manners, had invited them to a thorough union and coalition fortune had at last removed all obstacles,[1] and had prepared an expedient by which they might become one people, without leaving any place for that jealousy, either of honour or of interest,[3] to which rival nations[1] are naturally so much exposed. For the crown[2] of Scotland[6] had devolved to a female; that of England[6] to a male; and happily the two sovereigns, as of a rank, so were they also of an age, the most suitable to each other: that the hostile disposition[7] which prevailed between the nations, and which arose from past injuries, would soon be extinguished, after a long and secure peace had established confidence between them; that the memory of former miseries, which at present inflamed their mutual animosity, would then serve only to make them cherish, with more passion, a state of happiness and tranquillity, so long unknown to their ancestors.

Exercise LIX.

The year closed without any action with Hannibal. He had not recovered sufficiently from his late public and personal calamity to assume the offensive, and the Romans were in no mood to rouse the sleeping lion,[5] so overpowering, even in the collapse of all around him, was their sense[9] of his surpassing greatness. Indeed, it may be questioned whether his genius was not more marvellous in adversity than in success. For thirteen years he fought on an enemy's soil, at a distance from home, with chequered success. His soldiers were foreigners, the offscouring of every nationality, with no common tie of law, custom, or language. They differed in appearance, in dress, in accoutrements. They were aliens to each other in creed, ritual, worship, almost in gods. Yet so

---

[1] 41.   [2] 105.   [3] 170.   [4] 35, 182.   [5] 31.
[6] 158,   [7] 44,   [8] 29-31.   [9] 41,

happily did he weld[1] together this heterogeneous mass, that
no instance occurred either of dissension among their ranks
or of mutiny against their general.

Read Introd. **25, 26,** with the examples of Latin structure there
given ; and compare Exercise I.

EXERCISE LX.

(*Continued from* EX. XXXVI.)

1. Then seeing the need of instant action, at the suggestion
(with the sympathy and co-operation) of a famous physician
who in his father's lifetime had lived on terms of the closest
intimacy with the royal household, and after his death had,
against the wishes and efforts of the queen, been banished on
the pretence of using poison, he devised the following plan.
Having caused[2] a rumour to be widely circulated that he had
fallen suddenly and dangerously ill, he confined himself for
some days to the palace, and even to his bed. At last an
announcement was made that the disease was increasing
and that the king was at his last gasp. Believing the
story, and far from suspecting the truth, the nobles assembled
at the palace, some from real, some from pretended, sorrow at
their sovereign's untimely fate. When all had been admitted
to a sumptuous chamber, where the kings of Castile were
accustomed to entertain the ambassadors of foreign states,
the doors were ordered to be closed upon them, and the king
suddenly entered, having laid aside all appearance of ill-health,
and, with his sword drawn and a countenance of unusual sternness, took his seat on a platform at the extremity of the
apartment.

2. Turning[3] to this threatening apparition, the nobles
looked at each other in alarm, and asked in silence what this
scene portended. At last the king, rising from his seat, asked
a noble of the highest rank who stood nearest him how many

---

[1] **29-31.**   [2] **116.**   [3] **98.**

kings of Castile he had seen. Though wondering at his
meaning the noble answered " Four " To the same question
another replied " Five." The others, when asked the same
question in turn, made similar answers, some two, some three,
no one more than five. Meanwhile the king, after hearing
their answers, stood for a while speechless, and with his naked
sword in his hand gazed fiercely round on those standing
round him. It was like a second Telemachus looking on his
mother's suitors and his father's foes. Then, on his giving
a concerted signal, armed guards entered, led by an aged
soldier who, in the late king's reign, had been conspicuous
for his loyalty and courage. At the same time was seen
the executioner bearing the axe and other implements of
punishment. Then the king raised his voice and, "How is
it," he said, "that you have seen one or two or three
sovereigns, and none of you more than five, while I, almost
a boy, have known more than twenty ? You have seized on
the privileges, power, and resources which, had the laws been
respected, would have been in your monarch's hands : stripped
of my patrimony, you have succeeded in making me scarcely
command the necessaries of life."

3. The dismayed nobles, with death before their eyes,
throwing themselves at his feet, tried to pacify his anger
and implored his pardon : some turned and appealed to the
veteran general under whom many of them had served
against the Moors. They promised instant and entire resti-
tution of the fruits of their rapacity and embezzlement.
They did not however obtain their prayer till,[1] having
agreed to give up their persons as hostages, they had sworn
to restore all that during the last ten years they had by force
or fraud taken from the Crown.

Whether the story be true or false I do not venture to say.
But, whether it be true or false, it is an evidence of the state
of the monarchy at the beginning of the fourteenth century.

Consult Introd. 99, 100 (Ablative Absolute).

---

[1] 122.

Exercise LXI.

Therefore the Prince took a gallant resolution to give the enemy a brisk charge with his own regiment upon their advance,[1] whilst the Earl rallied his, and prepared to second him as there should be occasion. This was as soon, and fortunately, executed as resolved: the Prince at the head of his regiment charging so vigorously that he utterly broke and routed that part of the front that[2] received the impression. But almost half the enemy's horse, that, being extended longer than his front, were not charged, wheeled about and charged the prince in the rear; and at the same time the Earl of Carnarvon with his rallied regiment charged their rear; and all this so thoroughly performed, that they were mingled pell-mell one amongst the other, and the good sword was to decide the controversy.

Exercise LXII.

1. Things being in this state, Crassus, instead of[3] fearing for his army and himself, began to be more sanguine in his hopes, owing to the news brought him by his scouts, that after riding several miles ahead they had seen no single enemy; they added that from the many tracks which they had found of horses and men all pointing in the opposite direction, they felt sure that the whole array of the Parthians had taken to flight. And seeing that it was the will of Heaven that Crassus should lead the gallant troops of Rome to destined and fatal disaster, it seemed as though his self-confidence and rash presumption of success waxed greater in proportion to the need of thought and deliberation. The soldiers also, forasmuch as they had advanced so far without any opposition, began to hold the enemy in contempt, under the impression that[4] they had not the courage to encounter them in the field.,

---

[1] 98.　　　　　　[2] 113.　　　　　　[3] 107, 117, 148.,
[4] *Under the impression that:* use *quod.*.

But their General's hopes and their own belief were alike mistaken, and both he and they were destined to feel the real power[1] of the Parthians, even in flight, sooner than he had hoped or they expected.

For Orodes had divided his army into two divisions; with one portion he had invaded Armenia to wreak vengeance on Artavasdes for having made overtures of[2] alliance to the Romans. The rest he had placed under Surena, with a charge to[3] make head against the Romans as best he could. Not that[4] the king despised the Romans or thought it a fairer field of honour to make war upon Artavasdes and lay waste Armenia; for Crassus was, he knew, one of the most powerful men whom Rome had produced, and in no way an adversary whom Orodes could despise : but he seems, on the contrary, to have deliberately removed himself to a distance, whether from an apprehension of danger, or from wishing to watch the rising event.

2. Accordingly, as Surena was a person of no ordinary condition, but the first after himself in rank, blood, and military distinction, he despatched him to make[5] a previous trial of the prowess of the Romans, and to prolong the compaign by his stratagems. But the result turned out otherwise than he had intended. For Surena brought the matter to an issue sooner than either the king had hoped or his nation expected. For though not venturing[6] to face the Romans in fair fight, yet, inasmuch as he was greatly superior in cavalry, he entertained the design of[7] drawing off the Romans by a pretended flight from the river Euphrates, on which their supplies and all munitions of war were brought up, into the open and desolate plains of Assyria, where they would be cut off from all means of procuring either forage or water or fuel, and become dispirited, not only for want of provisions and all necessaries, but from the cheerless and gloomy landscape. since there was no object there that could refresh the

---

[1] **42, 1.**   [2] *Made overtures of* render by an adverb.
[3] **102.**   [4] **114, 3.**   [5] **110, 111.**   [6] **148.**   [7] **102.**

traveller's eye, neither trees nor hills, nor streams nor crops, nor even herbage, but a boundless and monotonous waste of sand spread round on all sides like a sea.

This Exercise illustrates the use of Causal Conjunctions (*quod, quia, quoniam, quum:* see Introd. X. **114.**)

EXERCISE LXIII.

We read in Polybius, an historian of at least respectable authority, that after the battle of Cannae Hannibal sent ten of his prisoners to Rome, after extorting from them an oath to[1] return to his camp, if they failed in[2] inducing the Senate to ransom those of their countrymen whom the fortune of war had left in his hands. On the refusal of the Senate, nine, he says, returned. One, who had gone back to the camp a few minutes after leaving[3] it, on the pretext of having forgotten something, remained at Rome. The Senate passed a resolution that he should be sent in chains to Hannibal. But the most striking[4] point in his story is yet to come. Hannibal had in his hands no less than 8000 men. They had neither laid down their arms on the field, nor been guilty of pusillanimous flight. They had simply capitulated in their camp to overwhelming forces after being abandoned by their generals. The Senate, however, decided against their ransom, though the sum demanded by Hannibal was trifling. Their motive was to make the Roman soldier feel that he must either conquer or die. The undaunted courage displayed by the Roman Government in her darkest hour struck with dismay, he says,[5] even the heroic spirit of her great enemy.

---

[1] **74.**

[2] *If they failed* . . . : think what the Latin idiom would be in *oratio recta ;* and cp. **84, 136.**

[3] **118.**   [4] **160.**   [5] **88, 130,** end.

Exercise LXIV.

If we may [1] place implicit confidence in the Italian historians, no period of society [2] has exhibited a character of darker deformity than that of Alexander the Sixth. Inordinate in his ambition, insatiable in his avarice and his lust, inexorable in his cruelty, and boundless in his rapacity, almost every crime that can disgrace humanity is attributed to him, without hesitation, by writers whose works are published under the sanction of the Romish Church. He is also accused of having [3] introduced into his territories the detestable practice of searching for State offences by means of secret informers, a system fatal to the liberty and happiness of every country that has submitted to such a degradation. As a Pontiff he perverted his high office [4] by making his spiritual power on every occasion subservient to his temporal interests, and he might have adopted as his emblem that of the ancient Jupiter, which exhibits the lightning in the grasp of a ferocious eagle. His vices as an individual, although [5] not so injurious to the world, are represented as more disgusting; and the records of his court afford repeated instances of a depravity of morals inexcusable in any station, but abominable in one of his high rank and sacred office.

Exercise LXV.

When the conqueror, having passed within the lines, saw the most beautiful city of his age stretched beneath his feet, the sense alike of his own magnificent success and of that city's glorious past overcame him, and he burst, it is said, into tears of mingled joy and emotion. A crowd of associations rose before him : the navy of Athens engulfed beneath those waters ; the annihilation of her two splendid armies, with two illustrious commanders; the prolonged and fierce struggle

---

[1] See 132, 138, 139.   [2] 32.   [3] 108.   [4] 35.   [5] 148.

with Carthage; the long roll of tyrants and sovereigns; in their foreground, the prince whose memory was still green, the fame of his virtues and his prosperity second only to the splendour of his services to Rome. And as in the midst of these memories came the thought that in one short hour all he saw would be wrapped in flames and reduced to ashes, he paused before he launched his legions to the assault, and despatched some of the townsmen, whose presence in the Roman quarters has been already noticed, to endeavour by a friendly appeal to win the enemy to a capitulation. But the gates and walls were manned mainly by deserters, who, hopeless of any terms that would secure them an amnesty, forbade all approach or parley; and the General after the failure of, this attempt withdrew his troops.

Exercise LXVI.

When the envoys reached the castle, the unanimity of the populace, the seizure[1] of the forts, and the loss[1] by treason of the strongest portion of the city, had made no small impression upon the Duke. But the Duchess, the daughter of a reigning prince, preserving[2] still all the high spirit of a princess and the pride of a woman, met the message which summoned him to meet the deputation by quoting to him a favourite saying of the great Duke : "A king may drop the reins of power when dragged by the heels, not while still in the saddle." It was easy, she bade him remember,[3] to resign a great position at any moment; to build it up and achieve it was a work of toil and time. Let him[4] obtain from the envoys some hours for deliberation. Let him take advantage of the delay to bring his Condottieri from Pisa; he had but to promise them the late Duke's treasures, and he was master of the situation. These suggestions the Duke neither absolutely rejected nor immediately accepted. The safer course seemed to lie in a temporising policy. He desired the envoys

---

[1] 43.   [2] 98.   [3] 93, 130 end, 158.   [4] 128.

to take back word that he would place himself at the earliest moment at the disposal of the civil authorities and of the people. If he saw [1] that those who had given their country her freedom were ready also to maintain that freedom, if disinterested counsels prevailed, he would not hesitate to restore to the people all that had been confided to his honour and keeping, since he who had conferred the trust had fallen a victim to his own madness.

Exercise LXVII.

While the commissioners were [2] enjoying a prosperous voyage to their native land, the camp of Cortes was the scene of so dangerous a conspiracy that all his hopes, alike of fame and success, were within an ace of being nigh shipwrecked. There were among his soldiers men who, [3] whether from disgust at their novel mode of life, home-sickness, or from some cause or other, had become disaffected towards their General, and were conspiring with one another with a view to seize on one of the ships and return to Cuba, from whence the greater part of them had come. Most fortunately a soldier, who had been reluctantly persuaded to join the cabal, was so disturbed by his conscience that on the very night on which they were to sail he could not refrain from disclosing the whole matter to Cortes

It was impossible for Cortes, after hearing his story, to doubt that if these men once accomplished their design nothing could enable him to prevent the contagion from spreading to a larger number Nor was he blind to the fact that there was absolutely no reason against his exerting all his authority against men who had acted in defiance alike of honour and of discipline. Nor was he a man [4] to be deterred by any danger from carrying out what seemed to him the right course. Fearing, therefore, lest if he let slip the

---

[1] What would *oratio recta* be? and what would this become in *oratio obliqua*? [2] 120. [3] 113.

opportunity he might be too late in parrying so fatal a blow, he ordered the parties indicated to be at once seized, and, without even an hour's interval, tried by court-martial. Their acquittal was impossible, and two who seemed the ringleaders were condemned and instantly executed. This was the first conspiracy which we read of among the soldiers of Cortes.

This Exercise illustrates the use of *quin, quominus.*

EXERCISE LXVIII.

Whilst these diplomatic negotiations were being carried on between France and Spain,[1] the other European governments (monarchs, potentates) were animated by various feelings. As each in turn received successive intelligence of the imminent crossing of the Alps and invasion of Italy by Charles, of the great army that he had already formed, and of the additional forces of both arms that he was raising throughout his kingdom, they were none of them unwilling that so formidable a prince should squander his resources in a remote and chimerical struggle. The most experienced statesmen were the most convinced to believe that, blinded by a spirit of ostentation and self-confidence, he was hurrying to his ruin.

But, provided that he had no intention[2] of crossing their own frontiers, they had no objection to[3] his rousing the easily-excited suspicions of Ferdinand, or that the two kings should prove another's prowess in a strife which, whatever the issue, would probably undermine the excessive and predominating position of both. —There was therefore a general inclination to wait till the game of war should be in some degree decided, and to charge their ambassadors to make neither promises nor threats till they saw what course would be pursued by the government of Venice, by the Florentine republic, and by the

---

[1] 158.   [2] 67.
[3] *Had no objection to:* " did not take it ill that " (*quod*).

Pope, whether they would form a league to protect the threatened existence of the Neapolitan crown[1] or in self-isolation consult merely their own interest.   Even Ferdinand, so long as he thought it possible that Charles, after descending from the Alps, while entangled among the marshes and streams of Lombardy, might be surprised by the Italian forces and sustain a check disastrous to his prestige and power, remained inactive; but finding that his rival, after an almost bloodless campaign, had traversed the Papal States almost without resistance, and, in defiance of the Pope's appeals to Europe, had entered Rome without[2] breaking a spear or pitching a tent, he recognised the importance of no longer waiting till his rival had seized on Naples and made himself master of Italy.

See Introd. XI. 115-122 (Temporal Clauses).

EXERCISE LXIX.

With this stern reply the allies were dismissed,[3] and the envoys summoned to an audience.   At the sight of their age and rank the remark was general that the propositions[4] for peace were at last sincere.   Conspicuous among them was an aged man, whose invariable advocacy of peace and steady opposition to the war party gave additional weight to his efforts to shift the responsibility of the rupture from the nation[5] to an ambitious clique, and to his warnings[6] to the conquerors to practise moderation and self-control in the hour of triumph.   [7] "Had his countrymen listened to himself and his friends, had they turned their opportunities to account, they might have[8] dictated the terms of the peace for which they were now petitioners.   Seldom, alas! did mankind receive the double gift[9] of good fortune and sound judgment.   The secret of the unbroken success of Rome lay in the wisdom and thoughtfulness which had marked her triumphs.   It would

---

[1] 31.   [2] 122.   [3] 99.   [4] 41.   [5] 35, 182.   [6] 40.
[7] See Introd. XII. (*Oratio Obliqua*).   [8] 74.   [9] 32.

have been strange had it been otherwise. It was the novice
in success who was intoxicated by the unwonted taste of
prosperity. To Rome the joys of victory were familiar, and
wellnigh exhausted. She owed the extension of her empire
less to her victories than to her mercy towards the vanquished." The language of his colleagues was still more
pathetic. They spoke of the high estate and present humiliation of their country [1]; but late mistress of the world, now
with nothing left her but her city's walls! Even that city
and their homes they could only retain on the condition that [2]
the conquerors would refrain from wreaking their wrath on
these their last possessions.

A movement of compassion was manifest in the audience.

Exercise LXX.

The public excitement reached such a height that the
magistrates were obliged to summon a meeting of the town
council. Many leading members, who had for some time [3]
absented themselves from its discussions, were openly threatened that, unless they attended the meetings, the people
would [4] surround their houses and drag them all out by force;
and the fear of this secured the magistrates a full attendance.
The general topic of discussion was the question of sending envoys to the commander-in-chief of the enemy. But the original
instigator of the revolt, on being asked his opinion, reminded
them that those who spoke of envoys, and peace, and surrender,
must have forgotten what they meant [5] to have done had they
got [6] the king in their power, and what must be the fate that
awaited them now. "What!" he said, "think you that it will
be a case of a surrender such as once we made to the king—a
surrender of ourselves and of our all to [7] secure his help
against the pressure of an enemy? Has it already slipped
your memory at what a crisis of his fortunes our revolt took

---

[1] 28.   [2] 105.   [3] 58.   [4] 124.
[5] 67.   [6] 84, 4.   [7] 101.

place? Have you already forgotten how in that revolt we put to death with cruel ignominy the garrison that we might have [1] let go? Have you forgotten our many hostile sallies [2] against the besieging forces, our attacks [2] upon their camp, our invitation [2] to a foreign ally to crush them—or, last offence of all, our despatching that ally to attack the capital? Look now at the other side of the picture,[3] and recall the determined hostility [4] of their proceedings against us, and learn from *that* what to expect. When a foreign enemy was at the gates, and the country ablaze with war, the king left everything else alone, and sent both field-marshals and two full *corps d'armée* to attack our city. This is now the second year of the close blockade that has worn us out by famine. They, as well as we, have endured the utmost peril and severest hardships, slaughtered many a time around their ramparts and trenches, and at last wellnigh spoiled of their camp. But all this I pass by."

Oratio obliqua and *oratio recta* to be employed, as in the English.

Exercise LXXI.

1. Ferdinand and Isabella were now on the point of [5] receiving the submission of Granada, when news was brought them that Columbus, despairing [6] of ever prevailing [7] upon either these monarchs or any of the grandees of Spain to assist him in his great enterprise, had resolved to have recourse to the King of France, that ruler having invited Columbus to come to him with all possible speed, with a promise that [7] every proposal should receive full attention at the French court. The limit of his toils and anxieties seemed now close at hand; and no Spaniard could have [1] complained that one so tenacious of his views as Columbus, wearied with the procrastination of several years, was ready [8] at last to turn elsewhere and put faith in the French King's invitation.

[1] 73.	[2] 41, 42, i.	[3] 30.	[4] 53.
[5] 67.	[6] 98, 116.	[7] 74.	[8] 73.

2. But, thanks to a happy chance or a kind Providence, it happened that on the eve of his departure for France, he was paying a visit to his old and tried friend, Juan Perez, to whom in friendly confidence he communicated the purport [1] of the King's letter, adding that had [2] he not so often failed in Spain, he never would have [2] craved for the aid of any other power. Perez was deeply touched, both by indignation at the proceeding and by the approaching loss [1] of such a personage to himself and to his country. But his sagacity was equal to the occasion; and, having [3] great influence with the queen, he persuaded Columbus not to [4] leave La Rabida till [5] he had made his way in person to the royal camp, with the intention [6] of urging Isabella as strongly as he could not to [4] lose unadvisedly such an opportunity as might never again present itself. Any one may easily imagine that, had not Columbus yielded to his earnest entreaty, the whole story which I am going to relate would have [7] had a different issue.

---

[1] 41   [2] Cp. 133, 143.   [5] 98, 116   102   [7] 122.
            [6] 67.   [3] 74.

PART III.

Oratorical.

EXERCISE LXXII.

1. And remember, gentlemen, that the case before you is not one of ordinary homicide, but of the murder of a parent. No theory has been started by the other side as to the motives which could have led my client to so detestable a crime. In other proceedings, even in the case of those minor delinquencies which are, I fear, on the increase, and are becoming of almost daily occurrence, the first and main question is the motive for the criminal act. Into this point the counsel for the prosecution on the present occasion does not feel called upon to enter. Yet surely in the case of so revolting a charge, even supposing that[1] a number of motives seemed to unite their forces, and a string of circumstantial evidence pointed in the same direction, we should not give a hasty assent, or leave the decision to inadequate inferences, or listen to any doubtful witness

2. Nor, again, ought the verdict to be ruled by the character of the accused. We should[2] demand proof, not merely of a series of past offences, nor even of a thoroughly abandoned life, but of unexampled recklessness, a recklessness amounting to insanity and lunacy. And even in the presence of such evidence, we should insist on clear indications of guilt,—

---

[1] 144, 145 ; cp. 138.   [2] 103, *Obs.*

evidence as to the place, the date, the means, the agents.[1]
Such evidence must be abundant and unmistakable, or so
hideous and revolting a story can never be accepted. And I
congratulate my client, in the absence of such evidence, that
the case is tried by so intelligent a jury, who are well aware
that even the smallest crime is not committed without a
motive.

EXERCISE LXXIII.

Bitter personalities [2] and fierce invectives are intolerable in
private intercourse; they are somewhat discreditable, I venture to think, within the walls of this House; but they can
and must be endured by all who wish to take part in political
life.[3] I therefore, sir,[4] with your permission, will pass by all
the personal part of the right honourable gentleman's speech,
and address myself to what he did not wholly omit, the real
question at issue. We cannot afford to deal with our allies
on the one principle that we are never to give a shilling more
than we receive. Such a theory is simply fatal to any alliance
between independent nations.[5] There are innumerable
political considerations, real, solid, and substantial, which you
cannot formulate in figures, or balance their loss and gain in
a ledger. There is a whole world of ideas closed alike to the
huckster in politics and to the self-seeker in private life.

In the latter part of this Exercise bear in mind what has been said
above (Introd. II. 27 *seq.*) on metaphors and metaphorical expressions ; and cp. Exx. IV, V.

EXERCISE LXXIV.

But at the very moment when my unfortunate client was
in the state of dejection natural to so crushing a disaster, and,
as though the sun of his life's happiness [6] had sunk for ever,
was in despair as to his future course, it seemed on a sudden

---

[1] 41. [2] 42. [3] 36, A. [4] 171. [5] 35, 182. [6] 31, 164.

as though a gleam of light had crossed the dreary horizon [1] Within the last two months a witness, whose presence at the former trials would have been invaluable, and whose sudden death in the most distant quarter of the Continent had been reported, has returned home safe and sound, as though he had obeyed a summons from the grave. In accordance with the affection which he has always borne my client, he is eager to do all that may aid his friend in his hour [1] of affliction, and he hopes soon to give such evidence in court as will put a final close to the unmerited obloquy of years ; and, for fear that you should think that I am speaking with confidence and boldness rather than with truth, and am unduly relying on the evidence of a single witness, I pledge my word in the most solemn manner—may no Englishman ever place the least reliance on my word if I speak other than the truth,[2]—that I shall very soon succeed in opening your eyes to the fact that I have not spoken otherwise than I have ascertained to be simple truth, and that you must do anything rather than allow an innocent man to be crushed under so undeserved a weight of odium.

This Exercise illustrates the use of expressions of *Comparison :* see Arnold, rev. ed , 488-497.

Exercise LXXV.

1. But I am told that my language for some time past has been [3] irreconcilable with the policy which I urged some five or six short months ago , as though, considering the entire change of times and circumstances, such divergence were incompatible with absolute consistency. And again, had I, it is said, instead of [4] standing aloof from public affairs,[5] as sullen, let us suppose, if not as valiant as Achilles,—had I, I say, given

---

[1] 31, 164.
[2] *May no Englishman,* etc. : *i e.* "may they only place strict confidence in me on condition of . . . ;" see 105.
       [3] 58.   [4] 107, 117.   [5] 36, A ; 171.

the present Ministry the cordial support of my advice, my speeches, my vote, I should not have taken my seat here, to use the words of the last speaker, as a broken-hearted and despairing man ; I should have retained [1] the influence in this House which I once enjoyed, but which now has sunk to zero, or lower still.   In short, if once you give [2] credit to these and similar invectives of the honourable [3] gentleman, the House will be ready to believe that the advocate has thrown up his brief in a manner perfectly shocking, that the general has gone over bag and baggage to the enemies' camp.

2. If, sir, these charges contained even an element of truth, I should indeed be put to the blush for an amount of inconsistency and want of principle, not to say of treachery, such as has no precedent, at all events within the present or last generation, in the records of Parliament. It would have been [4] far better, if I was doomed [5] to end the cares and toils and efforts of so many years with so ignominious a collapse, to have studied my own reputation and the interest of my country by bidding long since an eternal adieu to political [6] life. For it seems to me, sir, that the nation [7] is deeply interested in the character of its public men.

3. He was no dreamer, but one of the keenest thinkers who ever lived, who remarked that the morality of its statesmen is a fair key to the morality of a nation ; that if these are corrupt and unprincipled, the nation's hour has sounded. And therefore, if the House will bear with me, I will not treat with indifference even my own insignificant reputation, which is, if we may trust so eminent an authority, in some way a matter of public interest.   And if I know anything of myself and my past career, I shall not only disappoint the hopes of malignity and envy by easily disposing of the charge of inconsistency ; but I shall convince you that while others have trimmed their sails to the breeze,[8] or run before the gale, I

---

[1] 82, 135.   [2] 136.   [3] 179.   [4] 140.
[5] 67.   [6] 36, A ; 171.   [7] 35, 182.   [8] Cp. 30, 31.

have retained to this moment all my early political predilec-
tions, and that through every tempest of Parliamentary strife
I have adhered to the line which I marked out for myself
when first I embarked in the service [1] of the nation.

Consult Introd. XIII. (Conditional Sentences).

EXERCISE LXXVI.

But if your position as the friend of the accused bars [2] your
path, if you hold that the claim which I am now making
forms no part of your province, I will step forward as your
deputy and discharge your office taking upon me a task which
I never recognised as my own. Only let us hear no more
murmurs from right honourable gentlemen and noble lords [3]
at the readiness of this nation, now and in all ages of its history, to intrust high office [4] to untitled energy. [5] It is no
matter of complaint that the claims of merit should be para-
mount in a land which owes to merit its imperial position.
We do not grudge the peer his ancestral portrait-gallery; [6]
we are content that he should shine in the borrowed lustre of
departed greatness and renown : the character, the services
of the illustrious dead give them a title to the affections not
of a single household, but of an entire nation. [1] And, sir, if
he who now addresses you finds some work to do in life, it is
because he belongs to a land which men like these have raised
to fame, to power, to greatness; not least of all because he
has practised, to the utmost limits of his strength, qualities in
which they stood pre-eminent,—fair-dealing, industry, self-
control, the protection of the distressed, the detestation of
the bad,—an affinity of habits scarcely, I imagine, less close
than that of which noble lords can boast, community of
blood and identity of name.

---

[1] 36, A ; 171.   [2] 137.   [3] 36, A.   [4] 34, 35.
[5] *Untitled energy* think of what the phrase means, and remember
what has been said (Introd. p. 7) of the comparative characteristics of
Latin and English.
[6] Think of the Roman equivalent for this idea.

EXERCISE LXXVII.

But, to say nothing of your youthful proceedings [1] in this House, eight years have now passed during which you have made it your one object to [2] make every respectable member of the Conservative party [3] unpopular, odious, and suspected ; the effect of your speeches here, of your harangues elsewhere, has been to raise up such a cloud of confirmed misapprehension and unmerited obloquy, that a sound judgment is now rendered almost impossible to the mass of Englishmen, [4] and those who have the best interests of the nation [5] at heart have neither power nor courage left. To think, [6] sir, of such a man, one who has shown himself in such colours alike to us and to this nation, being now seated at the helm, and inspiring the revolutionary and destructive party [3] with fresh confidence, courage, and strength !

EXERCISE LXXVIII.

Did any one ever plan such crimes as the defendant has not only planned but undertaken and completed ? Has he ever spared his friends, or been grateful to the numbers who have loaded him with favours ? [7] Does any one remember any instance of his either loving good or hating bad men ? Do not all of us know that, as in his boyhood he imitated the worst crimes of manhood, so in his old age he has surpassed the cruelty and savage temper of the most terrible (savage) wild beasts ? Where and when can we find a parallel for such a monster ? What human being has he ever aided in his hour [8] of darkness ? What evil deed has he ever shrunk from ? Is it his brother who will

---

[1] **41.**   [2] **104.**
[3] Avoid *factio*, and render the meaning of *Conservative.*
[4] **182.**   [5] **35, 182.**   [6] **87, 151,** note.   [7] See **34.**
[8] **164.**

intercede for him against your anger? Do I say anger? it
is not your anger, but your justice, your honour, your sense
of religion, that he fears and shrinks from.

This Exercise illustrates the expression of Direct Interrogative ; see
also Introd. XV. (on Rhetorical Questions).

EXERCISE LXXIX.

(*Columbus before Ferdinand and Isabella.*)

For many years I have been [1] endeavouring, both before
you and elsewhere, to secure the goodwill of the powerful, and
enthusiasm of Spaniards, towards my intended undertaking.
Bear with me therefore of your grace, as I shall once more bring
forward facts which I have repeatedly urged before Almost
in my boyhood I felt a strange persuasion of the existence [2] of
lands beyond the ocean, which either I, or some one else more
fortunate, was destined [3] to visit; and destined, not only to find
there regions abounding in unheard-of wealth, but to bring to
thousands of mankind our own arts and civilisation. When
I name these I name also our religion, which the monarch
and the queen whom I address hold, I know well, dearer than
either. There was a time when, day by day, turning [4] to the
sinking sun, I dreamed [5] that I discerned the shores of an un-
discovered India gilded by his setting beams ; so, too, when
each dawn arose, [6] I would weep that another day was going to
be wasted. I do not care [7] to recall at this time the evidences
on which I placed and place my full belief in the reality of
those visions. It is one thing to convince one's-self by what
seems demonstration ; it is another to carry demonstration to
other minds. And I first appealed to you when, immersed in
the gravest crisis of the war with the Moors, you were unwilling and unable to turn your attention to other cares.
You pleaded the absorption of your thoughts, the exhaustion
of your resources in a long and perilous war ; your nobles

---

[1] 58.　　[2] 42.　　[3] 67.　　[4] 98.　　[5] 115.　　[6] 72.　　[7] 89.

whose enthusiasm I might (I thought) arouse were eager in proportion to their wealth to plead against my incentives their poverty and debt; in proportion to their zeal for religion to insist on the heterodoxy of my views and proposals.

In this Exercise *quum* is as a rule to be used with the indicative mood, except where the subjunctive is required by Latin usage (Introd. XI. 115).

Exercise LXXX.

For myself, sir, were I to[1] see once more, what the experience of our own generation and the voice of history[2] alike declare to be no idle dream, the supreme government of this empire[3] lodged in the hands of the vilest and most profligate of the nation, I might venture to undertake that neither interest, a motive which has never weighed with me, nor even that regard to personal security which does sometimes touch even the stoutest heart, would tempt me to join their ranks. But seeing as I did[4] the Cabinet presided over by one like our present Prime Minister,[5] one who[6] had reached that post of power and honour by unequalled public services and heroic achievements, one whose advancement I had myself supported from my youth, one, too, who had lent me in this very House the support alike of his vote and of his influence, I never dreamed that I need fear the charge of inconsistency if, in this point or in that, I somewhat modified my own views, and tendered the poor homage of my own support to one so eminent in himself, and with such transcendent claims, alike on my own and on the nation's[7] gratitude.

---

[1] 133.   [2] 32, 36, B; 41.   [3] 36, A.   [4] 98, 115-117.
[5] *Cabinet, Prime Minister:* are there any Latin equivalents?
[6] 113.   [7] 35, 182.

Exercise LXXXI.

He who died yesterday was doubtless a great man: stars
of such magnitude[1] do not often appear more than once in
a generation.   In the present generation he had no superior
in literary activity, in knowledge, in judgment, in ability;
perhaps no equal in character, certainly none in eloquence.
Indeed, his whole career[2] seemed, alike in success and in
reputation, to have almost reached perfection   But do not
hastily place him on a higher pedestal[1] than those whom the
last generation[3] of our countrymen looked on as its heroes.[4]
After all, his reputation will rest mainly on his words, theirs
is founded on deeds.   Which of these titles to fame is the
better I leave to the decision[5] of our descendants ; for myself[6]
I decline to pronounce.

Exercise LXXXII

I am told that a change[7] of opinion is dishonourable, to
listen to entreaties a vice, to feel compassion nothing less than
a crime.   Far other the teaching of those great masters under
whom I studied the laws of morality.[8]   They taught me that
the wise man is not always deaf to the voice of friendship ;
that mercy is the accompaniment of goodness ; that as offences
differ in kind, so their penalties vary in severity ; that a strong
character is not necessarily unforgiving ; that even a philosopher, if I may venture to say so, is satisfied sometimes with
an opinion where knowledge is denied him ; nay, is sometimes
moved to anger, is open to entreaties, capable at times of
modifying, if truth demands it, his statements, of abandoning
occasionally his views ; in short, that all excellence lies in a
balance between extremes.

---

[1] 30.   [2] 33.   [3] 31.   [4] 36, B.
[5] 66.   [6] 180.   [7] 42.   [8] 33.

Exercise LXXXIII.

I know the limits, the very narrow limits, of my own powers. Yet for all that, so far as I can trace the far-off horizon[1] of the past, and recall the faintest recollections of dawning life, I may claim to have earnestly and passionately devoted myself to the utmost of my ability to the systematic pursuit of the highest studies,[2] and to speak with all frankness, to have turned aside from no single subject which tends to elevate and purify mankind. And if my boyhood fell in with the halcyon days[3] of a long peace, and was spared the storms[1] and convulsions of these later days, yet all who care for literature or philosophy[4], nay, the mere pretenders to either, will allow, what even envy and malice[5] will scarce deny, that all my leisure and all my enthusiasm have been devoted to ennobling studies.

Exercise LXXXIV.

I never failed him in any time of need, or let slip any opportunity of promoting his interest and comfort; I never envied him his power and wealth; I forgave him, in consideration of his youth and royal station, his intolerable pride and vulgar insolence, which I ought to have[6] rebuked, and might have chastised; I rarely gainsaid his wishes, scarcely once crossed his pleasures; I unduly smiled upon his vices; I refused to desert him when his star was on the wane[7], and to join the standard of one who was basking in the sunshine[8] of fortune. Yet, somehow, I could not persuade him to[9] regain his senses even for an interval, or practise self-command even for a single instant; and the only reward which I reaped for long subservience was the displeasure of my countrymen and the suspicion of my prince. Such, indeed, was the spell

---

[1] 31.   [2] 34, 166.   [3] 30-32.   [4] 36, B.   [5] 40.
[6] 73.   [7] 29-31.   [8] 164.   [9] 102, 103.

which the grossest of pleasures cast upon him, that if life and honour and every other consideration in the world were placed in the opposite scale, they either seemed trifles light as air, or were not recognised at all.

EXERCISE LXXXV.

1. I, who in my youth was a keen politician,[1] have seen the times change, and men change with the times. I am, I feel, changed myself; for[2] in my old age I rarely and unwillingly enter the sphere of politics. Nevertheless I hope that neither my abilities, nor my opinion. nor my age, are entirely worthless in the eyes of the many who daily ask my advice, for[2] with them, thanks to long familiar intercourse, in spite of my extreme old age, I have, I know, some influence. [3]

2. Though[2] in your private capacity you reluctantly obeyed those whom the constitution[4] had placed over you, though, when in office, joining with the most abandoned of the nation,[5] you made war upon your native land, yet you now pretend to be of sound mind, and to disavow every one of your traitorous and monstrous[6] acts. You are ready[7], I am to believe, to be reconciled to me, whom you have long hated, to please the many friends of mine whom you have repeatedly outraged, to serve your country. which you have always done your best to injure.

3. Of the handful of men who, on that dark day's morning twilight, saw your ill-starred relative hurried to a degrading execution, the only one who could restrain his tears was his only and much-loved son. The other bystanders wept, the soldiers who guarded the victim were affected, he alone, such was his strength of nerve, unmoved by the general grief, silently swore to[8] inflict one day a righteous punishment on those unjust judges and traitorous rulers

---

[1] 36, A ; 171.   [2] *For I*, 111.   [3] 41.   [4] 36, A.   [5] 35
[6] 53   [7] *Are ready*. think of the meaning.   [8] 74

4. Those familiar [1] with your want of principle and consistency will scarcely, I imagine, be surprised at your having gone over, as I hear you have done, bag and baggage, to the other side. It is an event which I shall do my best, I hope, to bear with equanimity. Your new friends will, I presume, rejoice that so distinguished and so useful a character is to join their ranks.[2]

This Exercise illustrates the ordinary use of Relative Pronouns ; see Introd. IX. **109-113.**

Exercise LXXXVI.

1. I warn you, my Lords, and I would that I could impress upon you in more persuasive accents [3] my clear conviction,[4] that the present occasion is one mercifully vouchsafed to you by a kind Providence for ridding this House [5] of very foul stains, and freeing us from very ugly imputations. We have for some time, I blush to say, stunk in the nostrils [5] of this nation.[6] It is not the craving [7] for novelty that leads men to applaud and follow and aid with their suffrages the incendiary and the revolutionist. It is the sense that we have compromised the dignity of this great empire in allowing [8] a magnificent dependency to be pillaged and oppressed. And to-day the whole nation is in an attitude of strained attention. Men are watching the conduct [4] of each one among us, our care for conscience, our regard for law.

2. Yes! it is a trial in which he who stands at the bar awaits your verdict; but you also, my Lords, stand at the bar [9] of public opinion. All are agreed that never in the history of England,[10] never certainly since these functions were conferred upon you, did so splendid, so imposing a judicial

---

[1] **98, 2.**   [2] **29-31.**   [3] **53.**   [4] **42.**
[5] Think of the meaning of this phrase.   [6] **35, 182.**
[7] *It is not the craving* . . *that* . use a causal clause, **114.**
[8] **120.**   [9] Think of the meaning, and cp. **29-31.**   [10] **36, 158.**

assembly fill the seat of justice. And if you fail [1] to-day, the conviction will be universal that the power you wield must be intrusted to other hands. Remember, I implore you, who you are, and how high you stand, all that your country, [2] all that your ancestors [3] have a right to ask of you And I pray Heaven that you may do so, before it is too late.

Exercise LXXXVII.

If any one, as is easily possible, asks the reason [1] of my summoning you to my presence, I believe that no one, when he has once heard [5] something of what I am going to say on a really difficult question will doubt any longer whether I have acted wisely or the reverse. You are all aware that there is a person in the island of Cuba who, for some reason or another, will leave nothing undone in order to frustrate our present enterprise. Any one, therefore, of you can understand, nor can a soul gainsay it, that we must take care to prevent any enemy, whether he be mine or yours, from interfering, against our will, with our projects, and our achievements, whether he choose to have recourse to fraud or force. The greater the peril in which a man stands, the greater the promptitude and courage which he should use. I have resolved, and I incline to think [6] that no one here will blame me, to send to the Emperor and the government at home such a quantity of gold and other valuable objects that no one can say that we have reached some mere desolate region, where Nature offers nothing that can be of use to mankind, or that we are tempting brave men to encounter either the rage of the elements or the uncertainty of fortune

This Exercise illustrates the use of Indefinite Pronouns (*aliquis, quis, quisquam, ullus, quidam, quivis*).

---

[1] 136   [2] 28.   [3] 31, 182.   [4] 42.   [5] 65.   [6] 166

Exercise LXXXVIII.

1. In reliance on your honour and good sense I will bear this burden as long as I can,[1] and will do my utmost to perform my duty to my client, who stands to-day in an almost unprecedented extremity. Do you who are to try the case hear me with attention and indulgence. When I have said[2] all that I am about to say, then let a reply come from the other side; till[3] I have done this, let my opponent keep silence; then it will be for you to decide which of us has the stronger case, whether riches, interest, power, audacity, or the clearest evidence of an innocent life are of most weight with you.

2. Do you intend,[4] he says, to offer yourselves as marks to the weapons of your enemies, without defence or retaliation? I would fain know the meaning of those arms which you carry, or why we came here to wage an offensive war? It would have been[5] better to have stayed at home, and, as we might have done, asked for peace. Do you fancy that some god is going to succour you, or hurry you hence home? Let those of you who mean to see their homes, their parents, their wives, their children, follow in the direction in which they see me to go before them. He who strikes[2] down a foe will do well; he who shrinks from the din and danger of battle will be in equal danger. The bravest and the most cowardly must alike die when his hour strikes,[6] as regards life or death. Behave as you may; what is to be will be. It matters not whether you give way or attack, but he wins the day who proves[2] himself the more worthy of victory.

Chiefly illustrating the use of Future Tenses (Introd. V.).

Exercise LXXXIX.

My client might have[7] denied with impunity that he had either ever seen or knew by name, or by sight, the man whom

[1] 64.   65.   [3] 121, 122.   [4] 67.   [5] 140.   [6] 30.   [7] 73.

you assert him to have so seriously assaulted. For who could have refuted[1] him, or on what evidence could you to-day prove that he spoke what was untrue ? If I am[2] mistaken, let us hear your eye-witnesses, whom you ought to have[3] called yesterday; I could have[2] wished you had done this, for who would have dared to come into this court and in the presence of these judges have incurred such guilt as must needs cling to those who do their utmost to put out of the way an innocent man ? But it would be tedious to follow minutely all the charges which you have invented and brought against the defendant. The prosecutor who, without intending it[4], puts on his trial an innocent person, may be pardoned, but what punishment are we to[3] name for him who knowingly tries to use the tribunals of his country to put out of the way an innocent and blameless youth, as whose advocate I have appeared to-day ?

EXERCISE XC

My own sentiments are, I confess, not the same as yours; you put confidence in men who say that no man of ordinary good sense will take part in the present political[6] strife ; that they will do no more than the necessity of the hour demands : but will wait for better times, endure present trials in silence, and seek the friendship of the few good patriots who survive.

For myself, I hope that my influence with you will be as great as it has always been ; I know that our present evils are more numerous than those of the last generation[7], of a kind such as neither you nor I have ever experienced ; but those friends of yours are, I suspect, entirely wrong who say that these political storms are quite unprecedented, and that he can be a good patriot who makes no more effort, no more resist-ance, than he is compelled to do.

---

[1] 82, 134.　　　[2] 138, 139.　　　[3] 73.　　　[4] 53.　　　[5] 80.
　　　　　　　　　[6] 36, A ; 169.　　　[7] 31

Exercise XCI.

The matter has reached such a point that it can no
longer be concealed or glossed over. Let each man speak
out freely what seems good to him ; and do not let us to-day
think in concert of our common safety, and to-morrow place
ourselves each in turn in the General's hands. Is there[1] a
single one among us who wishes to renew the siege ? But
perhaps some one will[2] say that he disapproves both courses,
and advises us to steer a middle course, so as neither to
abandon our General or undertake a march (which will be)
exactly like a flight, for the basest course is often the most
dangerous. For myself I have no wish to think otherwise
than the majority of you, and, if this is your general opinion,
let us seize the first opportunity. As soon as it is light let
us all go to the General, each with his arms and ready for the
march ; only let us make him well aware that we are resolved
to take one of two courses, to march at once either with or
without him. It is idle to remind him how destitute we are
of provisions, fortifications, allies, weapons, I had almost said
of everything needful for men in such an emergency. The
most skilled in war among us know best how forlorn and
destitute we are. It is agreed, I think, among us, that it
would be better for us all together to put fortune to the
proof by an instant march than to perish singly in a succession of bloody combats.

This Exercise illustrates the use of *quisque, uterque, singuli*, etc.

Exercise XCII.

The Queen and Parliament of Great Britain have sent me
to thank you for services to our armies and civilians greater
than those of any other Indian prince ; at the same time to
congratulate you, first, on having[3] for the last eleven years

---

[1] 150.　　　　　　[2] 65, cp. 80.　　　　　　[3] 108.

past so governed your people as to have won both their affection and the respect of your neighbours ; secondly, on having crushed an enemy of such extreme animosity to both of us, that his existence was incompatible with either our safety or your own. Personally, I feel it difficult to express the satisfaction with which I heard of your having passed safely through this late storm, and that one who was bent upon your ruin had effected his own. I trust that his fall will prove a lesson to his neighbours to maintain and defend their own possession, rather than go out of their way to attack those of others, and to remember the truth that true glory is to be sought in right actions, that a good prince attends to the interest of his subjects, and will not make an unprovoked attempt to rob others of the fame and possessions which they have honourably won.

This Exercise illustrates the use of Supines , cp. Arnold, rev ed , 401-404

Exercise XCIII

Whether this course was legal or not, I leave to[1] others to decide. For myself, I hold that every step that has been taken was, however unconstitutional[2] on a superficial view, as constitutional in reality as it was valuable as a precedent for the future. It was not, as was the case a generation back[3], a question of the private whispers[4] behind closed doors of a dozen disaffected nobodies ; disaffection had almost risen to the dignity of insurrection : and the evil was too great and too serious to be remedied by the hands of county justices or legal discussions. The nettle had to be firmly grasped[5], and traitors treated with such a sternness as to give immediate, if tardy, relief to the nation[6], and to secure that in time to come the party of order should have no dread of similar enterprises.

---

[1] 66. [2] 36, A. [3] 31. [4] 41. [5] 29-31. [6] 35, 182.

Exercise XCIV.

1. Whether you wish for peace or war is a question which you must now decide, and that at the eleventh hour.[1] But whether you wish for one or the other, you have no alternative left but either an honourable peace or a necessary war. Peace is the greatest of all blessings; but on the one condition[2] that it is just, honourable, compatible with the national existence and honour. War is a miserable and dreadful scourge; but one that we must face if it is a defensive war, if we have no object[3] but to secure freedom, to avoid slavery, to hand down safe, unimpaired, and untarnished, to our children, nay, to our children's children, the laws, the privileges, the constitution, which we received from our forefathers.

2. For all this[4] you are still, I am told, uncertain as to your course[5], and are asking one another, it may be, to-day the reason of[5] my wishing you to endure every extremity of war or famine rather than abandon your present rebellion, as your enemies style this most righteous of wars, and return to your former so-called[6] peace and tranquillity. For myself, I will speak my real sentiments. I do not pretend to be ignorant of the amount, the number, and the kind[5] of dangers which he must face who counts all things but dust[1] in comparison with the freedom and well-being of the community. But whether we are to prevail, or to try the chances of war in vain, I for one[7], who am quite aware of the hazards of our position, entertain no doubt whatever as to whether the asserting my country's freedom, even at the peril of my life, or the dragging on my days at the mercy of the conqueror,

---

[1] Think of the meaning, and cp. 30.   [2] 105.   [3] 104.
[4] 116.   [5] 42.   [6] *So-called:* an adverb.   [7] 180.

if he will permit me, to an old age of slavery and dishonour,
be the better and more honourable course   It is for you, my
brother Hollanders, to decide[1] whether you prefer death in
battle or to live as slaves.

Consult Introd XIII. 131-143 (Conditional Sentences)

Exercise XCV.

You will ask, gentlemen, the secret of my enthusiasm[2]
for my client   It is this   I owe to him, and to men like
him, the tonic[3] that braces my spirits after the din of these
Courts, the opiate[3] that gives rest to nerves jaded with the
wrangling of the bar.   Do you imagine[4] that I could possibly
plead day after day on such a multiplicity of subjects, if I
did not cultivate my powers by study[5], or that without the
relaxation of study they could bear the strain to which they
are daily exposed ?   For myself[6], I frankly own that I am a
fellow-votary of these same pursuits   Let those blush to
make the avowal who have buried themselves for long years
in their books without finding[7] there any one thing which
they can contribute to the common good, aught which will
face the daylight of the outer world.[8]   But for me[6], why
should I blush, living[9] the life that I have lived for years ?
Never have I allowed my own interest or my own repose,
never have I suffered the seductions of pleasure, nor even
the calls of sleep, to prevent me from aiding a single client in
his hour of need.

---

[1] 66   [2] 40, 41
[3] *Tonic, opiate* think of the meaning, and cp. 30.   [4] 150.
[5] 34.   [6] 180.   [7] 105.   [8] 28.   [9] 111.

Exercise XCVI.

You will find, gentlemen of the jury, that the facts of the case correspond with the history which I have laid before you. And as you have thus far given me the indulgent and attentive hearing required by so obscure and perplexing a case, I hope that I shall have no difficulty in giving you a perfect key to the circumstances which I have still to bring[1] before you. I have attempted,[2] and shall continue so far as in me lies to do so, to speak not only according to my brief[3], but in a manner due to the past and present deserts of a client whose case I undertook at the eleventh hour[3] and with diffidence and reluctance.[4] I am aware that I have taken upon me an arduous part. It is always difficult to stem the tide of public opinion, of a general impression, and of long-standing prejudice. In the case of my client it is at once unpleasant and difficult to act as the advocate of a perfectly innocent client in the teeth of the views, if not of men of sense, at all events of the uninstructed mass of society,[5] and of all who take their tone from the uninstructed. So unfavourable, indeed, had been the decisions which on two former occasions had been pronounced, whether fairly or unfairly, on his case, that the feeling against him had reached such a pitch, that, but for the holding of this fresh trial, and but for the late yet entire confidence in his cause with which a reliance on overwhelming evidence inspired myself and others, my client could never have ventured to show his face in any respectable circle of Englishmen.

---

[1] 67.   [2] 104.   [3] Think of the meaning, and cp. 30.
[4] 54.   [5] 34.

Exercise XCVII.

It is not my intention[1] to set before you some theatrical or romantic standard of perfection, such as we see[2] on the stage or read of in romances, but such a measure of goodness as is compatible with human nature, and attainable by any of us poor sons of Adam[3]; for he of whom I am to speak was no perfect or ideal being, but one of those specimens of humanity who meet us in flesh and blood, one of the characters familiar alike to modern life and human history[4], and it is on instances of this class that we must base our induction[5] if we are to lay down any general law[6] that affects our race.

Bear in mind the direct and literal tendency of Latin as compared with English (Introd pp 7, 34).

---

[1] 67.   [2] 113.   [3] Think of the meaning, and cp 30
[4] 36, b.   [5] 30, 33.   [6] 30, 41

PART IV.

Miscellaneous.

EXERCISE XCVIII.

1. A mind like Scipio's, working its way under the peculiar influences of his time and country[1], cannot but move irregularly; it cannot but be full of contradictions. Two hundred years later the mind of the dictator Caesar acquiesced contentedly in Epicureanism[2]; he retained no more of enthusiasm than was inseparable from the intensity of his intellectual power, and the fervour of his courage, even amidst his utter moral degradation. But Scipio could not be like Caesar. His mind rose above the state of things around him; his spirit[3] was solitary and kingly; he was cramped by living among those as his equals whom he felt fitted to guide as from some higher sphere; and he retired at last to Liternum to breathe freely, to enjoy the simplicity of childhood, since he could not fill his natural calling to be a hero-king.[3]

2. So far he stood apart from his countrymen, admired, reverenced, but not loved. But he could not shake off all the influences of his time: the virtue, public and private, which still existed at Rome, the reverence paid by the wisest and best men to the religion of their fathers, were elements too congenial to his nature not to retain their hold on it: they cherished that nobleness of soul in him, and that faith in the invisible and divine, which two centuries of growing unbelief rendered[4] almost impossible in the days of Caesar.

[1] 28.   [2] 36, B.   [3] 41; cp. 36, B.
[4] *Two centuries . . . rendered impossible:* see 32.

Yet how strange must the conflict be when faith is combined with the highest intellectual power, and its appointed object is no better than[1] Paganism?

Exercise XCIX.

But I find that I have unconsciously assumed a tone of dictation quite different to my original purpose in addressing you. Why should I lay down rules for one[2] whom I know to be, above all in matters of the present kind, my equal in knowledge, my superior in experience? Yet, for all this, I suspect that you will feel more enjoyment in any course which you pursue, if you find it stamped with my approval

To express myself shortly, you will find essential a firmness and dignity of demeanour that will be proof, not only against partiality, but against the faintest breath[3] of suspicion. You must show yourself also a kindly and ready listener; for the purest spirit of justice may wear an air of austerity and harshness, unless softened and toned down by a due admixture of the sweets of courtesy.

Remember too, day by day, that your authority is given you not in fee, but in trust[4]; that it emanates from laws which must be your standard; in short, that you are responsible for it before God. For myself[5], I cannot but think that the one rule[6] of those who are in authority should be the happiness[7] of those whom they govern, and I rejoice to feel that this is and has been your very first consideration. For it is surely the duty of all who rule, whether over Englishmen at home, or over natives in our dependencies, to strive for the welfare and interest[8] of those who[9] are subject to their authority.

For the general tone and style see Cicero, *Ad Quintum Fratrem,* i. Ep. 1.

---

[1] *Its appointed object is no better than* i.e. the only condition of religious belief is acceptance of such fictions; see **105.**
[2] **113.** [3] **30.**
[4] Think of the meaning, and beware of any attempt at literal translation. [5] **180.** [6] **104.** [7] **33, 41.** [8] **170.** [9] **113.**

Exercise C.

But let us return to the earth our habitation ; and we shall, see this happy tendency [1] of virtue, by imagining an instance not so vast and remote ; by supposing a kingdom or society of men upon it perfectly virtuous for a succession of many ages : to which, if you please, may be given a situation advantageous for universal monarchy.[2] In such a state there would be no such thing as faction [3] ; but men of the greatest capacity would of course all along have the chief direction [2], of affairs willingly yielded to them : and they would share it among themselves without envy. Each of those would have the part assigned him to which his genius was peculiarly adapted, and others who had not any distinguished genius would be safe, and think themselves very happy by being under the protection and guidance of those who had.

Exercise CI.

Dishonesty and fraud are discountenanced alike by the legal code and by systematic morality. But the moralist and the legislator strike at fraud by different methods. Law deals only with what is tangible and palpable ; the range of Ethics is co-extensive with that of the reason and understanding. Now reason requires us never to act in a designing, hypocritical, or fraudulent spirit.[4] Such acts are, I am quite aware, thanks to our lowered moral tone, too often but faintly reprobated by the public opinion [5] of our age, and entail no penalty at either common law or equity.[5] But not the less are they condemned by the law of conscience.[5] And yet how few will you find who, if they can look forward to escape exposure and punishment, are capable of refraining from wrong-doing There are times, indeed, when [6] duty

---

[1] 42   [2] 36, A   [3] 170.   [4] 53.   [5] 34.
[6] *There are times when.* use an adverb, and express the emphasis by position ; see 7-12.

and expediency are apparently at variance It is not really
so The law of conscience is also the law of utility. And
the "righteous man," he whom we feel instinctively to be the
ideally good and perfect type of our race, will not dare to put
asunder things which God and Nature have joined together
He will not allow himself a thought[1], far less an act, which he
dare not avow. But I will not pursue the subject further.

This Exercise illustrates the treatment of abstract terms in Latin and
English See Introd **33, 40, 163 168**, and cp Exercises IV, V

EXERCISE CII.

Early in life he attached himself to the school of the Stoics,
and became an ardent champion of their system and doctrines
He never could induce himself to[2] become an atheist '; and
the Epicureans, and those who maintained that the world[4]
and all else came into being through a fortuitous combination
of molecules, always moved him either to ridicule or scorn.
A genuine votary of science', he found a charm in pure study
and in thought, and shrunk from all idea of entering upon
politics[6] or active life. He always made it his aim[2] to
insist on a scientific treatment, not only of the study of nature,
but also of modern and ancient history it may be[7] that, in
applying on too rigid a logical system the laws of natural
science[8] to subjects which fall within the domain of moral
and practical life, he fell into the error of those who demand
demonstration and mathematical evidence where such reasoning is quite inadmissible

On the rendering of abstract and philosophical terms, see Introd
33, 36, B ; 163-168

---

[1] **41.**   [2] **104**   ' *Atheist* render the meaning
[4] **28.**   [5] **34, 166.**   [6] **36, A ; 175.**   [7] **166.**   [8] **34.**

Exercise CIII.

For myself, of all the blessings which I owe to Nature or to Fortune, I know of none which I can place beside his friendship. Sympathy in politics[1], guidance in my private affairs, a repose from either that was always delightful, were all comprised in that one precious gift. I never gave him pain, so far as I was aware, in the merest trifle. I never heard from his lips a word that I could have[2] wished recalled. We lived beneath the same roof, we partook in happy partnership of the same fare. War, travel, rural retirement, found us side by side. It were idle to dwell on the passion for study[3] and for knowledge, for the sake of which we shunned the gaze of the public, and to which we devoted every moment of our leisure. Ah! had these memories and associations passed away with him whom they recall, the loss of the most sympathetic, the most affectionate, of friends, would be a burden too heavy for me to endure.

Exercise CIV.

He was a man of singular force of temperament and character, one of those who[4] seem destined[5], in whatever rank they enter life, to carve[6] for themselves a career. An adept in all the requirements alike of statesmanship and of business, he united in himself the able city functionary and the skilful agriculturist. The heights of office[7] are scaled by different paths[6]; legal lore, eloquence, military fame, alike lead their votaries to eminence. We have in him one whose happy genius followed every track with like success; the employment of the hour seemed the one purpose which had called him into being. A gallant soldier in the field and the hero[8] of a hundred encounters, no sooner[9] had

---

[1] 36, A. [2] 82, 134. [3] 34, 166. [4] 113.
[5] 67. [6] 30. [7] 34, 35. [8] 36, B.
[9] *No sooner than,* 118, cp. 68.

he won his way to a higher rank than he was unrivalled as a general. In the pursuits of peace he was at once the most erudite authority on a legal question and the most effective pleader before a jury. Nor can can it be said of him that, powerful as was his oratory in his lifetime, he has left no enduring record of his gifts. His eloquence is still a living power, enshrined in writings of universal range.

EXERCISE CV.

His ridicule on the poetry is misplaced, on the manners is inelegant. Euripides was not less wise than Socrates, nor less tender than Sappho. There is a tenderness which[1] elevates the genius; there is also a tenderness which corrupts the heart. The latter, like every impurity[2], is easy to communicate, the former is difficult to conceive. Strong minds alone possess it; virtuous minds alone value it. I hold it abominable to turn into derision what is excellent To render[3] undesirable what ought to be desired is the most mischievous and diabolical of malice. To exhibit him as contemptible, who ought, according to the conscience of the exhibitor, to be respected and revered, is a crime the more odious, as it can be committed only by[4] violence to his feelings, against[4] the reclamations of Justice, and among[4] the struggles of Virtue

EXERCISE CVI.

1. I always find a strange and mysterious charm[5] in reading the life of this prince; indeed his character seems to me to deserve universal honour at the hands of posterity: not only because at the height of his triumphs and successes he added the jewel[6] of mercy to the laurel[6] of military glory, and, abhorring cruelty himself, held back his followers to the

---

[1] 113.   [2] 33, 40.   [3] 106   [4] 99   [5] 41.
[6] *Jewel, laurel,* etc.   avoid literal translations, and see 30.

utmost of his power from all severe retaliation ; but because, from the moment that he mounted the heights of power and state, he not only refused to water the grave[1] of his murdered brother—murdered with every accompaniment of torture and insult—with the blood of his deadliest enemies, a course which would have involved no difficulty, no infraction of either law or honour[2], and no shock to public opinion[2]; but was content to be subject to the same laws as the meanest of his countrymen, and to measure everything by the standard of the national[3] good, rather than of his own passions or interests.

2. Nor must we forget that, tracing his descent from an obscure and foreign source, and born in lowliness and indigence, denied also in youth every advantage of culture and education, he showed himself as proof against the charges of flattery and wealth as against those of power. He suffered neither the influence and caresses of the great, nor his own popularity with the masses, to seduce him to consent either to a change of laws which he felt to be essential to the constitution of which he regarded himself as the trustee, or to the hounding on of the populace, maddened with the craving to avenge its own wrongs, to massacres and violence. He aimed rather at throwing oil[1] on the waters that were still heaving with the recent storm[4] of civil strife and warfare.

Nor did he so bury himself in the administration of[5] the state as to release himself from the responsibilities of family life. He saw carefully to the initiating of his son, not in frivolous and unprofitable pursuits, but in all honourable employments and princely habits ; and it is to him that we must trace the dawn alike of our present national[3] tranquillity and material prosperity, which surpasses the hopes and even the dreams of the last[4] generation.

This Exercise illustrates the use of the ablative case in Latin ; see Arnold, rev. ed., Exx. XXXIII.-XXXV.   Exercise CIX. may be employed as a preliminary exercise upon the same point.

---

[1] *Jewel, laurel,* étc. : avoid literal translations, and see 30.
[2] 34.   [3] 34, 35.   [4] 31.   [5] 36, A.

Exercise CVII

I must repeat once more, what I have already stated more than once. There is a social bond, to use the word in its widest sense, which exists between man and man, as between fellow-creatures; within this is a bond which unites those who are of the same race, a closer tie binds together members of the same nation [1]. In accordance with this principle our forefathers drew a broad line between international and municipal law. The enactments of the latter do not necessarily extend to the former, but any principle which holds good in the larger sphere should be recognised in the smaller. We however possess no solid and clearly defined ideal of true law and absolute justice; we have but a vague and shadowy outline; well would it be did we make this our model, for it reflects the highest types of conscience [2] and of truth.

Exercise CVIII

I never knew any one who at all came within the circle of successful speakers so absolutely untrained in every branch of a liberal education [2]. He was profoundly ignorant of poetry: he had never read an orator; he had amassed no store of historical [3] knowledge; law in all its branches was a sealed book [4] to him. His language, too, was barely grammatical, quite unfit for any cultivated circle; his gestures and action a constant theme for caricature; his style a strange medley of tropes and figures [5], pathos [6] and absurdities. Yet somehow or other, though when he held his first brief [7] his words were almost drowned in the titters of his audience, by degrees he so won upon the feelings alike of the jury and of the bystanders, that he could scarcely have been more successful had he been [8]

---

[1] 35, 182.   [2] 34.   [3] 36, b; 179.   [4] 30.
[5] Greek τρόποι, σχήματα   [6] 40.
[7] Think of the meaning of this English phrase.   [8] 133.

V. W. L. P.   8

the most finished orator whom the world has seen. He had a wonderful knack of gaining the confidence of the educated, and touching the hearts of the ignorant; and he deserves all honour for this, that in spite of[1] his humble origin he never stooped[2], even on the hustings[3], to the bitter personalities[4] in vogue with those who court the favour of mobs. He was a character indebted wholly to himself for his fame, without ancestry, without patrons[5], rough, untaught, uncouth, yet for all that deservedly respected.

Exercise CIX.

1. I rescued him in his infancy with my own hand from a burning and stranded vessel; I gave the shelter of my roof and all hospitable entertainment, as far as the circumstances permitted, to himself and those of his relations who had survived that terrible night; I supplied him in boyhood with all the necessaries of life, and had him carefully trained in all the branches of a liberal education; discharged, in fact, the whole duty, nominally of host, really of an affectionate guardian, or rather, of a father. To-day he sails before the favouring breeze[6] of fortune, enjoys what some call the height of human happiness, rolls in weath, has abundance of resources, and wastes his energies in costly banquets, and wallows in every form of luxury and pleasure. I, by whose aid he was snatched from the stormy sea and threatening destiny, have suffered shipwreck in my career and my hopes, am denied almost my daily bread, while I live on no resources of my own, but on the compassion of others.

2. If[7] at the commencement of your tenure of office you suffered such heavy afflictions that you would gladly have[8] bartered rank and power for privacy and obscurity, while now your industry, energy, and courage have enabled you

---

[1] 116, 146.   [2] Avoid a literal translation, and see 104.
[3] Think of the meaning of this English phrase.   [4] 40.
[5] 34.   [6] 30   [7] 138, 139.   [8] 67.

to surmount innumerable perils, and feel the ground so safe under you that, free henceforth from apprehension, and able to disregard your enemies, you believe the seals [1] of the highest office to be within your grasp, what possible need can you have of my advice? I would have you follow your own judgment, walk in your own course, only show yourself as proof against success as against failure.

This Exercise illustrates the uses of the Latin Ablative ;
see note to Ex cv.

EXERCISE CX.

1. If we estimate the character of a sovereign by the test of popular affection, we must rank Edward among the best princes of his time. The goodness of his heart was adored by his subjects, who lamented his death with tears [2] of undissembled grief, and bequeathed his memory as an object of veneration to their posterity. The blessings of his reign are the constant theme of our ancient writers not, indeed, that [3] he displayed any of those brilliant qualities which attract admiration while they inflict misery. He could not boast of the victories which he had won, or of the conquests which he had achieved : but he exhibited the interesting spectacle of a king, negligent of his private interests, and totally devoted to the welfare of his people. To him the principle [4] that the king can do no wrong was literally applied by the gratitude of the people, who, if they occasionally [5] complained of the measures of the Government, attributed the blame, not to the monarch himself, of whose benevolence they entertained no doubt, but to the ministers [6], who had abused his confidence, or deceived his credulity.

2. It was, however, a fortunate circumstance for the memory of Edward, that writers were induced to view his

---

[1] *Seals of office* think of the meaning, and see 30, 34, 35.
[2] 43.   [3] 114, 3.   [4] 160.   [5] 72, 139.   [6] 34.

character with more partiality from the hatred with which they looked on his successors and predecessors. They were[1] foreigners, he was a native : they held the crown by conquest, he by descent : they ground to the dust[2] the slaves whom they had made, he became known to his countrymen only by his benefits. Hence he appeared to shine with a purer light amid the gloom[3] with which he was surrounded ; and whenever[4] the people under the despotism of the Norman kings had an opportunity of expressing their real wishes[5], they constantly called for the "laws and customs of the good king Edward."

EXERCISE CXI.

It always strikes me, often as I have observed the fact, with fresh wonder, that the very men who, when the seas are[6] calm, allege their incapacity[7] to act as steersmen, from[8] having neither learned the art nor ever cared to study it, are yet ready and eager to volunteer their services at the helm when[6] the winds of some political hurricane[9] are at their wildest and the waves at their highest. But, surrounded as I am by state-quacks and nostrum-mongers[10], I feel confident that I have in you one whose[11] judgment and insight I should accept as final, even in preference to my own. I therefore repeat the request which I urged upon you in a former letter, that if in these darkest of days[12] you can discern any course which you think I ought to take, you will give me a friendly intimation.

---

[1] 130 *ad fin.*, 156.   [2] Avoid a literal rendering, and see 54.
[3] Cp. 31, 164.   [4] 72, 139.   [5] 42.   [6] 99.   [7] 41.
[8] Use a causal conjunction, and see 114.   [9] 31.
[10] *State-quacks* and *nostrum-mongers* : render the *meaning* of these phrases.   [11] 113.   [12] 31, 164.

Exercise CXII.

In youth he attached himself passionately to the popular side, and was for some time a strong opponent of the aristocracy; but he never condescended to become a demagogue or a flatterer of the populace, nor would it be easy to find in his whole career a single unconstitutional word or act. At the moment[1] of his entering political life the government was in the hands of a narrow and powerful oligarchy, and the rest of the community were denied all equality in law or voice in public policy. For himself he made no secret of his preference, as compared with all other forms of government, for a republic, in which all legislative, judicial, and executive authority should rest either immediately or ultimately in the hands of the people. But perceiving[2] that such a form of government was not to be realised in his own days or his own country, he made it his aim to [3] replace on the throne[4] the banished sovereign, and to establish a mixed form of government, removed alike from the excesses of democracy and the tyranny either of despotism or oligarchy. To accomplish this required not only a true patriot, but a heaven-born genius; and though he was far the first man of his nation[5] in judgment, in power of expression, and in influence, yet he attempted a work too great for his own capacity or the condition of his countrymen.

On the expression of political terms and ideas, see Introd. **36**, A ; **169-184** : and cp. Ex. III.

Exercise CXIII.

1. It is impossible for our ideal and perfect orator to be formed without scientific training. Without it the processes of classification, definition, division[6], are beyond our reach;

---

[1] Cp. **34** and **115**. [2] **98.** [3] **104.** [4] **31.** [5] **34, 35, 182.**
[6] The *meaning* of these abstract terms must be thought out and rendered ; see **33, 41,** etc.

we cannot distinguish the true from the false; we cannot see
either what follows from our arguments or what is fatal to
them, nor can we detect a verbal fallacy. I need not speak
of the physical sciences, and the wide fields of matter [1] which
they open to the orator. Nor again of practical life, moral
duties, virtues, habits. A very considerable training in these
subjects is essential to the mastery [2] of either the principles or
the practice of oratory.

Nor is this formidable list exhaustive. In addition
to them the aspirant to the highest type of oratory must
avail himself of a vast store of what may be called orna-
mental aids. Indeed it was instruction in these which
formed, at the time I speak of, the whole repertory of those
who were looked on as the leading professors of the art of
eloquence.

2. The result is, that the ideal and true standard of
oratory was reached by none, owing to the wide distinction
made between the teaching of principles and of practice; and
because the student must needs go to one class of teachers
for a knowledge of things, to another for that of language.
For this reason one, to whom the last generation awarded the
highest place among its speakers, a man of native shrewdness
and good sense, remarks, in the one literary production which
he has left behind him, that he had met with many good
speakers, but not a single man of eloquence. The words indicate [3] that he had nursed in imagination a purely ideal type
of eloquence, of which his mental vision [4] was cognisant, but
which had never been realised in practice.

N.B.—Such a passage as this cannot be satisfactorily attempted
without at least some acquaintance with the style of Cicero's treatises
on Oratory (e.g *De Oratore*, or *Brutus*) : a few chapters of which
might be read with or translated by pupils before attempting this
Exercise.

---

[1] 30, 33, 34.   [2] 41.
[3] An adverb will express this phrase; 54.   [4] 30.

Exercise CXIV.

Let us consider you then as arrived at the summit of worldly greatness; let us suppose that all your plans of avarice and ambition are accomplished, and your most sanguine wishes gratified in the fear as well as the hatred of the people; can age itself[1] forget that you are now in the last act[2] of life? Can grey hairs make folly venerable? And is no period to be reserved for meditation and retirement? For shame! my Lord; let it not be recorded of you that the latest moments of your life were dedicated to the same unworthy pursuits, the same busy agitations, in which your youth and manhood were exhausted. Consider that, although you cannot disgrace your former life, you are violating the character of age, and exposing the impotent imbecility, after you have lost the vigour of your passions.

Exercise CXV.

My dear Friend,—A dearth[3] of materials, a consciousness[3] that my subjects are for the most part and must be uninteresting and unimportant, and, above all, a poverty of animal spirits, that makes writing much a great fatigue to me, have occasioned my choice of smaller paper. Acquiesce in the justness of these reasons for the present; and if ever the times should[4] mend with me, I sincerely promise to[4] amend with them.

Homer says on a certain occasion, that Jupiter, when he was wanted at home, was gone to partake of an entertainment provided for him by the Aethiopians. If by Jupiter we understand the weather or the season, as the ancients frequently did, we may say that our English Jupiter has been absent on account of some such invitation: during the whole

---

[1] 32   [2] 167   [3] 41.
[4] On the tenses to be used, see **74, 136.**

month of June he left us to experience almost the rigours of winter. This fine day, however, affords us some hope that the feast is ended, and that we shall enjoy his company without[1] the interruption of his Aethiopian friends again.

I have bought a great dictionary[2], and want nothing but Latin authors to furnish me with the use of it. Had I purchased them first, I had begun at the right end. But I could not afford it. I beseech you admire my prudence.

Yours affectionately,
WILLIAM COWPER.

The first sentence should be rendered by a principal and dependent (causal) clause in Latin : see on the order of such a compound sentence, Introd. **15-20**.

EXERCISE CXVI.

Our business is[3] to attain knowledge, not concerning obvious and vulgar matters, but about sublime, abstruse, intricate, and knotty subjects, remote from common observation and sense; to get sure and exact notions about which will try the best forces of our mind with their utmost endeavours; in firmly settling principles, in strictly deducing consequences, in orderly digesting conclusions, in faithfully retaining what we learn[4] by our contemplation and study. And if[5] to get a competent knowledge about a few things, or to be reasonably skilful in any sort of learning, be difficult, how much industry doth it require to be well seen in many, or to have waded through the vast compass of learning, in no part whereof a scholar may conveniently or handsomely be ignorant; seeing there is such a connection of things and dependence of notions, that one part of learning doth confer light to another; that a man can hardly well understand any-

---

[1] **99.**   [2] Use a Greek term   [3] **104.**
[4] **65.**   [5] **138, 139.**

thing without knowing divers other things, that he will be a lame scholar who hath not an insight into many kinds of knowledge; that he can hardly be a good scholar who is not a general one.

Exercise CXVII.

Peace of mind is, they tell us, the first constituent of happiness [1]; a man's own affairs are a more than sufficient burden; to entangle himself in other people's cares is mere vexation; friendship [2], they add [3], may be cultivated with a view to obtain protection or assistance; but it is not reasonable that a well-ordered mind should set such empty feelings as inclination or affection above its own solid interests. When once they have begun, they go on in this strain *ad infinitum*. For myself, as I listen [4] to their arguments, I feel disposed to ask what will [5] remain of the human being when you have [6] weeded him of all that is human; in what, when [7] all affection, all feeling is gone [6], man differs, I will not say from an animal, but from stocks or stones or any inanimate matter? But I leave the question to [8] wiser men.

Exercise CXVIII.

Philanthropy [9] admits of two forms. It can be displayed in acts of kindness either to the individual members of society [10], or to society at large. The Philanthropist [9] need hardly be reminded of the obvious truism that he must be on his guard against injuring one class while he relieves another. He must remember that, desirable as are all efforts to promote the happiness of individuals, these exertions need to be so guided as to conduce to the welfare, at all events not to tend to the detriment, of the community. The statesman [11]

---

[1] 33. [2] 44. [3] 158. [4] 97, 98. [5] 67. [6] 65.
[7] 99. [8] 66. [9] A periphrasis must be employed; see 33.
[10] 34. [11] 36, A.

on his part must study the claims of the individual, and not
allow the State to encroach on the rights of property. After
all it was for the preservation of these rights that political
society was originally organised.   Man is gregarious by
nature ; but it was in the hope of calling what he possessed
his own that he conceived the idea and sought the protection
of civil government.

The style should be that of Cicero's philosophical treatises,
e.g. *De Officiis*.

EXERCISE CXIX.

Plutarch says very finely, that a man should not allow himself to hate even his enemies, because, says he, if you
indulge [1] this passion in some occasions, it will rise of itself in
others ; if you hate your enemies you will contract such [2] a
vicious habit of mind, as by degrees will break out upon those
who are your friends, or those who are indifferent to you.   I
might here observe how admirably this precept of morality [3]
(which derives the malignity of hatred from the passion itself
and not from its object) answers to that great rule which was
dictated to the world [4] about a hundred years before this
philosopher wrote ; but, instead of that, I shall only take
notice, with a real grief of heart, that the minds of many
good men among us appear soured with party-principles,
and alienated from one another in such a manner as seems to
me altogether inconsistent with the dictates either of
reason or religion.   Zeal for a public cause is apt to breed
passions in the hearts of virtuous persons, to which the
regard of their own private interest would never have
betrayed them.

---

[1] 136.   [2] 113.   [3] 33, 36, E.   [4] 28, 29.

Exercise CXX

Put yourself in my place, conceive an impossibility, imagine yourself to be me If you find[1] it easy to decide on your course[2], no longer give a moment's quarter to my indecision[3]. But if, in spite of treason and disaffection all around you, you think[1] you see some promise at least of a closer union among the sounder[4] portion of the community, some symptoms of growing strength and rising courage among the loyal, and if, therefore, you hesitate[1] for a moment between a temporising policy[5] and an attempt to stake the very existence of the country on an effort to[6] crush the guilty by condign punishment · you will have to confess, allow me to tell you, that my administration has not been so wholly irrational, and that if, as you warn me, there has been some lack of vigour[2] for the passing moment, there has been no small insight[2] into the requirements of the far-off future

Exercise CXXI.

The existence of God has been asserted, questioned, categorically denied. The doctrines of rival schools[7] are so conflicting, that while it is possible that all may be wrong, it is scarcely possible that more than one can be right. Yet the question is obviously one of enormous and practical interest. If it admits of no solution, mankind are doomed to remain plunged in the profoundest darkness[8] on the most important of all subjects. Yet on that which is the real and vital point of the problem, the question whether a Divine person takes any part in the government and administration of this world[9], there has been and is every variety of opinion, the utmost disagreement among the uneducated, the keenest

---

[1] 65, 136   [2] 41, 42   [3] 40.   [4] 174
[5] Think of the meaning, and cp. 41.   [6] 104.   [7] 36, A.
[8] 30.   [9] 28.

controversy among thinkers. One thing is clear : if the
Deity has neither the will nor the power to aid us, if our
actions are not only indifferent to him, but do not even come
within his cognisance, there is an end at once of all the
outward forms and all the inward feelings of religion.
Prayer and worship are based on the assumption that their
object is interested in the welfare of the human worshipper;
that the material universe[1] is ordered and ruled by his
intelligence and wisdom ; that, in a word, some influence[2] can
pass from the Divine to the human being.

The question therefore between the believer and the atheist
is no light matter, it concerns most closely the very existence
and constitution of human society.

EXERCISE CXXII.

The first suggestion[3] then that I would venture to offer is
this, not to[4] let your heart fail or your courage sink, or suffer
yourself to be overwhelmed by the tide[5] of responsibilities ;
but rather to rise to your full height and face them, or even
meet them half-way. The post to which you have been
called is one from whose sphere[6] the element[7] of chance has
been entirely eliminated ; intelligence and application are all
in all ; everything depends, depends in my judgment
absolutely, upon your own ability, rectitude, courage, and
self-control. You have nothing, so far as I can see, to dread
from the issue of battles, or from the hostility of open or
concealed enemies. No wavering allies, no empty military
chest, no failing commissariat, no mutinous regiments, need
enter into your calculations. Yet these are disturbing
causes to which the most far-sighted statesmen have been
repeatedly exposed. They have failed to sustain the blows
of Fortune, just as the skilful pilot fails to weather the fury

---

[1] **28.**   [2] **34.**   [3] **41.**   [4] **102, 103.**   [5] **30.**
[6] *From whose sphere*, etc. : think of the meaning of this expression,
and cp. **30.**   [7] **34.**

of the elements. To you, my Lord, a far different lot has been vouchsafed ; an horizon[1] without a cloud, a sea without a wave ; where, though he who slumbers at the helm may suffer shipwreck, the watchful pilot will find enjoyment in his task.

EXERCISE CXXIII

The limits within which the orator may permit himself the use of sarcasm[2] require very careful consideration Neither signal depravity, such, I mean, as is associated with actual crime, nor signal misfortunes, are fit subjects for ridicule. Great criminals men[3] would fain see struck down with some heavier weapon[4] than that of ridicule ; they do not care to see misfortune satirised, unless there be an ostentatiousness in misfortune. We must deal tenderly with men's affections, lest we send a random shaft[3] against some object dear to them. And thus the most natural marks for ridicule are things which move neither strong dislike nor deep compassion. Hence it follows that the satirist finds his true material in the blemishes which mark the lives of men who are objects neither of affection nor of pity, still less of those whose crimes seem to demand instant execution ; and these failings, if handled[5] with tact and skill, will afford free scope for ridicule.

EXERCISE CXXIV.

The preachers and apostles of the new creed[6] of the divine right of republicanism claim a superiority[7], not only in theoretic excellence[7], but also in the solid advantages of freedom and of happiness[7], for a form of government which lodges the supreme legislative and judicial powers, the absolute control of all financial and all foreign policy, the disposal of the life

---

[1] **31.**   [2] **40.**   [3] **38.**   [4] **30.**   [5] **65.**
[6] Think of the meaning of this expression, and cp. 30.   [7] **33, 40.**

and property of every individual member of the State, in the hands of the natural and proper guardians of all these interests. They protest against drawing from the failure of a single people, a universal inference against the system of free and popular government; and they assert that no organisation is so durable or so conservative as that of a people at entire harmony with itself, and subordinating its whole policy to the national security and freedom.

On the rendering of political terms, see Introd. **36, A ; 169-184.**

Exercise CXXV.

1. The public services[1] of this personage certainly exceeded those of any of his contemporary statesmen, and I incline to[2] think that in his long tenure of office he conferred greater benefits on his country than any, I had almost said all, of those who before his time had held the reins of government. Not only did he succeed in the difficult task of bringing under the control of law a haughty and defiant nobility[3], but, what was far more difficult, he accomplished this without[4] either lowering their position, or impairing any of their just and salutary privileges, or even incurring more than their momentary displeasure. Not that[5] he was wanting in courage or strength of will, but that beyond all other reformers, he impressed men with the conviction of his entire disinterestedness, of his intense and enlightened patriotism. Under his teaching the highest grandee learned that in a constitutional country the true strength of an aristocracy[3] lies in setting a voluntary example of self-control and submission to law. With the masses, towards whom he had presented at one time a somewhat stern and forbidding aspect from his intense dislike, though the kindliest and most open-handed of mankind, to all the arts of the demagogue, he

---

[1] 161.   [2] 166.   [3] 36, A.   [4] 105.   [5] 114.

was long rather powerful than popular. He was honoured, valued, respected, but scarcely loved and rarely applauded. But in proportion to men's knowledge of his true character and inmost feelings was their enthusiastic admiration [1] for qualities whose existence they had never suspected, and which they seemed each to have discovered for himself.

2. As he advanced in life he became so endeared to all classes, that it seemed as though his popularity with the lower orders kept pace with the growing favour bestowed on him by the aristocracy. The result was that when, at the age of more than threescore and ten, he resolved, in spite of [2] the tears of his sovereign, the entreaties of the nobles, and the louder protestations of the people, on laying down the burden of office, he retained in private life an influence beyond that of the most powerful of his successors, and found the rest and leisure for which he had so long sighed absolutely unattainable. For though [3] he had determined no longer to take any part in public affairs, yet no young aspirant, whose views rose above an ordinary level, would [4] enter political life [5] without [6] using all means to visit and consult one who was looked on as, beyond all rivalry, the wisest and most experienced of the national statesmen And thus he never shared the lot of so many who have retired from statesmanship [5] to private life, and who have outlived, not perhaps their fame, but their influence and their authority. His country [7] mourned his death with tears of [8] genuine grief, and the nation [9] will cherish his memory as long as the national existence shall endure

This Exercise illustrates the use of Comparative and Superlative expressions; see Arnold rev. ed, 488 seq

---

| [1] 41. | [2] 99. | [5] 145. | [4] 69. | [5] 36, A, 171. |
| [6] 175. | [7] 28 | [8] 43. | 35, 182. | |

Exercise CXXVI.

The young aspirant[1] to the highest office[2] in the State was undoubtedly the possessor of striking gifts; but, besides this, he had from childhood studied the art of their effective display. Whether there was some vein[3] of superstition in his own temperament, or whether it was with the aim of[4] insuring for his commands and suggestions the unquestioned authority of inspired utterances, he rarely spoke in public without[5] pretending to some nocturnal vision or supernatural intimation. In order to impress public opinion in this direction, he had made a practice from the day that he reached manhood of never entering on any business, political[6] or personal, without first[7] paying a visit to the Capitol. There he would[8] enter the sanctuary, and pass some time in entire solitude and seclusion. This habit, from which during his whole lifetime he never deviated, made converts in some circles to a belief, to which accident or design had given wide currency, that his origin was other than human. He himself lent countenance to the notion by the course which he adopted of neither wholly disclaiming the story, nor openly asserting its truth. There was much besides of the same tendency, partly genuine, partly counterfeit, which in spite of his youth had early made him an object of something more than admiration; and it was under the influence of these feelings that the nation consigned to one who had not yet reached maturity an enormous responsibility and an unlimited authority.[9]

Exercise CXXVII.

There are two maxims of this philosopher which the future statesman will do well to observe. The first is to devote himself to the interests of his country, and, forgetting all

---

[1] 33, 171.   [2] 34, 35.   [3] 30, 34.   [4] 102.   [5] 175.
[6] 36, A; 171.   [7] 122.   [8] 69.   [9] 157.

selfish aims, to make these the one test of all his policy. The
second is to minister to the needs of the whole of the body [1]
politic and not, while [2] devoting himself to some individual
portion, to be indifferent to the claims of the rest. For it is
with statesmen as with guardians : the trust is to be adminis-
tered not for the benefit of the trustee, but in the interest of
those for whom he is bound to act. And those who study
the interest of a single class, unmindful of other classes,
expose the community to the deadly evils of party-spirit [4] and
disunion. And as a result of this, while society [5] is divided
between the popular party [6] and the partisans of the aristocracy, the general good finds few advocates. This is a fault
which the earnest and sterling [3] patriot, one worthy of the
highest place in the political world[7], will avoid with aversion.
He will devote himself wholly to his country, and, making
neither wealth nor power his aim, he will embrace in his
political horizon [8] the interest of all. He will not by un-
founded aspersions expose any one to odium and unpopularity;
in a word, he will hold so firmly by the rules of justice and of
honour, that he will rather suffer any loss, yea, face death
itself, than abandon the principles which I have indicated.

For the political terms here used, see Introd. 36, A ; 169-184.

EXERCISE CXXVIII.

There is no subject more conducive to the gratification of
the reader than the vicissitudes of life, the ebb and flow of
Fortune. These, though [9] in our own experience [10] we have
found them far from pleasing, will nevertheless give pleasure
in the perusal. For there is a charm in the tranquil recol-
lection of past sorrow, and those who have encountered no
personal distress, and who watch the misfortunes of their
neighbours with no sense of pain, find a pleasure in the mere

---

[1] A corresponding metaphor is admissible.   [2] 120.
[3] Think of the meaning, and cp. 30.   [4] 170.   [5] 34.
[6] 172.   [7] 29.   [8] 31.   [9] 145.   [10] 97.

indulgence of commiseration. Who of us is there whom the'
scene[1] of the Theban hero dying at Mantinaea does not touch
with something of a melancholy pleasure? that waited to bid
them extract the spear till his inquiries had been answered,
and he knew that his shield was safe, so that, in spite of the
torture of his wound, he passed away with resignation and
with honour! Or who can read, without[2] being spell-bound
by the tale, the banishment and the return of Alcibiades?
The mere chronology of history has something of the languid
interest of an almanac[3]; but the hazardous and chequered
fortunes of its heroes[3] inspire wonder, suspense, joy, trouble,
hope, fear; and if[4] they are wound up by a signal catastrophe,
their perusal satisfies the mind with the keenest sense of
gratification.

Exercise CXXIX.

These wars are narrated by Virgil, who softens[5] whatever
is harsh in them, and alters and accelerates the succession of
the events, in the latter half of the *Aeneid.* Its contents
were certainly national[6]; yet one can scarcely believe that
even a Roman, if impartial, could receive any genuine enjoyment from his story. To us it is unfortunately too plain how
little the poet has succeeded in raising the shadowy names,
for which he was forced to invent characters, into living beings,
like the heroes of Homer. Perhaps it is a problem[7] which
defies solution, to form an epic poem on an argument which
has not lived for centuries in popular songs and tales, as the
common property of a nation, so that the cycle of stories
which comprises it, and the persons who act a part in it, are
familiar to every one. Assuredly this problem was beyond
the powers of Virgil, whose genius was barren in creating,
great as was his talent for embellishing. That he himself

---

[1] 34, 35.　　[2] 175, 177.　　[3] 36, n.　　[4] 138, 139.　　[5] 99.
[6] *Its contents*, etc.; render by a concessive clause, and cp. 144, 145.
[7] Think of the meaning, and cp. 30.

was conscious of this, and was content to be great in the way
suited to his endowments, is proved by his practice[1] of
imitating and borrowing, and by the touches he intersperses
of his exquisite and extensive erudition, so much admired by
the Romans, but now so little appreciated.

Exercise CXXX.

These wire-drawn discussions have little bearing on the
general wellbeing of mankind. They may be left[2] to philosophers and professors; while for ourselves we shall do well
to turn aside[3] from such dreams and aspirations[4] and confine
our speculations to subjects which lie within the sphere of
practical and daily life. Whether such a man is now enjoying
an immortality of happiness[5], or whether his soul, if your
materialistic[6] philosophers will any longer allow me the
expression, passed into nothingness with his latest breath,
we must needs rejoice that he was born unto the world, and
England[7] will cherish his memory with a joyful gratitude till
the last moments of her existence.

Exercise CXXXI.

To be dear to one's countrymen, beloved by one's friends,
things which are instinctively pleasing and welcome to every
one, you, it seems, count cheap. The being satisfied with
yourself, and the entertaining the same views and aims[8] in
office[9] as in private life, seems to you right and honourable. You prefer leisure to activity, enjoyment to patriotism.[10] I do not care to refute your views in detail; I will
only say that you are doubtless the same man that I always

---

[1] 108.   [2] 66.   [3] 99.   [4] 41.   [5] 33.
[6] Think of the meaning, and render as nearly as you can.
[7] 158.   [8] 41.   [9] 34, 35.   [10] 33.

believed you to be, but that such sloth and such indifference
to the welfare of the community are beyond what I had
looked for even in you.

This Exercise illustrates the substantival use of the Infinitive ;
see Introd. 89.

Exercise CXXXII.

Wickedness [1] in high places is doubtless in itself a serious
evil; it becomes still more serious from the tendency of mankind to imitate their superiors. Turn over the pages of history [2], and you will find the law [3] to hold good, that, given the
character of the leading men in a nation [4], you have the
national character, and that no moral revolution has occurred
among the upper classes which has not been reproduced in
the mass of the people. Indeed this principle comes nearer
to the truth than Plato's maxim. "Change," says he, "the
national airs, and you change the state of nations." "Change,"
say I, "the habits and life of the great, and you change the
character of the nation."

It is this that makes vicious rulers doubly ruinous to a
country; ruinous not only from the vices which they contract,
but from those which they propagate in society [5]; they are
injurious not only as corrupt, but as corrupters; their example is more mischievous than their practice. Give but rank
and fame and office [4], and a small, wonderfully small, section
of society may raise or lower the moral tone of a whole
nation.

Exercise CXXXIII.

You understand then the transformation of the King into
the Despot; and the steps by which an excellent form of
government [6] was, by the crime of an individual, converted

---

[1] 42.   [2] 36, B ; 171.   [3] 30, 34.   [4] 35.
[5] 34.   [6] 36, A.

into the very worst. Such indeed is the government of the
Despot, to whom the Greeks gave the name of Tyrant. The
title of King they confined to him who has a paternal care for
his people, and maintains to the very utmost the wellbeing
of those who are intrusted to his care. Doubtless an excellent form of government, as I have already said; but, for all
this, with a tendency to gravitate towards a condition of all
others the most fatal. For no sooner has the sovereign of
whom we speak stooped to any act of unrighteous tyranny,
than from that moment he becomes a tyrant. This, however, is a question for enlarging on which I shall find a more
natural opening when the course of my subject shall [1] remind
me to raise a protest against those who, even after [2] political
freedom has been secured, have aimed at establishing arbitrary
government.

Exercise CXXXIV.

1. *[In the history of this country the aspirants to political
life and to political eminence have always fallen into two
classes. Of these the one has practised and professed the
principles of a popular, the other those of an aristocratic,
party. Those who aimed at gratifying the masses by their
measures and their language were classed among the former,
to the latter were assigned, as their very name imports, those
who so shaped their conduct as to win for their policy the
approval of the best members of the State.]

2. I am asked for a definition[4] of this last expression. Those
to whom I refer are in number beyond my reckoning; were
it not so, our ruin were inevitable. They are to be found
alike in the leaders of our public policy, and in the residents

---

[1] 65.	[2] 99.	[3] 36, B.

* The first paragraph of this Exercise has been translated in the
"Specimen Lecture on Latin Prose Composition,' 171-174; see also
36, A.

[4] 179.

of our provincial boroughs and rural districts; nay, even in our commercial circles. But wide and varied as are the ramifications of this party, a short statement of its limits and characteristics will obviate misapprehension. All belong to it who are neither the enemies of the Constitution, nor inherently corrupt, nor fanatics, nor entangled in pecuniary embarrassments. This is tantamount to saying that it is composed of the upright, sound-minded, well-to-do portions of Society.[1] And those statesmen who defer to the wishes, interests, and views of this class, are the champions of the aristocratic party, and in its rank and file are enrolled the most influential and most distinguished members of the State, and the leaders of our country.

What then is to be the end and aim of a ministry[1] formed from this class? What is to be the pole-star[2] by which they are bound to shape their course? It is that best of all blessings, the prayer of all the wise and all the good—the union of tranquillity and honour.

∨   EXERCISE CXXXV.

I should like next to quote the authority of one who was in my judgment the greatest master of political[3] wisdom in that old world[4] which you so respect. A prophetic insight taught him that the sea-board was no favourable site for cities whose founders aspired to permanence or dominion. Such states, he felt[5], must in their soft and callow immaturity be exposed to innumerable and even invisible dangers. On the mainland no invader could swoop suddenly down without[6] a thousand signs betraying his intention and his approach, to[7] give due warning, not merely of his coming, but who and whence he was. But the corsair or the pirate might present himself before a soul had even dreamed of his approach; he

---

[1] 34.	[2] 30, 31.	[3] 36, A; 169.	[4] 28.
[5] 88, 123 *seq.*	[6] 175.	[7] 102.	

need carry no flag to mark his nationality, his home, or his destination[1]; and till[2] he had actually touched the shore, it might be impossible to distinguish whether he were friend or foe.

Exercise CXXXVI.

Great as was the reputation that had preceded our friend, he has been found to surpass it. He has great command of language, with a rich and abundant vocabulary; always speaking extempore, yet with the appearance of careful preparation. His style is of the purest, his introductory observations pointed, elegant, and pleasing; sometimes weighty and elevated. He propounds several subjects for discussion, and gives his hearers their choice, often without any preparation at all: then up he rises and begins directly. Every idea seems to come at once with almost equal readiness; recondite thoughts present themselves, and language—ah, what language! —carefully chosen and polished. His impromptu utterances show[3] plainly the result of much reading and much writing. His prologues[4] are appropriate, his narrative clear, his attack incisive, his conclusions bold, his rhetoric of a high order: and he ends by teaching, charming, and affecting you—you hardly know which the most. His memory is incredible: he can recall at some distance what he has spoken extempore, without[5] failing in a word. This power he has acquired by persevering practice: night and day he does, hears, or says nothing else. He has passed his sixtieth year, and still is a scholar *pur et simple*—the simplest, most guileless, and best class of men in the world. For we, who have the rough work of the courts and practical law learn a great deal of ill-nature, however little we wish it.

The style is Epistolary.

---

[1] 42.   [2] 122.   [3] 32.   [4] 41.   [5] 105.

Exercise CXXXVII.

For when the soul, having once recognised and compre-
hended virtue, has forsaken [1] its obedience to and indulgence of
the body, and trampled pleasure down like some disgraceful
stain, and dismissed all fear of death and pain; when it has
entered into a fellowship of love with its kind, regarding as
such all those of kindred nature; when it has embraced
divine worship and a pure religion, and has sharpened its
mental vision [2] to refuse the evil and choose the good,—what
happier state can tongue express or thought conceive?
Again, when it has learnt the secret of the heavens and
the earth, of the sea and universal nature, and has seen
whence all things spring and whither they return, when
and how they are doomed to perish, what is the mortal and
decaying element in them, and what the divine and ever-
lasting; when it has almost grasped the knowledge of their
great Ruler and Governor, and feels [1] itself a citizen of the
whole universe, not hemmed within the walls of a single spot,—
amid all this glorious world [3], in this its survey and study [4] of
nature, O heavens! what self-knowledge [5] will it gain! [4] how
will it despise, look down upon, and count as nought all that
the world [6] calls greatest! and it will protect all this knowledge by a rampart of logical method [7], by a power of distinguishing truth and falsehood, and by an art, so to speak,
of understanding the consequences and the opposites of each
several point.

Exercise CXXXVIII.

Fellow-countrymen! it is your gentle and upright character, the source of so much power and reputation abroad, that
now makes me most apprehensive in the struggle with
tyranny at home. I am afraid that your unwillingness to

---

[1] 65.   [2] 30.   [3] 28, 40.   [4] 34, 35.
[5] 41.   [6] 28, 29.   [7] 36, P.

believe of others what your own judgment condemns as disgraceful, may lead [1] you astray—the more so, as all our tyrant's trust is in crime and treachery, and his only hope of safety lies in becoming even more detestable than your fears suggest, so that your very misery may extinguish in you all regard for freedom : while, if you do take [1] any steps, I am afraid that you may be too much occupied in avoiding danger to think of vengeance. As for his minions, men of high lineage, with examples of noble ancestry before them, I cannot wonder at them enough—men who purchase power over you at the price of their own subjection, and prefer such power and such slavery in the cause of wrong to their unquestionable right of freedom , noble scions indeed of good old houses, born to upset all that their ancestors' valour won ' For what, I ask, was it that our fathers saved from King or Pope ? What but freedom, and the sacredness of home, and our right to own no master but the law ? Yet all these liberties your tyrant is now clutching in his grasp, like spoils wrung from foreigners ; nor is he glutted with the blood of all those armies, and all those leaders of our country, whom the chances of war have swallowed, but is only more savage at a time when success turns most men's hearts from wrath to pity. Nay, he alone in all human history[2] has ordained punishment for children yet unborn, to assure them[2] of wrong even before life · and hitherto the very atrocity of his guilt has insured him a disgraceful security, while[1] the fear of still heavier slavery has deterred[2] you from reclaiming your freedom.

EXERCISE CXXXIX.

1. Men who are in the habit of finding fault with the present generation and with men of the present day, who are always extolling our ancestors, and sounding the praises of the good old times, are, it seems to me, like those who hate

---

[1] 65.   [2] 36, n.   ' Use a relative pronoun, and see 111.
[4] 120.   [5] 32.

our own climate, and are always inveighing against our rain, our cold, our gloom, our fogs, and sighing for the brilliant sunshine and light of Italy or Greece. Both the former and the latter are in my opinion very wrong ; it is better to make a good use of things which are our own, than to praise and crave for those of other people or another generation.

2. The great Plato, who lived in a Greek city, and that Athens, refused to mix with the politicians and statesmen of his day. Doubtless he so acted not without reason : yet the modern student of Greek history[1], while rejoicing[2] that so great a philosopher had leisure to write so many immortal works, will be dissatisfied at his having[3] refused his aid to his country in her old age and dotage.[4]

3. I am not the person, to quote your own words, to[5] abandon my best friends in the extremity of peril. Life, and fame, and honour, are I confess dear to me ; danger and pain most offensive : but you and I have as young men faced the latter together, and in these latter days we know that the former, and everything which can be dear to honest men, is at stake. I hope, therefore, or rather I promise soon to[6] share all those troubles with you, and to make some return for the innumerable acts of kindness which I have received from you.

4. The defendant says that he is under no obligation to these excellent brothers, whose cause I have, according to him, unwillingly undertaken. But those fraudulent and dishonest partners of yours, I reply, thought otherwise ; they returned him thanks[7] not once but repeatedly. You are the only one who feels no gratitude[7] for so many favours. And yet much as you have spoken about the past, you are it seems either incapable of distinguishing truth from falsehood, or are pretending to remember little, to hope everything.

This Exercise illustrates the use of the pronouns *hic, iste, ille* (see Arnold, rev. ed., 335-348.)

---

[1] 33, 36, n ; 166. [2] 98. [3] 89. [4] 40.
[5] 113. [6] 74. [7] 161.

EXERCISE CXL.

1. And it would have been well if the current[1] of events had been arrested at that stage of its progress, instead of sweeping us into the hands of a party whose cry is no longer for Reform, but for Revolution. 2. Confidence[2] in a Ministry is a plant[1] of slow and cautious growth. It can be secured only by two conditions. we must impress the nation[1] with a belief alike in our wisdom and in our fair dealing. 3. It is one thing to use what is clear to throw light on what is questionable : quite another to employ what is questionable to throw a cloud over what is clear. 4. Great as may be the influence on our intellectual and emotional condition, of matter evolved from day to day in the laboratory[1] of the body, the analogy, whether real or imaginary, does not warrant the conclusion that soul and body have a common origin and are destined[4] to a simultaneous extinction. 5. The difficulty[5] of forming any clear view of the nature and properties of the soul led men to a categorical denial of its existence. 6. That older world[6] stood nearer to the dawn, and saw truth, it may be, with clearer eyes than we. 7. He would often quote the well-known[7] words, "Our birth is but a sleep and a forgetting."[8] 8. It was not that[9] he claimed to belong to the school which denied the existence[2] of all truth.[10] But he held with those who believed that, while all truth, as presented to and attainable by human faculties, was combined with some admixture[2] of falsehood or uncertainty,[10] yet there were many principles which rested on sufficient evidence to claim to guide men's lives and mould their characters.

---

[1] 30.   [2] 42.   [3] 35.   [4] 67.
[5] *The difficulty . . led* use a causal construction, and see 114.
[6] 28, 29.   [7] 160.   [8] 42.   [9] 114.   [10] 40.

Exercise CXLI.

1. The orator should also be master of the whole domain of history[1], and of its rich treasure-house [2] of illustrations, and he must not omit the study [3] alike of municipal and international law.   2. He reminded us that the true cause of your unpopularity [4] in old age was to be found in your having devoted [5] the prime of life to heap every wrong and every insult alike on the most exalted and the humblest of your countrymen.   3. But the high-spirited and undaunted chief, though [6] surrounded on all sides by armed foes, turned to Cortes and [7] heaped reproaches on the cowardice of his followers, for [8] having tamely surrendered to the conquerors, and flung away the priceless jewels [2] of freedom and of honour.   4. Nor should we gloss over but avow the fact, that ambition exercises a magnetic [2] force upon all mankind, and that it is sometimes the noblest natures for whom fame has the most attraction.   5. If we supply [9] those who are destitute of morality with the gift of utterance, we shall find that instead of making them orators, we have put arms into the hands of madmen.   6. One would have [10] thought that no one worthy of the name of Englishman would have allowed himself to [11] tide over a pecuniary embarrassment by the sale of his ancestral portrait-gallery.[12]   7. Had there been [13] any sense of honour in hearts where it should have been [14] most keen, we should never have been exposed to this distress.   8. If this was [15] to be the result of all your exploits, you might have spared yourself all this toil and trouble.

---

[1] 36, B : 171.   [2] 30, 170.   [3] 34, 166.   [4] 41.
[5] A causal sentence, see 114 ; and for *oratio obliqua*, 123-130.
[6] 99.   [7] 97.
[8] Use a relative pronoun, and see 110, 111.   65.
[10] 82, 134.   [11] 74, 104.
[12] Think what the corresponding Roman idea would be.
[13] 134.   [14] 73.   [15] 138, 139.

EXERCISE CXLII.

1. No one can aspire to rank as a great writer of history without [1] sometimes in the thick darkness [2] of remote antiquity trusting to an instinctive insight into truth and falsehood. But he must be on his guard against importing an element of fiction into the region [3] of facts. 2. It is a common practice for those who wish to bring good tidings to add some detail of their own imagination to [4] enhance the value of what they announce. 3. With the actual words and expressions of this discussion I have not troubled myself; the ideas I had long since enshrined [5] in my memory, and have reproduced according to my own judgment. 4. He was at that time the leading member of this House alike in ability and in character. 5. You have repeatedly urged me to write a history of England during our own and the last generation [6]; I have invariably declined to attempt such a task, feeling myself unequal to it alike in ability, knowledge, and leisure. 6. You will [7] confer on us a great kindness if you will [7] put before us your views [3] on the present war; what you think of its origin and real cause, and of its probable duration and result. [8] You ask me, he replied, to play the part of a prophet rather than of a philosopher. 7. To catch the cheers of popular assemblies, composed as they are of the most ignorant members of the community, by honeyed words and truckling speeches, is beneath the dignity of one who [9] aspires not to follow but to guide the policy of a nation. [10] 8. The highest excellence is proportionally rare, and nothing is harder than to find anything which reaches the full perfection of its own type.

[1] 175-177.   [2] 31, 164, 165.   [3] 30, 34.   [4] 102.
[5] 97.   [6] 31   [7] 65, 137.   [8] 42.
                [9] 113.   [10] 35, 182.

Exercise CXLIII.

1. [1] "Once," he said, "let us accept a falsehood as a truth, and we no longer retain any criterion for distinguishing truth from falsehood." 2. It is a great comfort to be able to reflect that even if success has been denied you, yet that your views have been at once well judged and upright. 3. I say nothing of the entire readiness which you have shown to brave any storm [2] of unpopularity, had I permitted it. 4. The good man, he said, does his duty and keeps his word. 5. He replied that he would [3] use the utmost exertions both to keep their communications [4] secret, and to obtain a favourable answer to their wishes. [4] 6. No sooner did [5] the emperor see the commissioners stand before him in his camp, than, in the presence of [6] his whole staff, he burst forth [7], " What brings you to me ? Do you come as spies ?" He stopped every attempt at reply, and ordered them at once into arrest. 7. The course he took in the war betrayed a wish to serve France [8], combined with a reluctance to come to a rupture with Germany. [8] 8. [1] " It was better," they said, " if things have come to this, to die fighting while striving [9] to win our country's freedom, better to endure any extremity of fortune, than to be tortured to death by those among whom we have lived as masters." 9. To this the General replied : [1] " If you wish for a conference, you can have one. As to the lives of your men, I hope I can obtain them from my Government [10]; for yourself, no harm will be done you—for that I pledge my word."

Exercise CXLIV.

1. And therefore I repeat the request which I made when I wrote to you before, that if in these darkest of days [11] you can discern any course which you think I ought to take, you

---

[1] Use *oratio obliqua*, 123-130.   [2] 30, 31.   [3] 74.   [4] 41, 1.
[5] 4, 116.   [6] 99.   [7] Use *oratio obliqua*, 130.
[8] 158.   [9] 120.
[10] Use some equivalent Roman idea.   [11] 164.

would give me a friendly intimation. 2. It always strikes me
with fresh wonder, in spite of long observation, that men, who
when the seas are [1] calm, allege their incapacity [2] to act as
steersmen, as having [3] neither learnt the art, nor ever cared
to master it, are yet ready to volunteer their services at the
helm, when the winds are [1] at their loudest, and the waves at
their highest. 3. He would often quote, with approval, the
traditional saying [4] of King Tarquin, that exile had taught
him to distinguish between true and false friends only when
it was too late to repay either. 4. Do not judge every aim
of life by a conventional [5] rather than a true standard.
5. The moment that you deprive [6] a fellow-creature of anything from a selfish motive, you cease [6] to act as a human
being, and violate a law of Nature. 6. I may remind [7] your
friend that political sympathy [2] does not necessarily imply
personal regard [2], and that noisy professions [2] of patriotism [8]
are quite compatible with the most mercenary and self-inter-
ested motives. 7. I am aware that the utmost weight should
be given to the judicious advice of friends; that such advice
should be resorted to when circumstances require [6] it, and
when resorted to should be obeyed. 8. He always had a
fancy while in office that the eyes of all society were turned
specially upon him, and that he was acting his part on a
world-wide stage. [9] Yet, it is fair to say, that when advanced
to the post of First Minister, he treated his dignity not as
a prize [3], but as a sacred trust [3], and fully realised its great
and solemn responsibilities. [2] And, welcome as [10] were the
smiles of the great and the applause of the crowd, it is a
question whether the enjoyment he derived from greatness
ever equalled its anxieties and burdens.

---

[1] 99.   [2] 41, 42   [1] 97.   [4] 160.
[5] Think of the meaning of this term.   [6] 65, 137.   [7] 83.
[8] 33.   [9] 29, 30.   [10] 146.

I.—GRAMMATICAL INDEX.

[The references are to *pages* of the Introduction.   Roman numerals refer
to the *numbers* of the Exercises.]

A. W. L. P U

II.—INDEX OF LATIN AND ENGLISH WORDS AND PHRASES SPECIALLY NOTICED IN THE INTRODUCTION.

III.—INDEX TO EXERCISES

Edinburgh University Press.
THOMAS AND ARCHIBALD CONSTABLE, PRINTERS TO HER MAJESTY.

RIVINGTON'S EDUCATIONAL LIST

Arnold's Henry's First
Latin Book. By C. G. GEPP. 3s.
[The original Edition is still on sale.]

Arnold's Latin Prose
Composition. By G. G. BRADLEY. 5s.
[The original Edition is still on sale.]

First Latin Writer. By
G. L. BENNETT. 3s. 6d.

Or separately—
First Latin Exercises. 2s. 6d.
Latin Accidence. 1s. 6d.

Second Latin Writer.
By G. L. BENNETT. 3s. 6d.

Easy Latin Stories for
Beginners By G. L. BENNETT.
2s. 6d.

Second Latin Reading
Book. By G. L. BENNETT. 2s. 6d.

Selections from Cæsar.
By G. L. BENNETT. 2s.

Selections from Vergil.
By G. L. BENNETT. 1s. 6d.

Cæsar de Bello Gallico.
Books I.—III. By J. MERRY-
WEATHER and C. TANCOCK. 3s. 6d.
Book I. separately, 2s.

Gradatim. An Easy Latin Translation Book. By H. R. HEATLEY and
H. N. KINGDON. 1s. 6d.

Excerpta Facilia. A Second
Latin Translation Book. By H. R.
HEATLEY and H. N. KINGDON.
2s. 6d.

First Steps in Latin. By
F. RITCHIE. 1s. 6d.

Arnold's Greek Prose
Composition. By E. ABBOTT. 3s. 6d.
[The original Edition is still on sale.]

A Primer of Greek
Grammar. By E. ABBOTT and E.
D. MANSFIELD. 3s. 6d.
Separately—
Syntax. 1s. 6d. Accidence. 2s. 6d.

A Practical Greek Me-
thod for Beginners. THE SIMPLE
SENTENCE. By F. RITCHIE and E.
H. MOORE. 3s. 6d.

Stories in Attic Greek.
By F. D. MORICE. 3s. 6d.

A First Greek Writer.
By A. SIDGWICK. 3s. 6d.

An Introduction to Greek
Prose Composition. By A. SIDG-
WICK. 5s.

An Introduction to Greek
Verse Composition. By A. SIDG-
WICK and F. D. MORICE. 5s.

Homer's Iliad. By A. SIDG-
WICK. Books I. and II., 2s. 6d.—
Book XXI., 1s. 6d.—Book XXII.,
1s. 6d.

The Anabasis of Xeno-
phon. By R. W. TAYLOR. Books
I. and II., 3s. 6d. Separately, Book
I., 2s. 6d.; Book II., 2s.—Books III.
and IV., 3s. 6d.

Xenophon's Agesilaus.
By R. W. TAYLOR. 2s. 6d.

Stories from Ovid in
Elegiac Verse. By R. W. TAYLOR.
3s. 6d.

Stories from Ovid in
Hexameter Verse. By R. W. TAY-
LOR. 2s. 6d.

Waterloo Place, Pall Mall, London.

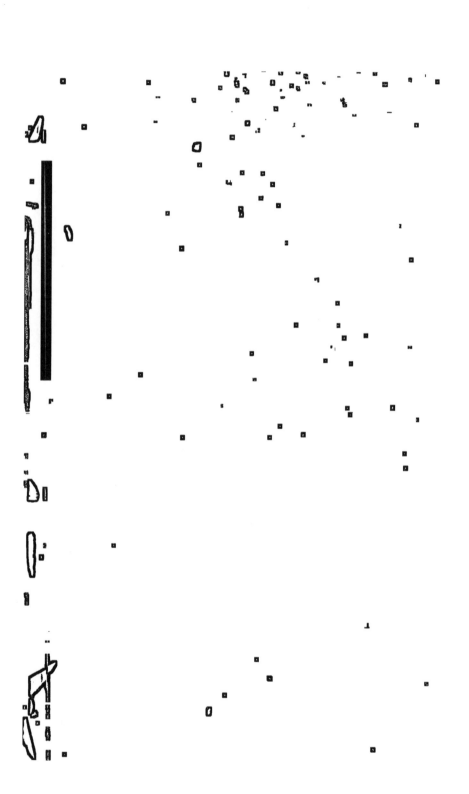

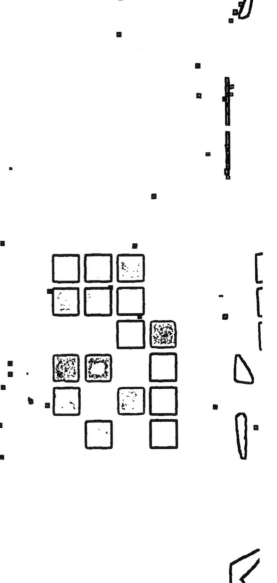